DICK
JOHNSON

DICK
JOHNSON

DICK JOHNSON and _JAMES PHELPS_

EBURY
PRESS

An Ebury Press book
Published by Random House Australia Pty Ltd
Level 3, 100 Pacific Highway, North Sydney NSW 2060
www.randomhouse.com.au

First published by Ebury Press in 2013
This edition published in 2014

Addresses for companies within the Random House Group can be found at
www.randomhouse.com.au/offices

National Library of Australia
Cataloguing-in-Publication Entry

Johnson, Dick, 1945–
Dick Johnson: the autobiography of a true-blue
Aussie sporting legend/Dick Johnson.

ISBN 978 0 85798 259 9 (pbk)

Johnson, Dick, 1945–
Automobile racing drivers – Australia – Biography

796.72092

Cover design by Luke Causby/Blue Cork
Front cover photos: Mark Horsburgh, Edge Photographics
Back cover photo: Getty Images/Staff
Internal design by Midland Typesetters, Australia
Typeset in 12.5/17 Minion LT by Midland Typesetters, Australia
Printed in Australia by Griffin Press, an accredited ISO AS/NZS 14001:2004 Environmental
Management System printer

CONTENTS

1

IT ALL STARTED WITH
A SPLASH

The Deep End

'Wake up!' he screamed.

I shuddered to attention, almost headbutting the man who was standing over me, pulling at my arm.

'Wake up, Richard,' he shouted again.

I looked towards the noise, trying to make out the face in the dark. I didn't know what was going on, trapped in a trance-like daze.

And then it hit me . . . time to swim.

I might one day go on to become a race car driver, a great one some say, but back then I was a seven year old destined to swim at the Olympics.

Or so Dad thought.

'Get up, Richard, we're going to be late!'

I tried to roll over, but he grabbed me in a vice-like grip and tore me from the sheets.

'No, Dad, I'm tired. Let me sleep.'

My father wanted me to become an Olympian. That was his dream – Dick Johnson, the world 100-metre freestyle champion.

Dad bundled me into the car, a brand-new FE Holden, all sparkling chrome and fresh vinyl. It was the only good thing about the early morning wake-up call. My two sisters, Robyn and Diané, bright-eyed and bushy-tailed, were already in the back.

Splash!

I dove into the pool and my body shuddered again, this time from the numbing cold. The sun was peeking through the sky, eating away at the shadows, but the water was still more black than blue.

'Swim,' my coach Joe Emerson, also the Queensland sheriff at the time, cried through his cardboard megaphone.

And with that I was off. For the next hour or so I threw my arms into the water, kicking until the black-blue churned white. And I stared at that damn line until I hit my mark: four miles.

'Good job, Richard,' Dad said as he chucked a towel over my shoulder, sun now throwing a brilliant shine on the 50-metre pool.

In hindsight, having this sort of routine was a fantastic start to my life and gave me great grounding, but back then, looking at that black line every morning . . . well, it bored the shit out of me. In the 1950s, there were no fancy lane ropes, no speed suits, and certainly no heated pools. Hell, we didn't even have goggles.

'Don't rub them,' Mum said as I sat at the breakfast table

in our suburban house in Queensland following the early morning swim. 'They'll only get worse.'

My eyes were red-raw, and I was mashing at them like mad.

I then went to school – a place I didn't like much – and fell asleep. Smack-bang on the old hardwood desk, I was out in a pool of drool.

Every morning was the same. Dad would be standing over me, shouting as he tried to pry me out of bed. He became sick of it at some point, so he found a solution that would have had people today ringing DOCS.

'Do you want to drive?' he asked.

As quick as a lightning bolt, I hit the floor and stood magnificently bright. I was wide awake.

'Yeah,' I replied.

Yeeeeees!

Dad knew I loved cars, and I guess he did too. After a stint in shipping yards, working all the way up and down the east coast, the old man became the sales manager at a big car dealership in town. They mostly dealt Holdens, and I couldn't get enough of whatever he would bring home.

Dad always had the latest model Holdens. He also got his hands on Pontiacs and Buicks and so on. They seemed like such magical things. I used to wait for him out the front of the house every day. At the end of the driveway, a touch past five o'clock, I would pace, kick rocks and stare down the street to spot his car.

Dad would pull up, inches from my feet. 'Jump in, son.'

On his lap, I would grab the wheel, shove it into gear and negotiate the rest of the drive.

I used to love Saturdays because that was when I got to visit his work. It was typically a movie day, but sometimes I got to work with him and I would just drool all over the shiny, perfectly buffed machines.

So Dad figured out an easy way to stop the morning torment: the pushing and pulling; the shouts and slaps; the me going back to sleep 15 times. He let me drive us to the pool. It would keep me happy and his Olympic dream alive.

Or so he thought.

I grabbed my pillow, threw it onto the seat of the Holden and climbed in. Grinning from ear to ear, I started the old girl up.

Brrrrrr.

How good is this? I thought, not worrying one bit about the prospect of swimming or the warm, soft bed I had left behind.

The rumble of the six-cylinder engine was music to my ears. The smell of burning petrol, the clunking sound of metal on metal – a glorious assault on my senses.

My little hands grabbed at the stick shift and I used all my might to shove it into gear. Three on the tree.

My sisters were in the backseat, unconcerned. Our destination: the Valley Baths, one of only two 50-metre pools in Brisbane at the time, 20 kilometres or so away.

And with that I was off.

I pulled out onto the street, pillow propping me up just high enough to see the road. My feet barely touched the floor. I searched with my right foot, found the pedal and slammed it to the ground.

This is the best, I thought. *Here I am with my old man next to me, driving. I am* driving!

It was as if the cool morning breeze amplified the car's speed. Window open, the wind smacked me right in the face. It felt like I was doing 100 miles an hour. There was nobody else on the road, just me and my dad's Holden.

I don't think it would have turned too many heads. They were different times, early 1950s Brisbane. Today this would be unthinkable: dangerous, illegal and bloody stupid. Nonetheless, it gave birth to my dream. I didn't have the guts to tell Dad, but I didn't want to be a swimmer, an Olympian.

I wanted to drive a car.

Lights Out

Again I was being woken, but this time not by Dad.

'Rich, it's Christmas,' my sister whispered as she pushed and pulled and punched me to get out of bed.

My childhood house was at Coorparoo, a small working-class neighbourhood on the southern side of Brisbane, and on this morning, tinsel and the crisp smell of pine filled our home.

This was the third house from my childhood I can really remember. It was on Shire Street and was quite big, even almost grand, for that time. The house's exterior was nailed with neatly painted weatherboard, and inside were airy hallways and stained wooden floors.

I didn't have my own bedroom. None of us did. There were simply too many of us to have our own room. Aside from me and my two big sisters, Robyn and Diane, I also had two little brothers, Peter and David, or Dyno as he was later known.

We slept out in an old verandah that had been converted into one long hall. There were five single beds lined up, like in a hospital ward. We were close enough to touch each other with an outstretched hand. We called it 'the sleep-out'. And it was mob rules.

'Get up, Richard,' she shouted.

Before going to bed we had connected all our toes with a piece of string. It was supposed to have acted like an alarm clock; when one moved, we all did. But on this morning it hadn't worked.

I rolled out of bed and it was pitch-black. What was it with early mornings in the Johnson house? It must have been about 3 am, but that didn't matter because there were presents to find. I thought about the wrapping paper, all the ripping, tearing and what lay beneath, as we ventured off into the deathly quiet house. My sister was fumbling round in the dark.

CLICK, click.

'The light doesn't work,' she said.

We grabbed each other, held hands and negotiated our way through the black nothing.

CLICK, click.

'Neither does this one.'

Like most kids, we couldn't wait until Christmas Day. It annoyed the hell out of Dad, who was no doubt desperate for a good night's sleep before a rare day-off.

CLICK, click.

'Nup, this is out too,' my sister said.

We had no idea, as we bumped and barged our way through the dark, that Dad had come up with an ingenious plan to stop our early morning raid, probably after one drink too many at the annual Johnson Christmas Eve house party. All wobbly legged and light-headed, bravely with stepladder in hand, he must've pulled out every light bulb inside, hoping to force us kids back to bed.

All except one.

CLICK.

'This one works!' my sister said. 'Go and get the presents.'

The bathroom light must have been too high for Dad, even with his ladder. He probably thought we would give up before finding it. Wrong. So Mum woke up and there were the five of us, sitting in the bathroom on a *very* early Christmas morning, ripping presents open.

She smiled.

The 1950s were a wonderful time. The tallest building in Brisbane was the Town Hall, which is now dwarfed by an even larger house. The thriving city wasn't more than dust and dirt back then. It was a big country town, a bit like Townsville is today. Places like Sunnybank and Mount Gravatt were out in the sticks.

As kids we could do anything. We could roam around at night without a care in the world. There were few dangers, and we had little to worry about. We knew everyone in the street. Even the local police sergeant knew us by name.

Our biggest fear was Mum. One day I came home sucking on lollies while coins rattled in my prodigiously pleated pants. She looked at me with a fierce frown.

'Where did you get that from?' Mum demanded. 'No boy of mine steals.'

She proceeded to belt my bum three shades of blue.

I hadn't been stealing. I used to get on my billycart and collect sugar bags. I would head round to all the paddocks and pick up cow shit, horse shit and whatever other stinking delights I could find and sell them for a shilling a bag. I was only about nine then. I wouldn't say I was a budding entrepreneur; I just didn't get pocket money and that was the only way I could make an earning.

Though Mum did have every right to suspect I'd flogged the lollies. I had some history when it came to five-finger discounts.

The shopping centre at Stone's Corner was about seven kilometres away, and to get there we had to walk about 400 metres to the main road and catch the tram. (Believe it or not, Brisbane used to have the old clunking bits of metal that clung to the rails.) I was with Mum one day and I made a massive mistake.

For whatever reason it caught my eye. I can't say I was into what was considered women's work, but I flogged a crotchet needle. It's not like I wanted to throw together a doily, but I nicked it all the same. I whacked the thing in my pocket and tucked it under my pillow when I got home. I was sure Mum wasn't going to find it there. But she did.

'Richard,' she screamed. 'What is this? Where did you get it from?'

'I took it, Mum,' I replied, shaking at the knees. 'I nicked it.' I had to tell her the truth. She wasn't going to accept anything less.

'Right,' she said sternly, her soft, tender hands finding

brutish strength as they tightened around my forearm. 'You're coming with me.'

I can't remember her ever being that angry. She dragged me over to the phone and wound the thing like mad before getting the dial tone. The manager from Woolworths picked up at the other end and she told the man that her son was a thief, that he had stolen from the store and would be there within the hour to face the music.

Mum marched me back to the tram; it was the longest ride of my life. The whole time she didn't talk, just clutched at my arm with the force of a boa constrictor squeezing the life from a rat. I was shaking, sweating and red with embarrassment. Mum was fuming.

Then she dragged me through Woolworths before finally releasing my arm. I looked up. We were standing in the manager's office, and there was a big man behind the desk, staring at me through his glasses. Next to him was a police officer, decked out in blue. I almost shat myself.

I was about five then, and I was scared silly. I seriously thought I was going to jail. They made me admit what I did and I think I was even threatened with a cell. I'm not sure what was worse: being lectured by a representative of the law or the cold, silent ride on the tram. I had never seen my mother so disappointed and I never want to again. I had learned my lesson. I would never steal again. Never.

Even with the occasional smack with the wooden spoon, Mum was the soft one. She had nothing but love for us and always put the family first.

Dad was a bloody good bloke, and it saddens me that I don't know much about his past; I never asked. All I know is that Dad, Bob Johnson, came over to Australia on his own when he was just 19. He jumped on a ship from Dublin and took the long trip to Australia, to the new frontier. I don't think he made this choice out of hardship because his family was very well off. His father, my grandfather, was a building contractor and they owned streets of houses in Ireland, farms . . . stuff like that. I don't really know why Dad had left. I guess he just wanted to do things on his terms and make his own name.

Dad could fix anything. He was a master with his hands and that's what got him jobs in the early years. He worked on ships, living wherever the work took him, which included places like India. He disembarked at Port Adelaide and moved on to Adelaide in 1920. He first worked as a boundary rider on a big sheep property on the Murray River, lived in Sydney for a bit, and by the end of the 1930s moved to Brisbane, where he ended up as a car salesman for Eager's New Cars.

I think that's where he met my mum, who worked there too. He did pretty well for himself because Mum was a lot younger than him. Dad was 39 when he got married and Mum was only 23. He got a fair bit of resistance from Mum's side of the family when they first met because of his age, but everything worked out. They were together from start to finish and that's all that matters to me.

I was the firstborn boy, so I guess I was the apple of Dad's eye. He was already 45 when I came along. I didn't feel like I was the favourite or anything, but we did do a lot of stuff together. We'd always work in the yard, go fishing and, of course, go to the pool.

I don't know if I was cheeky, more adventurous I guess, but I got into my own share of trouble. I can remember a few hidings pretty well. Dad was a man of routine and he used to bundle us kids in the car every single Sunday to take us to Redcliffe for a swim. I can remember one Sunday he came out and told us we weren't going. I'd suspected he had a big night and was too hung-over to bother. We were living at our first house in Mackay Street.

'We can't go today because I've run out of petrol,' he said, matter-of-factly. 'Sorry, guys.'

So I took matters into my hand.

'We're right now, Dad,' I said proudly, about ten minutes later. 'We've got plenty of petrol; we're full.'

He stormed out of the house and went red with rage when he saw the hose sticking out of the car's tank. I'd filled the bloody thing up with water.

The old FX Holden wasn't going anywhere.

'What have you done?' he screamed.

I got a good whack on the bum before spending the rest of the day helping him bleed the old girl dry, but we eventually got it going. And I got my way because we ended up heading to the beach that afternoon.

Another Saturday comes to mind, but this time it wasn't me getting into trouble. My old man had obviously been to the pub for a while after work. He came home and my sisters had weeded the two big garden beds out front. Robyn and Diane had barrows full of dirt and stuff they'd pulled from the ground with their hands. They went up to Dad and showed him the barrow and asked him if they could have a shilling for all their hard work so they could go to the movies.

'No,' he said bluntly. 'You're not going to the movies – don't ask me again.'

But they kept on pestering.

'No, this is final,' he said. 'You are not going anywhere. Full stop.'

The next thing I saw was my two sisters down at the front yard, planting the weeds back into the ground. I don't remember how old I was, but I know I was old enough to think it was funny. I was pissing myself with laughter. What a classic.

The Billycart Kid

Sparks flew from the cast-iron wheels as they desperately tried to bite into the asphalt. Wind smacking into my face, I was pulled to the left, almost violently, as I attempted the 90-degree turn at the bottom of the street. The front right wheel screeched, slipped and slid. I wanted to lean to the right, into the corner, to help the brakeless beast through, but already I knew better. So I leaned to the left, against all natural judgement, and the iron wheels on the outside hit the road, giving me just enough grip to avoid a high-speed spin that would have sent me into the gutter and into the lap of one of the cheering parents.

I was on the home straight; finishing line in sight. The Coorparoo Cup was mine.

Victory.

From as early as I can recall, we used to make billycarts and race them down the street. Old bits of timber were slapped together with nails, belted with hammers and ripped apart by saws. The crude carts were where it all began for Dick Johnson.

I started building billycarts when I was about nine. I would hunt through the neighbourhood, finding all the lumber I could, and come home and bang them together. But the wheels were the problem; there was just nothing available. I searched the yard for something that would do the job. Car wheels: no. Bike wheels: no. Wood carved into wheels: no. Mum's washing-basket trolley wheels: yes! They were perfect. About 12 centimetres across, lined with black rubber, they were the best-looking wheels I had ever seen.

So I got out my screwdriver, tossed the trolley on its side and went about taking them off.

'Richard,' Mum screamed, as she dragged the metal carcass along the neatly mown grass. 'What have you done?'

She needn't have asked. She already knew.

The first billycarts were primitive, but after a while I became more inventive. Everyone, including myself at that point, was steering the four-wheeled weapons with a piece of rope tied to the front axle. You tugged on the right-hand side to go right and the left-hand side to go left. Simple stuff. But that wasn't enough for me; I wanted a steering wheel, just like the one Dad used to sit me dead-smack in the middle of when I was nine months old. So, using my knowledge of Meccano sets and a childhood spent ripping machines apart, I went about building myself the best billycart on the block. It seemed pretty simple. I made a steering column, then grabbed some rope and pulled it around. I tied it to the front axle before throwing on an old Holden wheel I'd found in a wreck.

Then I started my descent, chest puffed, smug smile. The slow roll quickly turned into a healthy chug as my high-tech machine was helped along by gravity. Then–

Whack!

I was sitting on the ground bloody and busted following a spectacular roll. I had smashed into the gutter and had launched into the air, before sliding along concrete and grass. I had forgotten about the small design flaw – a minor but costly mistake. The thing had been hooked up backwards. It was all in reverse. You needed to turn the wheel left to make it go right. I knew this because we had tested it, but when I reached the corner my natural instincts took over and I turned right to go right. Ouch.

It would be the first of many mistakes, and certainly not the worst.

There were about six guys from the neighbourhood who I built and raced the billycarts with, and this included Anthony Eisler, Tony Newton and his brother Nicky. We were all good mates and got together and mucked about most afternoons.

I was always messing around with anything that had wheels and a motor. I just loved mechanical devices. To cut the grass we had one of those barrow mowers. I would take the muffler off and put a bit of pipe on there to make an open exhaust so I could fire up and down the yard, ears full of the engine.

Anthony Eisler's mother owned a foundry, where

craphouse components were made. I never knew Anthony's dad because he died before I was around. They used to make toilet cisterns; the big cast-iron tanks that sat above outdoor dunnies.

Anthony was a few years older than me and was just as mad for cars. What a team! We used to hang out at the foundry, and it didn't take us long to work out we could use all the high-tech machinery to make some wheels. With the help of some of the men, the hardworking factory types clad in blue overalls and dripping with sweat, we designed a pattern. We then built the casts and filled them with iron.

We raced on bitumen, so I'm not sure if they were such a great idea. But other than getting a smack on the bum from my mother, it was the best option we had. We would race down Woodhill Avenue, wheel to wheel, all gritted teeth and deathly stares. Everything was good until we got to the lane, when all hell broke loose because the shithouse factory wheels had about as much grip as a dog on lino.

We raced every fortnight. We'd marshal at the top of the street, fathers ready to push, and mothers lining the road, clapping and cheering. We even had a trophy, the Coorparoo Cup. I'm not sure who made it, but it was an old china cup, which had lost its handle, that was stuck onto an old board. And more often than not, it sat on my mantelpiece. I was rarely beat.

This is where racing began for me. On the road, mates by my side, a thrill a minute. And maybe it was in my blood too. Dad wanted me to swim, or go work in a sparkling white office, all shirt and tie. He didn't want me anywhere near grease and grime, but in a way maybe it was his fault I enjoy racing so much. I have no idea if it was true, I never checked, but he reckoned he did a bit of racing before he settled down. Dad said he used to do the old Mount Druitt circuit. And he worked in a car yard, so he couldn't blame me for loving everything engine and steel.

But when I was ten, I didn't dream of becoming a race car driver. Instead, I had my heart set on becoming a motor mechanic.

I was always good with my hands. We had a lot of lantana bushes around Camp Hill in the really early days. And I had this you-beaut idea to build myself a bow and arrow using these plants, inspired by the black-and-white cowboy movies we would watch on Saturdays.

Mum thought it was a terrible idea.

'No, Richard,' she said. 'You'll hurt someone. Go back and play with your cars.'

I didn't listen, of course. I sat there for a couple of hours with some tools and chiselled, whittled and cut until I had my bow. I then got to the arrow, sharpening the moist wood until I had fashioned it into a pointy end. With all my might, I pulled back on the taut string and shot the arrow into the air. I looked to the heavens, dreaming about the Indian I was about to bring down.

'Ouuuuch!'

I turned around and saw the arrow sticking straight out the top of Mum's head, blood trickling down her face.

I nearly died.

I ran around the corner and smashed the weapon into a thousand pieces. I tried to hide, but she found me huddling behind the shed. With a deep frown, she pulled the finely crafted arrow from her head. Thankfully, it was just a minor injury.

'Your mother is always right, Richard,' she said. 'Remember that.'

It was strange that I hit her because I was never a great shot. Just ask the old bloke who lived over the road at Coorparoo. He could never work out why his roof gutters leaked. We weren't trying to flood his yard, but we weren't too good with the old Daisy slug gun we used to shoot. We were aiming at pigeons, not the metal on his roof.

Playing war games, we found a small piece of water pipe and jammed a penny bunger inside. Then we shoved the wick through a drilled screw cap on the end. We rammed paper into the thing, some rocks too, and lit it.

Bang!

I'm glad Mum never stood in front of that one.

How we didn't kill anyone, I don't know.

2

OGDENS, PISS AND
HUMPY HOLDENS

Give Me Fuel, Give Me Fire

We needed an engine; there were no two ways about it. The old billycart, full of rusty nails and worn timber, hadn't lost its thrill, but boy, were we sick of pushing.

'Your turn to push,' one of the billycart crew members said.

'No, it's your turn,' said another.

I got the shits, sitting in the old girl, waiting to be fired down the hill. 'Let's just get an engine.'

They looked at me with a deafening silence, till finally it broke.

'Where the hell do we get one of them from?' Tony Newton asked.

'Well, your dad's lawnmower looks pretty good,' I said.

Tony Newton's dad had a state-of-the-art Ogden lawnmower, which he kept in the back shed. Tony didn't have

18

the slightest hesitation when I suggested we rip it apart and strap the engine to our wooden billycart. So I grabbed a screwdriver, some pliers and a wrench and went to work.

I was only ten at the time, but my mates had confidence in my abilities despite me being about two years younger than them. They knew I could do the job.

My parents had always encouraged my fascination for nuts and bolts, nails and washers. When I was six they bought me an old cuckoo clock that was in pieces and set me the challenge of rebuilding it. A yellow bird launched from its wooden lair and woke them the very next morning.

It took about ten minutes to pull the old Ogden apart. That was the easy bit.

But it took us a while longer to figure out how to get the thing on, and more importantly how to get the engine's power to reach the wheels. Once again the foundry proved our saviour. I had a pretty good grasp of engineering and knew that motorised go-karts used a chain to send power from the engine to the wheels. We couldn't get our hands on anything that high-tech, but there were plenty of belts and pulleys lying around at the factory. We worked out what we needed and went about flogging the parts.

After bolting on the engine with some old coach bolts we found in someone's shed, we went about hooking the kart up with a V-belt drive. It was crude, almost prehistoric, but I knew it would work.

So, hoping it would be the final push, the last of the heave-ho, we bent our backs and manhandled the thing down to the school for a test. We had to keep it top secret because the threat of a flogging loomed. Hopefully Tony Newton's dad wasn't in the mood to mow his lawn.

The Coorparoo State High School was about 500 metres away. The playground was mostly three acres of brown dirt. A concrete cricket pitch rose from the middle, and closer to the bricks and weatherboard was a small section of bitumen used for assembly. We weren't concerned about building a track, never thought to mark anything out, to move old bins or take off shoes to create turns. We just wanted to fire the thing up and go.

Brrrrrr!

With a momentous heave on the rope, the engine rumbled to life. The old wooden kart shuddered as the Ogden engine rocked and revved. But would it work? I jumped into the cockpit, sure and steady. I had no doubt I would soon be hurtling around the playground. So I grabbed at the throttle, a piece of metal sticking from the engine, with my right hand and steadied the reins with my left. I pulled the thing up and I was away.

Whoosh!

She had a top speed of about 20 k/h, but that was fine. We had a self-powered kart and the days of pushing were over. It was my first taste of mechanically powered freedom. And being the chief engineer of this machine, I felt an overwhelming sense of pride.

The racing bug got stronger and our bums got sorer when Tony Newton's old man found out he didn't have an engine on his lawnmower.

'Where's my bloody engine?' he yelled. 'What's happened to my lawnmower? *Tony!*'

He then found the kart in the shed. All pride of place, we had shoved over boxes of tools, old broomsticks and spades to clear a prime space for the machine.

We were told not to do it again, but, of course, we did. We just got a bit smarter about it and took the engine when the grass was short, returning it long before the lawn needed a trim. We might've even mowed the lawn ourselves at times to stop Tony's dad searching for the powerless thing.

Despite my love for anything with wheels, I never had a pushbike. My parents couldn't afford it then, so I used to borrow one from the guy over the back. It was only a half-size deal, but that didn't matter. I would push the bike until it would wobble and shake. I loved riding on it, the freedom and the speed, and I couldn't help racing everything.

One day I decided to race a tram. It didn't look that quick; I was sure I could take the rattling, rocking people-mover constricted to rails. So I took off. Pumped my little legs until my thighs burned. Arse out of the seat, I pounded at the pedals and shook the handles, trying to extract every ounce of speed. I looked to the left and the tram was edging out of sight. It was winning.

No! I thought. *I can't lose.*

I raised my bum further into the air and looked to the ground. I watched my knees bouncing up and down and willed them for more.

Splat!

The skin on my knees and elbows was ripped apart by dirt and gravel and I momentarily blacked out. I came to an excruciating halt as my neighbour's bike slid under the tram, sparking as it hurtled across the tar. I looked down at my arm, expecting to find blood.

But there was none. I was covered in white.

I turned to my left and saw an old Italian lady lying on the ground. The bag of flour she was carrying was torn apart, now all over me and her too. Evidently the tram had stopped and I had caught it. I'd also caught the poor woman, who had her groceries in hand. The poor bird didn't even make the footpath. Our run-in had clobbered her fair and square, the impact sending her bag of flour and sunglasses crashing to the ground. She was on her backside in a world of hurt, and started screaming in Italian.

'Gran disgraziato,' she swore. 'Mannaggia tua. Bastardo.'

She jumped to her feet, pointed at me and spat before leaving in a huff. She was rightfully pissed, but all I could think was that I had won. I had caught the tram.

High Voltage

Sitting behind my desk at school, daydreaming after another early morning swim, my thoughts of motors and mayhem were interrupted by a sudden warmth.

Mmm, what's that? I thought, as my second-grade teacher scribbled on the blackboard.

My delight turned to disgust when I felt the wet seep through my pleated shorts and onto my skin.

That's piss, I thought. *The girl next to me has* bloody *pissed on me!*

I jumped to the air screaming, 'What the hell?' and my

suspicions were confirmed when I saw yellow liquid pooling in the chair.

Back then we shared a bench seat. We sat behind old wooden desks built for two; the type with ink wells and lifting lids, and room for a sandwich and apple inside. The twin sit wasn't flat. It had a gentle slope that declined to the middle and that's what had sent the piss rushing towards my pants.

I'd sat there wondering about the warmth for too long. I was utterly soaked by the time I sprang to my feet, absolutely repulsed.

'Dick's pissed himself,' the other kids said and laughed, as I stood in front of the class drenched and stinking of foul.

I looked to the dirty little bird who had pissed all over me and gave her the stare of death.

It was one of the most embarrassing moments of my early life.

I was a terrible student. I just wanted to be a mechanic and I felt like I was learning a bunch of meaningless crap at school. I could never work out why they rewarded you for doing something well by giving you a job. The gun gig was getting to ring the bell. If you did well in a test, or paid attention for long enough, you would get the privilege of ringing the bell. It's fair to say I didn't usher in the school day all that often.

Most of the time, my job was to deliver the milk. Back in my day we used to have milk dropped off at school, but it would be rank by the time I got to it. Off and ready to curdle, thanks to the brutal Queensland sun. And the shit tasted absolutely terrible, but it must've been good for the immune system because we never got sick. What bacteria stood a chance when we were used to guzzling that crap?

When I was good I got to deliver the milk. When I was bad I got smashed over the palm with a taut piece of bamboo. I'd stand still, looking at the emotionless principal as he cocked his arm and drew the cane over his shoulder.

Whack!

The pain rippled into my palm. With gritted teeth I bore its brunt and looked down at my hand as the red mark rose and turned into a welt.

Getting the cane wasn't so bad – it was usually over in an instant. What was worse was waiting outside the bloody principal's office. They used to make you wait for an hour or more so you could stew in your menace, to think about getting whacked and how much it would hurt. The discipline was tough and I didn't mind it one bit. It kept us in line and there should be more of it today. Kids get away with far too much for my liking.

But we certainly weren't angels.

'AAAARGH,' the teacher screamed as he ran out of the brasco, pants around his ankles. He tucked his old fella in, his face a deep shade of red.

We were nowhere to be found.

The phones back in the 1950s used to have a big old handle sticking from the side. You needed to wind the rotary dial in order to generate the electricity to make the call. It was what they called a 'dynamo'. Anyway, being the cheeky little buggers we were, we used to rip the machines apart and hook them up to the tin urinals in the teachers' toilet. We would snake the wire from the pisser to our feet, far enough away not to be seen – and, more importantly, not to be caught – and wind like hell when we heard the sound of urine belting into steel.

The teachers didn't know what hit them. Piss all over their pants, electrical volts ringing in their manhood. No doubt it was worse than the cane!

My mates and I could be little shits at times. The street we lived in was only four houses or so down from Cavendish Road. We didn't get much traffic, but we came up with a plan to have a laugh at the expense of those brave enough to turn right. We would grab an old empty shoebox and wrap it up to the nines to make it look like a present: paper, ribbon and card. We would stick the thing in the middle of the road and hide behind bushes, letterboxes or whatever else would give us cover. And sure enough, some drivers couldn't resist.

Errrrrrr.

The brakes would squeal as they came to an abrupt halt. We would try to suppress our laughter as the driver sat in the cabin, looking right to left, wondering if they could pinch the package anonymously. Some would shake their heads before hitting the accelerator and taking off. Most would jump out of the car, scoop the thing up and leave like a thief in the night. It was hilarious.

But that wasn't enough for us ratbags. Once they left, our box of nothing was gone and we'd have to go about wrapping another. And we hated wrapping. So, being as smart as we were, we decided to tie a piece of string around the hollow gift and wrap the other end around our fingers. We would yank at the package just before their outstretched hands found their mark.

Whack!

They would jump into the air before turning bright red, waiting to be humiliated. Then we'd emerge, laughing until our stomachs hurt. Word of our prank spread, and one day the fire department turned up – we thought we were done. Instead, a strapping man climbed down from the lofty cabin and smiled. He gave us two bob each.

A bloke down the road didn't think it was as funny as the firefighter. He used to plough over our fancy boxes, sending them flying into a thousand pieces. We fixed that, and his Holden, one day by finally putting a present in the box – a four-kilo besser brick. Ouch.

Lighter Fluid

The old MG TF screeched and smoked as it hurtled from the track. I almost fell off Dad's shoulders as the 6000 or so people launched into a deafening roar. He grabbed at my legs, trying to steady me, but I fell towards the turf as the little red rocket gripped, spun and tore its rubber in an angry bid to rejoin the thunderous mob. I was in Dad's arms by the time the MG TF belted into the unsuspecting Triumph.

Not surprisingly, I used to live for the weekends; especially when I knew Dad was taking me to a race. With brown-bread sandwiches packed for lunch, Dad would throw me into the back of the car and take me to a place called Strathpine. It wasn't far away, but I couldn't stand the drive. I just wanted to get there and watch these guys race.

Strathpine was a dusty bowl with lashings of tar broken up from excessive use. An old airfield, with winged carcasses and relics galore, it was the home of motor racing in Brisbane. A high-speed racetrack for the weekend warriors and the early pioneers of an Australian sport that was very much in its infancy.

I think I went to my first race in 1957. I can remember blokes like Brian Tebble and Dennis Geary ragging their prehistoric beasts to the point of extinction. There were Porsches, MGs, Humpy Holdens and Triumph TR2s. Streamlined bits of metal, marvels of the time, were being riffled, revved and sometimes ruined. There were no roll cages or side intrusion bars. No aerodynamic advances or water-cooled brakes. No sequential shifts or race-bred rubber. These cars were pure production class, rolled off the showroom floor, tuned, tinkered and flogged. The biggest modification you would see back then was a sparkling MG slapped with an aluminium bonnet held down by chunky bits of leather strap. They would also put motorcycle mudguards on the wheels' arches. Why? Stuffed if I know.

The drivers were even less modified. They would rock up in a fancy singlet and their best pair of thongs. Yeah, they had helmets – if you could call them that – and their only other bit of protection was an archaic bit of strap they called a seatbelt.

Strathpine was little more than a runway with a couple of cones at either end. There was a frightening straight, all flat stick and blown engines, before a hairpin turn that would scorch the brakes and send the reckless brave hurtling into the dirt and debris. After that there was another breakneck straight, guarded by bales of hay, which were often sent flying towards the crowd. Another hairpin ruined the rubber, and back you went to the start.

Simple stuff, but more than enough to make me forget about billycarts and dream of becoming something more. I thought it was the best thing in the world. I also believed that one day I would become a race car driver, so I bought books and read up on the Formula One and everything happening overseas in the motor racing world.

Watching guys like Tebble, smoking his wheels and sending his MG sideways, sparked my lifelong addiction. It became more than a fantasy, a dream, and nothing was going to stop me. I suppose that's why I started fucking around with Anthony Eisler's car.

Anthony was a fair bit older than me. He was a great neighbour, loved hotted-up cars and was my best mate. He got his licence just before he went to college and his parents bought him a car – a brand spanking new Austin Lancer.

'What are you doing, Rich?' he asked.

'Mate, I'm just giving it a valve grind, you know,' I replied, my arms greased up to the elbows, cylinder head lying next to grimy boots.

'Oh, OK. Sweet.' Anthony joined in.

The car didn't need any work, but I couldn't help myself, and neither could he. We would be in the bloody thing at any given moment. Heads out the window, driving for the sake of ripping up the road. But our ambitions outweighed our piggy bank balance and we often didn't have enough money for fuel.

'Dick, what are we going to do?' Anthony asked one day, as the car spluttered before its untimely death.

It was pitch-black and we were in the middle of nowhere.

'OK, you stay with the car,' I said. 'I'll go and find some fuel.'

I jumped out and walked down the road, my path occasionally lit by the headlights of a passing vehicle. I stuck my thumb out, but no one stopped. I reckon I walked for three kilometres or so before I stumbled across a grocery store that happened to be open.

'I'll have some Shellite,' I said.

Shellite was an old fluid used for cleaning metals and filling lighters. It wasn't supposed to be put in cars, but it was cheap and I suspected it would do the job.

Brrrrrrrrrrr.

And I was right. The car fired to life and we were away. I thought I was a genius. It wouldn't be the last time the Austin got a dose of that stuff.

Sing and Swing

Anthony had a gardener whose name was Henry. And we used to give him the shits.

'*Around the corner . . . looking for Henry Lee,*' we would sing.

It was a song from decades back and we would launch into tune whenever we saw him. Gee, it drove him mad. The silly bugger would chase us all day. A man well into his 50s, he didn't stand a chance.

Henry was a proud war veteran and would strut around on Anzac Day, metal clinging to his chest. He was a good style of fella, but we used to get stuck into him all the same.

'*Around the corner . . . looking for Henry Lee.*'

Henry used to have a motorbike – well, not quite. It was one of those things that had pedals you'd have to pump to go up the hill. As Henry toiled away, digging dirt and pruning trees, we'd go to the shed and find some rope, keen to get back at him for making us run up the street. We would tie the rope to the back of his wheel and sit back, waiting for him to leave. Finally, he'd finish, get on his bike and chug away at the pedals, no doubt happy to be leaving a hard day's work behind.

Whoosk!

He was on the ground, swearing and out for blood.

'*Around the corner . . . looking for Henry Lee.*'

Henry grabbed the shovel out but couldn't catch us. Poor bugger. Next day he was arse over head again.

'*Around the corner . . . looking for Henry Lee.*'

Our neighbourhood was a happy place. We got into some mischief every now and then, but all in all, the people in the street were just like family. Well, apart from the mob over the back. The Woodrow family refused to have anything to do with the Johnsons and couldn't stand the ruckus we made. Maybe they were Churchies, certainly bookworms, and they didn't appreciate besser bricks and bungers, slug guns and shenanigans. We Johnson kids were on strict orders to stay clear. But one day we just couldn't resist.

Clang, clang.

The sound of metal smashing into wood caught my attention. I looked over to the Woodrows' yard and was captivated by a huge sleeper swinging into place. I stared through a tiny slit in the back fence, three or four of my mob by my side. The old Woodrow fella was building his little girls a swing set, the likes of which I had never seen before. All hardwood and concrete base, it was a towering marvel. With my sisters jostling me aside to get a view, I watched as he poured the last of the concrete into the hole before hitching the swing to the crossbar.

'Shit, we have to try this thing out,' I said.

So we waited until the Woodrows left, and we climbed over the fence. Once we reached the set and I got on the swing, my sister hurled me into the sky.

Woohoo!

She was up next and it was my turn to push. We went like maniacs, pushing each other and kicking our legs in the air for an hour or so before taking off the way we came.

The Woodrows returned a few hours later. I think I was back in our yard kicking a ball when I overheard them.

'Blast it,' the old Woodrow fella said. 'I didn't do a thing wrong.'

'Well, you must've,' said his wife. 'You can't tell me that's the way it's supposed to be.'

The big supporting sleepers were sitting at 40 degrees. I wasn't about to tell him, or his fuming wife, that we'd jumped on the thing before the concrete had set. Oh well. Karma . . . or something like that.

During the school holidays I was nowhere to be found.

'Where's Richard?' Mum would shout. 'Dinner's ready.'

And sure enough, not long after she worked out I was missing, I'd arrive home. Sometimes I'd be dropped off in a steam-roller, other times in a tractor, maybe even in a dump truck.

'He's been a great help,' the council worker would say. 'No trouble at all; better than the blokes I pay.'

Cavendish Road was always under construction when I was young and I was drawn to the heavy machinery and the men who made it happen. I would pack my sandwich, throw it into a tin and go to work. I reckon I was eight around then, and I'd take up a shovel as soon as I got there. They were putting road base in, shovelling shit into the manholes, and I'd help out. I got to sit on the machinery, pull on gears and levers – stuff you couldn't dream of today.

I was always going missing, and Mum would worry sick, to the point that she'd ring the police.

'You poor thing,' the local sergeant used to say to her. 'You're like the mother of Ginger Meggs – your boy's always getting into strife. How do you do it?'

3

DIRT AND DANCING

Drying Off

Bang!

The cap gun fired and I was a thrashing machine. I launched myself from the concrete block, a flash of arms and feet destroying the clear blue water that stood between me and victory. With cupped hands, I tore at the water and sent it rushing towards my hips. My chest heaved as I twisted my neck, launching my head into the air for a short gasp of air.

Whack!

Before I could even settle into a rhythm it was over. My wrist thundered into the wall and I pulled my head from the deep, watching on as my wake slammed against the end of the pool.

The other competitors were still swimming, but I was one hand on the edge, tossing the chlorine from my brow. I looked across the water and saw Dad, who was euphorically clapping and cheering. My coach Joe Emerson looked down at his watch. He smiled.

I had broken a metropolitan record. Only ten years old at the time, I'd clocked 31.7 to smash the 50-metre freestyle under-12s national record.

Dad pulled me from the pool and gave me an ecstatic embrace. He was as proud as punch. But me . . . well, I couldn't have given a rat's arse. I'd won by three body lengths, obliterated the competition, but I wasn't interested in swimming.

I quit soon after. The record may have stood for 25 years, but my swimming career was over. *Finally*. I'd always hated training, and it seemed to get harder as I got older, reaching a stage where the only thing good about the daily dawn trips to the pool was seeing sheilas in their swimsuits. Dad loved the pool and wanted me to continue swimming. My coach also thought the sun shined out of my arse and urged me to keep on going. Joe had a lot of very good swimmers in his squad, but for whatever reason he thought I was a special talent.

Quitting didn't happen suddenly. I didn't dig my heels in and refuse, it kind of just fizzled out. When I got to high school, swimming became a chore and got a bit too hard for everyone, Dad included. My sisters were older and they started to lose interest in the sport, which probably helped; one dropped off and the others followed. My younger brothers never got into swimming and all of a sudden it was all over. *Thank God.*

I was never going to be an Olympian, but I still admired those who were. Given the old man's obsession with the pool, I couldn't help but be inspired by the likes of John and Ilsa Konrads. They were everywhere in those days and were true role models of Australian sport. I think Dawn Fraser was also on her way to becoming a great champion, and I would bump into them at different meets. But for me, swimming was early mornings and burning eyes, endless black lines and sore shoulders.

Looking back, I'm very grateful for the lessons I learned from my swimming experience, gaining traits that would help me throughout my life and career in terms of discipline and fitness. Waking up at the crack of dawn and slugging it out in the deep taught me that you needed to work hard in order to get somewhere in life. You had to make sacrifices to become the best. I also learned how to smash through the pain barrier, to break through that point when you say enough is enough and want to pull out. Through swimming I learned how to ignore the pain and to push on, all gritted teeth and steely determination. I learned you can find another gear and things eventually get easier; the pain subsides and a second wind blissfully blows on in.

Swimming was about rhythm, timing, harmony and coordination. Finding that perfect balance and place where everything just works itself out – which wasn't too different from the sport I would turn to next. I remember seeing it in Kieren Perkins in 1992 – the ideal example of a man in his element.

Before the Barcelona Olympics, Kieren, his dog in tow, was out on the water one day, cruising around in a boat. I knew Kieren and steered on up to say hello. He was under a lot of pressure, copping it from the media and the public. Around that time, no one thought he was fit, and his performances had been poor leading into the games.

I thought I could help.

'Kieren, just ignore it, mate,' I said, as the water lapped at my boat's bow. 'You know where you are and you know what you can do. If you start listening to them, you might just believe it.'

He nodded.

As I watched him stranded in the outside lane in the 1992 Olympics 1500-metre final, I knew he was going to win after just 400 metres. His rhythm and timing were impeccable. You could count the strokes from one end of the pool to the other and they wouldn't change. His turns were identical, same hand thundering into the same spot. He was in the zone, and once you're there you are unbeatable.

Ties, Blazers and Two Tonnes of Dirt

In high school, there was a senior staff member who found great joy in making our lives hell.

It was time for some payback.

'We'll have two tonnes of dirt, please,' my mate yelled down the line. 'Yes, that's right, two tonnes. Can I please have it delivered right on the driveway? Yep, just dump it straight down. Oh, and just stick the bill in the letterbox. I'm good for it.'

Later that day, after rushing back from school, we waited at the other end of the street. The dirt had been delivered by then and it was everywhere, spewing all over the neatly manicured lawn. There was more dirt than we'd ever dreamed of. Everything was stained brown.

'What in the world?' he screamed when he finally got

there, his once-perfect yard now covered with tonnes of dirt. 'What is this? God damn it!'

His face went so red we half-expected for steam to rush out from underneath his collar. He launched his polished shoes into the mountain of dirt, kicking and yelling in a perfect fit of rage.

It was priceless.

We weren't there when he checked the mail, but I suspect it was equally as good, maybe even better . . .

Overall, though, high school was OK. It was a new adventure, with new people, and more importantly I was another step closer to entering the workforce. Even back then, on my first day of high school, I was planning my exit strategy. I was going to do what was asked: take the tests, study, learn all that crap. But as soon as I was 14 and nine months, I was out.

I was going to become a mechanic. End of story.

My parents, however, had other ideas. They didn't want their son becoming a tradesman, worst of all, a grease monkey. They were better than that. They wanted a doctor, a lawyer, even a teacher, so they made the ambitious and costly call to send me to Brisbane Grammar School. My parents had hoped that sending me there would kick the dirty dream of grease and gears out of me. A top-drawer school that had produced 24 Rhodes scholars, a deputy premier and even a Justice of the High Court, Brisbane Grammar was all ties, blazers and boring, and I was never going to last. It wasn't my cup of tea with its stone walkways, mahogany arches and grassy quadrangles full of lunchtime political debate. But I didn't whine once about not wanting to be there. I was happy to wear the tie, the blazer and do whatever ridiculous homework was set.

Evidently, it didn't take long for my parents to realise they were wasting their cash. I was never the sort of kid who'd be slumped in a chair reading a book or stewing over an equation. I was the little bloke out in the yard, ripping into whatever he could find. With two girls at Brisbane Girls Grammar, my parents were already financially stretched. For whatever reason, I really don't know why, they made the decision to pull me out and send me elsewhere after just two terms, much to my relief.

I ended up at the much cheaper, more practical Cavendish Road High School, and that suited me fine. I think my parents were a little disappointed, but it was the right place for me. I didn't mind my new school; there were new people to meet, new troubles to find. But it was still school, and choosing my subjects turned into a fight.

'Dad, I don't need to do French,' I argued. 'When am I ever going to use that? Let me do metalwork, woodwork, something with tools. I'm not planning on going to Paris.'

My pleas fell on deaf ears. Although I wanted to do trade-based subjects, my parents were still determined to set me on an academic path. I had bombed out of Brisbane Grammar, but my parents were still deadset against me ending up in a factory or a yard. I was good with my hands, not with my brain.

But I did like Maths because it was a subject that made some sense to me. I liked the fact that it was structured, and you couldn't progress to the next level until you'd mastered the first. But languages? What a waste of time! I also did art, which was pretty funny because I couldn't even draw a stick man, still can't. Even funnier was the fact that I passed.

We all liked Physics, not because of what we were being taught but because of who was teaching it.

'Miss, has this expanded at the right rate?' someone would ask, grabbing at a metallic stick.

'Is it big enough for you?'

She would slam down the penis-shaped object and we'd laugh. Despite her frown and blush, she was a pretty little thing. Very young, and her name was – wait for it . . . Miss Penell. It was worse than another teacher we once had, called Mr Condon. We gave her heaps, took the piss at every opportunity, and looking back I feel very sorry for her. But I'm sure we were tame compared to what some of the teachers cop today.

It was about this time that I'd started dancing.

Believe it or not, I used to shuffle, shimmy and step. It might sound a bit how's-it-going? but back then I attended dancing lessons. I'd go down to the School of Arts Hall on Cavendish Road every Thursday for lessons, and believe me, it wasn't because I wanted anything Broadway. I did it simply for the girls. All the good sorts were there, so I went chasing. I was always on the lookout for something.

One day at the hall the teacher's old gramophone failed to fire. He whacked and walloped the thing, screamed and shouted, but it refused to pump out a tune. He looked to the class.

'Does anyone have a gramophone at home?' he asked. He didn't want to cancel the lesson and refund the money we'd all paid.

'Yeah, I do,' one of the boys replied. 'My parents have the new whiz-bang one at home.'

'OK,' the teacher said. 'Who has a licence? I need someone to go pick it up.'

He was met with silence, not a hand in the air.

'OK, who knows how to drive?'

My hand shot straight up. He threw me the keys to his FB Holden.

It was probably a ten-minute drive but it took us half an hour. We went up to the school, smashing the car through the dirt and showing it off to the girls. Eventually we got back to the lesson, cranked up the gramophone, pulled the prettiest little things we could find in nice and tight, and waltzed the night away.

Not too long ago I got a call from Channel 7. They wanted me to be a contestant on the TV show *Dancing With The Stars*.

'Do you want to laugh at a geriatric with two left feet?' I shouted. 'Get stuffed. You've got to be kidding.'

Packed Lunch, Dashing Dave and Twisted Metal

The Cooper Maserati screamed off the line. Amidst a sea of gleaming metal and smoking rubber, it launched into the straight, turning and twisting as it jostled for position on the flat-out runway. The machine was red-lining as the former airforce runway extracted every ounce of power from the 1.5-litre machine. It darted and dashed, looking for the best line. What happened next would leave the 3000-strong crowd stunned and silent.

Until they began running for their lives.

Screams of terror filled the air as John Hough's $4000 race car collided into Clive Nolan's Lotus 20. The open-wheeled rocket then launched into the air, before slamming back to the ground and taking off again, this time quicker and totally out of control. Spilling into a barrel roll, the car was spat into the ground, then the air . . . ground again then air, spewing bits of metal as it hurtled from the track and towards the terrified crowd.

The spectators didn't know where to run. With a death machine blasting their way, they screamed and scattered, hopelessly trying to anticipate the trajectory of the metal hurricane, which was now on fire. The freewheeling Cooper tore through the fence before smashing into the turf and picnic boxes.

Crack!

The machine finally exploded into a parked car that had three people trapped inside. Pieces of glass, rubber, metal and engine flew into the sky.

I was at Lowood the day John Hough died. Remarkably, the people in the car his Cooper had hit survived, but Hough, an up-and-coming race star was dead – at 25.

Hough had just bought his Cooper Maserati from Dennis Geary. He had worked on the thing, hoping it would help him fulfil his dream of winning the Australian Drivers' Championship, maybe even one day earning him the coveted title. But his dream had ended tragically when he became another victim of open-wheeled madness.

Hough was killed instantly. I remember standing by horrified, watching the chaos unfold with my family. He was doing about 80 miles an hour when he turned in and collected a wheel. He never stood a chance with barely a seatbelt and a prehistoric roll cage to keep him alive.

The day had already been one to forget for the Johnsons. Dad had convinced Mum and the girls to come along for a rare race outing, which in itself was a big deal as they weren't really into that sort of thing. Not long after arriving at the track, an old airforce base in the middle of nowhere, Mum screamed.

'Where's David?' she said, panicked. 'He was just here.'

We all shrugged. I turned to my left and then to my right, but I couldn't see him.

'Where is he?' she continued, her forehead creasing with concern.

I looked straight ahead. 'There he is,' I said, pointing.

Dyno was on the racetrack, cars striking through like lighting by his side. He had dodged his way through the masses and was on the other side of the wire barrier that separated the crowd from the loud and deadly machines.

Mum almost fainted.

We rounded him up, smacked his arse, and Mum wanted to go home then and there.

'That's enough,' she said. 'Never again.'

But we talked her into staying, and then Hough died.

I had probably been to a half-a-dozen races before the horror of Lowood. Dad would take me when he could, but they were few and far between. I will always remember this day because even though we thought we could bring Mum round to liking the sport, after Dyno's dash and then

Hough's death, she was adamant she wanted nothing to do with it ever.

For me, Hough's fatal crash didn't dull the dream or put a doubt in my mind. Even back then, I was extremely confident in my own abilities. Sure, my experience was limited to homemade karts and joyrides in Dad's car, but I'd always felt in control. I also had no ambition to drive in an open-wheeled race car, and it was during this period that blokes were into the phenomenon, killing themselves left, right and centre.

Still, what chance did I have? Who was I?

It was about that time I quit school. I'd had enough. It was evident that I wasn't going to become a Rhodes scholar or a teacher, and my parents were no longer in a mood to argue. I felt like I'd let them down when I left school, and I suppose I did. But something I've learned is that you can't live your life for somebody else. You can't live your life through your kids. You have to let them go and do what they want to do, even if you don't agree. School wasn't me; it isn't for a lot of people. I certainly learned many valuable life lessons from my time there, but at that point of my life I realised school was holding me back from my real calling – using my hands.

I still have an affinity with Cavendish Road. The school recently changed the names of their sports houses from colours like blue and red and green, to famous Australian athletes who'd been at the school. Kids now run, jump and swim proudly for the Dick Johnson house. Who would have ever thought?

Red Face, White Overalls

Spewing out all kinds of hell, the nasty old boilers sprang from the floor. With fuel firing their insatiable bellies, the hulking metal giants sent soot and filth into the air. Heat filled every inch of the sprawling factory; grime and grot lined the floor.

'Look at that kid,' they said, pointing. 'Who does he think he is?'

I stood there, chubby cheeks erupting fluorescent red, palms oozing sweat, and I cursed my mum.

Looking more like an angel than a soon-to-be apprentice fitter and turner, I rocked up to my first day of work wearing an immaculate set of white overalls ironed to perfection.

'You are kidding, aren't you, mate?' one of the workers said. 'This isn't a hospital. And you're no doctor.'

The rest of them bowled over in laughter.

I never wanted to be a fitter and turner, but for some reason my parents thought it was a clean and respectable job. Not as good as a doctor or a lawyer, but better than a motor mechanic.

'No, Richard,' Dad had said, 'you are not going to be a grease monkey. No son of mine is getting into a dirty pair of overalls.'

That's probably why I was sent to A.E. Sergeants wearing a sparkling new set. It was a way to ignore the fact that I was destined to be in a trade. To be dirty.

But A.E. Sergeants was a horrid place, a vast factory of fire and filth. Across the road from the Botanical Gardens in Alice Street in the city, the foundry pumped out cast-metal monstrosities. I started out sweeping the floors and picking up shit. I also got lunches and ran whatever errand was needed.

Eventually I was competent enough to work on a lathe. It was a huge machine, spitting, spinning and slapping away. My job was to set fire-hydrant heads up in a jig. I would slap them down, lock them in and then go about cutting a groove big enough to fill with a rubber O-ring. Sounds OK? Sure, but the flaming-hot hydrants were pulled straight from a cast and dumped in thick, curdling tar. The seething black shit would fly at me at 900 revolutions a minute, covering me in dark muck and filling my lungs with searing caustic fumes.

I would stand there for eight hours a day, spat at by tar. My only respite was a pie and peas for lunch. I hated the place. My white overalls came home black and Mum would clean them every two days and return them to white. The work was filthy, hot and boring.

My first pay cheque was four pound two and six; about $80 today. It was terrible money, but I thought it was great. I'd hand the whole thing over to Mum. Half of it was for board – not that anyone under 40 would know what that is today – and the other half I would get her to save, my eyes already firmly set on buying a car.

I only had a couple of quid left over to spend, but that was OK. I didn't drink, that didn't happen until I was 26, so the remainder would go on movies, magazines and milkshakes.

Still, I hated my job, even to the point where I would skip college. We used to have to do two nights of the rubbish, where we were lectured on how to wield a tool. But I would always wag. Big steel box in hand, notepad by my side, I would rock up to the movies and demand a ticket to whatever it was that might be showing, That's not to say I wasn't a hard worker. I would always arrive on time – to work, anyway – and do whatever was asked and give it my all.

But apparently that wasn't enough for the foreman at the factory. He was just the grumpiest old man I would ever meet. He put the fear of God into every bloke in the place. He must have had a reason for being the way he was, maybe he had a bad upbringing or a bossy wife, but we couldn't work it out. We all toed the line and got the job done, so there was absolutely no need for the way he spoke to us, or the rubbish he would make us do.

He screamed and shouted constantly.

'You stupid idiot!' he would fire. 'You son of a bitch. What the hell did you do that for?! You are a retard.'

It was never: 'Hold on, mate, I'll show you how to do it properly' or 'Do you need a hand?'

It was just full-frontal abuse. He's probably one of the reasons why I eventually quit. All I wanted to do was work on cars, but I probably wouldn't have had the courage to throw in a potential trade had it not been for him. So I guess I should thank him, otherwise I still might be sucking tar.

I did about nine months of my apprenticeship. Then I quit and got a job in a spare parts house. I wasn't worried that I didn't have a trade because I knew what I wanted to do – work on cars. That was my dream, all I'd thought about since I could ever remember.

And I was going to make it happen.

4

ON THE ROAD

Cars and Cones

MGs lined the car park. Silver, green and cream, there were TFs, TCs and MGAs. Hardtops and convertibles, packing at most 100 hp thanks to the MGA and its ball-blasting twin cam. They shone under the streetlight. Young men, aged about 30 or so, checked them out like they were girls.

'She's a beauty,' one would say.

'What a body. Does she go hard?'

I was in the right place. I joined the MG Car Club when I was about 13, and I would spend the rest of my teenage years perving on the glittering pieces of metal and talking shit. Mostly we crapped on about cars, but of course, we also talked about girls.

Brrrrr! Rrooooom!

The sweetest sounding rumble, a perfect note, wafted across the lot. Our ears pricked and we turned. Completely captivated by the sound of mechanical perfection, we stared into the dark, waiting for the magnificent machine to reveal itself. We were suddenly blinded by high beams as the car lurched into the drive. We squinted and strained, seeing nothing but bright white light. The self-sprayed two-pack paint job of an old MG reflected the light, and revealed the machine: a brilliant, new Jaguar XK140.

Dennis Geary gave it a rev, the soft hum becoming a thunderous bark, before he slammed the brakes and sent the Jaguar to a screaming halt.

What a sight. With stunning arches, polished chrome and intricately spoked wheels, it was the envy of all. We ran over and looked, jaws to the floor.

Anthony Eisler had introduced me to the club, which he'd found out about through a friend, and I begged him to take me along. There was some paperwork and a joining fee. I had a paper run back then, so raising the cash was no problem. I would've given them everything I had if it came to it. It was the thing to do those days. As much a social occasion as a celebration of motorsport, the MG Car Club was a place to chew the fat and hang out.

The clubrooms were down in the Valley, now one of the trendiest parts of Brisbane filled with nightclubs and bars. Back then it was strictly a working part of town, jammed with factories and soot-stained men. The clubhouse was above an old radio shop in Wickham Street and it was mostly a Friday night affair. The guys would always be talking about their two favourite things: driving cars and rooting sheilas. I'm guessing that's where I got my education in both matters.

MGs were the dominant car back then; they were really popular, the must-have. But there were also other makes: Triumphs, Holdens and Chryslers, and of course, Dennis Geary's Jaguar. I didn't have a car yet, so I would marvel at them all, turning a shade of green.

The MG Car Club introduced me to the world of racing beyond what I'd read in books and magazines. Not only did I get to sit around and talk cams and clutches, but I also got to go to the gymkhana at Tingalpa.

Now forget about Ken Block and his donuts, drifts and death-defying jumps, back then a gymkhana was witch's hats, parallel parks and stopping on a painted line. It was very basic stuff. A bloke would start a clock, mostly his wristwatch, and you'd drive through an obstacle course on an old airfield. The most technical move was probably a reverse park. Still it was fun, and after watching for a few years, Anthony finally threw me his keys and gave me a go.

I was about 15 when I strapped down for my first attack and I went pretty well. I can't remember my time, or where it ranked, but I know I turned a few heads. Even then I was very precise. I knew not to rush, understood that smooth and accurate were better than fast and frantic. It was a long way from doing 300 k/h down Conrod Straight at Bathurst, but it was a start.

Enough for a young fella like me.

It was around that time Dad and I embarked on a father–son project that will forever remain with me, an experience that furthered my desire to get into mechanics and no doubt helped give me some of the skills I still use today.

Out of the blue, Dad brought a boat hull home. It was a

big hulking piece of wood, a five-metre skeleton begging for flesh and a heart. I'm sure my mother wasn't impressed, but we didn't care. Dad was with the SES voluntary rescue, an organisation left over from the war, and somehow he found a PT boat at Kangaroo Point. It was from a guy called Charlie Crowley, a renowned boat builder from Breakfast Creek, and for whatever reason it ended up in our yard.

'What's that, Dad?' I smiled, knowing it had to be something I could get my little hands into.

'A boat . . . well, it will be when we're done. What do you think?'

I beamed.

It was a big step up from lawnmower-powered karts and cuckoo clocks, but I was up for the challenge. Dad was good with his hands – which is probably where I got it from – and I envisaged us motoring along the water, wind parting our hair, in no time at all.

It was a huge project.

Scouring the paper and the local yards, we sourced a Studebaker motor, which was nothing but a block. We shoved an old modified Chevrolet gearbox up the boat hull's arse, bolted it on and then made the engine mounts by hand. We fabricated most of the parts ourselves, even a water-cooled exhaust manifold. We cut up bits of metal, mostly scrap, and plied them into shape. It was rude, crude but it worked.

We painted the boat white and blue, and made the interior with stitches and glue. I couldn't believe how well it ran when we finished, winding out to 22 knots, crashing over any wave that dared stand in its path.

As I said, the project was something I will never forget. It was great spending that time with my father. The project taught us that with a hacksaw, a piece of metal and a dream, we could make whatever we wanted. We could do anything.

Hill Start

The old sergeant looked at Dad.

'Bob, if he's anything like you, we won't have a problem,' he said.

'Chip off the old block.' Dad smiled.

'Well, get on in,' the police officer said, slapping me on the back. 'Let's see what you can do.'

I didn't need to be asked twice. With a grin from ear to ear, I jumped by the wheel and started her up. Supremely confident, I whacked her into gear and took off.

My dad booked me in for my driver's licence test the day after I turned 17. He picked me up from A.E. Sergeants and drove me down to the Kemp Place Police Station.

Back then there was no RTA. There were no L-plates, logbooks or computer tests available in the language of your choice. No, in 1962, there was a copper, a car and you. If you could show the policeman you could drive, well ... you could drive. Stuff up, and it was back to the bus.

The sergeant knew my dad; he knew everybody. Dad worked next door to the police station and I suspect he even sold him a car. That didn't mean the sergeant was going to go easy on me, probably the opposite.

'Good,' he said, as I rattled through the gears. 'Nice and smooth.'

Hell, I was doing this when I was four. Piece of piss.

'That's it,' he continued, as I geared down, feathered the brake and caressed the turn.

I cruised around the streets, shuffling through the gears, one hand resting on the windowsill, the complete pro.

Then we reached the hill.

'OK, now we're going to test you,' he said. 'This is the one that gets them all. Let's see you do a hill start.'

I was laughing inside as he suggested this might prove difficult. Sure, it was steep but seriously? Hard?

With my right foot hovering above the accelerator, I took my left foot off the brake and quickly found the clutch. I planted both feet down and danced for a moment, finding the friction point. I kept the car steady, feet shuffling to achieve the perfect balance. And then I took off. As I thought, easy.

I slowly wound my way back and pulled up on a dime outside the station.

The sergeant looked at me. 'Well . . . I'm not sure,' he said, shock in his voice. 'Most of it was pretty good.'

Good? I thought. *How about flawless?*

'That hill start was wrong and I should fail you,' he fired. 'I've never seen anyone do it without the handbrake, and that's the correct way. But, considering the car didn't roll back an inch . . . well, what can I say? I'll have to give you your licence.'

Phew. Yes! Wow. Finally, I was free. All I needed now was a car.

No, Thanks. I'll Have a Holden.

Clunk!

The entire vehicle rattled as race car driver Dennis Geary muscled it into gear. 'Don't worry about that, mate,' he said with a wink. 'They all do that. Just wait until you see her go.'

Geary had a car dealership near Stone's Corner: Dennis Geary's Sports Car World. For wannabe mechanics or lovers of all things motors and metal in Brisbane, this place was heaven. Every Friday night, after an evening talking women and wheels, a bunch of us would go down to Stone's Corner just to take a look. Peering through the wire gates, we would stare at the exotic wonders: MGs, Austin-Healeys, Sprites. We would leave a puddle of drool on the footpath.

'I'm going to get that one,' we would say.

'Na, maybe that other one.'

I'd been thinking about buying my first car from the moment I got a job. I used to hand Mum my pay packet, bulging yellow envelope after envelope, telling her to put it somewhere safe to give it to me the day I turned 17. I dreamed of walking into Geary's yard, handing him a wad of cash, and scorching out in an Austin-Healey. No, maybe a Jag.

Reality was, I barely had 200 quid. I couldn't even afford to buy a wheel. Mum kindly offered me a loan, giving me another 600 and taking my budget up to a whopping 800 quid. So I walked into Geary's yard, the Austin-Healey or Jag no longer an option. I thought I'd settle on an MG TC 1250; that would do me fine.

Vroom!

Geary, one foot still on the clutch, smashed into the accelerator with his right leg. The car sounded magnificent as the race star made it shake and shudder.

'Watch this little beauty go,' he said. 'You'll love it.'

We were waiting behind a tram. Dennis was going to put the thing to shame. Show me what the little MG had.

Ding. Ding.

Dennis was off. With a flick of his foot, he dropped the clutch and launched the TC to life. Off the line, he snapped through the gears, all accuracy and precision. He redlined the thing in first, second, third and fourth. And then we were at the next tram stop, still behind the old clunking machine.

The bloody thing had beaten us. As slow as it was, the people-mover was more than a match for Geary and his MG TC 1250.

'So what do you think?' he said with a salesman's smile.

'Um,' I muttered. 'Well, um, Dennis . . . I don't think it's the one for me. I better have a look around. It's nice and all, but.'

The MG was an absolute dogbox. There was no way I was going to drive something that got flogged by a tram. *A tram.* So I went home and enlisted the help of the old man.

'So, Dad, tell me about those Holdens you sell,' I said.

Dad grinned, winked and then went to work. Within a day or two he told me to meet him at the yard.

'What do you think?' he said, gesturing towards the FJ Holden, the sparkling cream exterior brought to life by the green upholstery.

'Yeah.' I nodded. 'It looks good but how does it go?'

'Better than the MG,' Dad said and laughed. 'Get on in.'

He was right. It was no race car but it was fine. The motor hummed, the transmission sang, and my feet danced away on the pedals to its tune. I took it for a quick drive and knew it had to be mine. Dad, of course, got me a deal. 800 quid. I paid him my money, got in and drove. Window open, foot flat, I wasted every ounce of fuel. It was magic, and I was in love with her by the end of the day.

But I thought I could make her better.

Every day at 4.30 pm, almost like clockwork, a bloke would drive up Cavendish Road with the sweetest sounding machine. It was different to anything else on the road; it was deep and powerful, a note that smacked me right between the ears. I just had to pull my FJ apart and tune it to the same degree. So on the jacks my FJ went. I only wanted to play with the engine, but I couldn't help fiddling with the rest. Off the springs went, hub caps and tailpipe too. And I strapped the extractors on, searching for its tune, lowered it and whacked on a gigantic exhaust.

This was all highly illegal, of course. You weren't allowed to modify your car back then. The coppers would pick you up if they sensed an air cap on the wheel had been changed, and off you'd go to machinery for a complete inspection and strip. It's fair to say I had a lot of hard work thrown in the bin during those times.

So there you have it. Dick Johnson, the Ford man, was actually a Holden man first.

5

HOLD IT FLAT

Creating Undue Noise by Manner of Operation

Cruising along, listening to the humming of my finely tuned machine, I jumped, a cold shudder ripping down my spine as the siren pierced through my open window. I gathered myself, eased my foot off the pedal, assuring myself that he wasn't after me. I glanced into the rearview mirror and caught a face full of red and blue.

Shit, I thought. *Here we go again. Another two days of work.*

I pulled over to the side of the road and waited. The copper heaved his big frame from the seat and waltzed my way. He didn't come straight to me: the shaking teenager with sweat now pooling in his palms. First he stopped about two metres from my door, eyes firmly planted on my car. Then he looked down at the wheels (hub caps missing) up to where the springs should have been (gone). And then to the driver: also gone.

'Hello, mate,' he said, coming closer. 'Do you know why I've pulled you up?'

I knew exactly why he had stopped me.

'Yes, sir,' I said. 'I've made some slight modifications to my car.'

He nodded.

I used to work on my car every weekend. I had the idea that I might race one day, and this was the beast that would start my dream. So every Saturday and Sunday, I would have my FJ up on jacks, making it a thrashing machine. First I whacked bigger valves in (more horsepower). It had three and a quarter bore, plenty more than what it was born with. I threw a bigger clutch in, strapped on Triple SU carburettors. I also tossed away the hub caps (unnecessary weight) and the springs were chopped. I did it all in bits and pieces. I didn't have the money or the time to do anything in one big whack, and she had to be on the road come Monday so I could get to work and earn more money to buy rubber and metal pieces.

My car was anything but standard and that was a problem.

'You know your car is highly illegal,' said the officer, now right beside my window.

'I do,' I replied, nodding.

There was no point lying to the police. They weren't fools and I'd learned long ago that nobody likes a smartarse. This bloke was no dope and treating him like one of Snow White's sidekicks would only make things worse. I had to show him the respect he deserved.

'OK, son, you're off to machinery.'

For a wannabe racer and a kid that lived for cars, the police were a huge problem. I was attempting to make my machine the fastest thing I could with the dream of soon racing it, and that didn't sit well with the law. They used to have an infringement called 'creating undue noise by manner of operation', and I was pinged for it at least six times. There was no fine, and they didn't beat you up. They just sent you to the machinery where you were made to take apart all your work.

The machinery was basically a workshop where an inspector would look over your car. He would pull out his fine toothcomb and list all the parts or adjustments you'd made that were not factory standard. After a couple of hours of standing around, watching him, hoping he wouldn't find the real good stuff, you'd be given a checklist.

'Son, come back when all these bits are gone,' the inspector would say, matter-of-factly, 'and when these standard bits are back on it. We'll talk then.'

It took a good whole day to tick the boxes off Mr Machinery's list. The hubs would have to go back on, the springs returned, the engine reconfigured. Thankfully, they never checked the size of the bores or the big fat carburettors I'd shoved into the FJ's guts. That would've been weeks of work and money I just didn't have.

'That's all good, mate,' he'd say once you returned, checklist ticked off. 'Back on the road and don't do it again.'

It would take me another day to fix it all back. Straight away, as soon as I got my FJ home, I'd put it up on the jacks. All in all, it was two days of work and a small price to pay for having a soon-to-be race car. Though it was a pain in the arse, it was just something we had to live through. You wouldn't believe it, but the same copper actually picked me up another time. He looked at me, with a shitty frown.

'Not you again,' he said. 'Don't you kids ever learn?'

Weeding Gardens and Mowing Lawns

I knew it was going to be tough. I was ready to race, but was Mum prepared to let me? I wasn't frightened a bit about the prospect of jumping into a race car and pushing it to its limits. But Mum? Well, she still scared me shitless.

So, first, I tried Dad.

'Dad, can you just scribble your name on here please?' I asked.

'What is it?' he asked.

'Nothing much. Just a form that'll let me go and do some laps in my car.'

He looked a little closer at the piece of paper. 'Race?' he shouted. 'Oh no, I'm not signing that. Go see your mother.'

I went to Mum.

'Not a hope in hell,' she said. 'Go see your father.'

Damn it. I knew it wasn't going to be as easy as that.

I had a problem. I was ready to race, old enough and good enough, but too young to control my own destiny. Back in my day, the age of consent to race was 21, and if you were any younger you had to get permission from your parent or guardian. After the horrors of Lowood, Mum was not keen to let her little Richard go racing.

I'd collected the entry form a couple of days earlier from the MG Car Club, where I had put my name down on a list and paid my five-quid entry fee. Racing was a very social event back then and all you needed to enter any race was a Confederation of Australian Motor Sport (CAMS) licence, a car and a pair of balls. It was more like going to play a game of golf than going to an event like a V8 Supercars race today.

There were three main racing categories in Australia: Open Wheelers, Sports Cars and Touring Cars. The Open Wheelers were probably the big deal, followed by the Sports Cars and then the Touring Cars. Open Wheelers and Sports Cars were fast and expensive. You had to have specialised cars, and big-name international drivers like David Myles, Graham Hill and Pedro Rodriguez would come over to race, which added to the glitz and glamour of those categories.

In the Touring Cars category, you could race just about anything, even an old FJ, so this was the one for me. There were three main levels in this category: local, state and national. We would have about ten local meetings a year between Lowood and Lakeside. They were very informal and the races were fought out between a bunch of mates. The state races were less frequent and a little more prestigious. Every couple of years there'd be a race at the national level, and this would either be a Touring Car Championship or an Australian Grand Prix that took place at racecourses such as Warwick Farm and Catalina Park. Even at these big national events, the only entry requirement was a CAMS licence. You weren't ranked and you didn't need to have a certain number of wins – just three stripes ripped off on the back of a card to show that you'd done three races.

The big races weren't very well organised and you could find yourself racing against anything. If there weren't enough entries in one particular race, they would mix up the categories and often put open and closed sports cars in with the touring cars to make up the field.

Brushes with Mr Machinery aside, my car was ready to race. By this time I was starting out as a mechanic and had an excellent grasp on motors. After leaving the first spare-parts house, I got a job at Martin Wilson Brothers, before ending up at Repco. The work was much the same as what I did before, just a bigger operation, where I made deliveries, sorted shipments and ran errands. The great thing about the job was that I got to study every conceivable car part for every known car. I would open the boxes, look their insides up and down, and figure out what they were. There were cams and shafts, exhausts and rings. I did my deliveries in a ute, blasting out to the workshops and parting with pieces of metal I'd studied and learned. I also got to serve on the spare parts counter.

'G'day, I'm Richard,' I'd say with a smile.

I liked the job – it was to do with cars, which was perfect for me. I learned about every model and make of car, and more importantly what was inside.

'So, Richard, why don't you come and work for me?' Ivan Bevanoff, a customer I delivered parts to, had eventually asked one day.

Ivan knew that I loved cars and worked on them at any given chance. He used to do a lot of secondhand car yard work and owned the BP service station in Greenslopes. I knew him well enough; he was the real deal.

I thought for a second, if that. The amount of money he was going to pay me was almost double and I was going to get to work on cars all day, not just handle the parts that were destined to be bolted onto them.

'Why not,' I said, downplaying my enthusiasm.

Shit, this is me, I thought, but didn't dare say.

It was 1964 and my first job was to put rings and bearings into a secondhand Holden. Cars back then weren't what they are now: these days a flogged Hyundai can still get you to work after 200,000 kilometres without a service, but back then even a finely manicured Jaguar would be done at 90,000. The old engines would just shit themselves, smoke and crap belching into the air. Our job at the BP servo was to straighten out the trade-ins thought by the owners to be done and dusted; we'd rip the tired cars apart and give them a new lease on life. Off went the head and the sump, the pistons too. I would give it a valve line and fit new rings and bearings, make it as good as new.

The job was supposed to take three days, but I could do it in eight hours. That gave me a lot of time to work on my other project: my race car, which was now ready. But I wasn't; I still needed to get that damn permission slip signed. So I went about becoming the perfect son. I washed cars, weeded gardens and mowed lawns. I did the dishes, folded clothes and generally made a very helpful pest of myself.

Eventually Mum cracked.

'OK, Richard, I'll sign it,' she said.

I did cartwheels in my mind.

'But you have to promise me one thing,' she continued. 'You must swear that you will never race an open wheeler.

Never. Not even after I'm gone. If you can promise me that, I will sign the form and you can race.'

I agreed and I've kept my promise. To this day I have never set foot inside an open wheeler.

Appendix J

Hold it flat.
Go on, you can do it.
Hold it flat.
What have you got to lose?
Hold it flat.

I couldn't get those three damn words out of my head every time I approached the Carousel at Lakeside during my first-ever race. Strapped down in my self-made racing FJ, looking every bit the Juan Manuel Fangio with my open-faced helmet and my thousand-yard stare, I roared off the line and held my position. I was up against experienced guys in tried and tested race machines. They were in Minis, Ford Cortinas and Holden FCs; there were even a couple of FJs like mine. I didn't know what they had under the hood, but I suspected they had plenty more than the 800-quid car, which was technically still owned by Mum.

But I didn't care. Not one bit. Here I was, a kid who had dreamed about rubber, rocket covers and pushrods since the day he was born, about to race.

I knew most of the guys I was racing against. Graham Lax was there, and so were Kevin Johns and Kerry Horgan, all good blokes who I knew well. It was a motley crew and this wasn't Formula One, WRC or V8 Supercars. This category was Appendix J, consisting of basically anything that wasn't open-wheeled or good enough to be called a sports car, a no-frills name for a black-and-white bunch.

Organised by promoter Sid Sakzewski, there were about 5000 people to cheer us on. And they were going to scream loudest for me because Laxy, Johnsy and Horgan were going down. Well, that's what I thought.

Hold it flat.

Barely through the kink, a bump threatening to launch me into a wall, I heard it again. I had qualified in sixth position and I was trying to size up the Cortina in front as I fired up the hill towards BP bend.

Before the race, with much bravado, I had talked it up. I honestly didn't have a fear in the world and thought I could do anything. I didn't have one nervous bone in my body. This is what I'd dreamed of doing my whole life and I was dripping with excitement. The thought of going out there and legally thrashing a car was like being a big-wave surfer in a thousand-year swell. And not only was I going to get to thrash my car – no speed limits or stop signs or Mr Machinery waiting at the bottom of a ditch – I was also going to get to race blokes. I knew I didn't have the best car there, but I didn't care. I just wanted to get out there and give them hell.

I guess my mates caught on to my confidence. They tried to shoot me down with a dare.

'Richard, I bet you can't hold it flat at the Carousel,' they said. 'No one can.'

Yeah right, I thought. *We'll see.*

I knew every inch of Lakeside like a conman knows a fool. I'd been at every race since the place had been opened.

The Carousel was a very interesting piece of road. It was a constant radius corner with a slight banking that gave you added encouragement – or fool's gold, as I'd liked to call it, because this was a section of tar that played tricks with your mind. All smoke and mirrors, the banking was a mirage. If you got greedy and took too much of it, you would put on your skates and slide over the back. There was no grip at the top, and many brave souls toppled right over the arch. Ouch.

But not me.

Hold it flat.

There were no sand traps, no kitty litter and no soft landings at Lakeside. A crash was a crash, which was likely to not only end your day but also your car. There were a couple of Armco barriers for aesthetics and to give us drivers a false bravery, but that was it.

After three laps, I felt in complete control. I had just about mastered BP Bend, a lightning-fast corner before a slight downhill left that would see your car launch into the air towards Dunlop Bridge. I'd been told that the daring could really make up time here and I had the old FJ screeching and screaming at its limits. Tyres were being chewed and I was being thrown to the edge of my seat, and the side of the track.

Hungry Corner, the next left-hander, slightly uphill, was also done and dusted. I had figured out my braking point, the negative chamber, and reckoned I had it pretty close to perfect, even though I would later learn this was a piece of road that took years to master.

And then there was the Eastern Loop, another constant radius corner that sloped downhill at the exit before hitting Shell Corner at the bottom. Piece of piss.

Lakeside was all up and down, gradients everywhere, which made for a fabulous track. You could really make a name for yourself here, because of the high degree of difficulty and risk. And that's what I'd intended to do.

Hold it flat.

After four laps, back in the midfield and going OK, I succumbed to the incessant voice in my head. Coming into the Carousel, I planted my foot flat. Every ounce of sense in my body – and there wasn't much of it – told me to lift, to get the pedal off the floor, even if just for a second. But I didn't. Ankle threatening to crash through the firewall, I kept my nerve. I thought I was going to make it. Knuckles clenched tightly upon the wheel, body at 45 degrees trying to tip it in, I thought I was there.

I wasn't.

The moment I knew I was fucked came and went. In a spilt second I went from hero to zero, grip gone and me spinning off the track. I didn't hit anything. The rear wheels grabbed and stopped me in a half-spin, but I was on the grass, facing the wrong way.

Hold it flat, indeed!

There were three races on that day. I can't tell you what happened in the second; seriously, I don't have a clue. But I can tell you about the third in crystal high definition. Some memories never fade.

Something to Lose

I sat on the line and glanced to my left.

FX, I thought. *I can take him.*

Then to my right.

FJ. Easy meat. I've been on him all day.

I slammed my foot to the floor and revved the guts out of the FJ, the tonne of metal shaking violently and threatening to edge forward, my left foot keeping it from going any further. With a flick of my leg, I unleashed the steel and the clutch sprang from the floor. I was a rocket heading towards the stratosphere.

I'd started in position four for race three, but already the FX was gone, a blur in my rearview mirror. The FJ was next and I was looming. Without even thinking, eyes set firmly on the end of the straight, I pulled from his slipstream and sailed on by. Perfect.

With a blast-off for a start, I was extracting every inch of power from my car. I had no idea how fast I was going, but I'm guessing it was about 95 miles an hour. But speed in these cars wasn't the problem – pulling them up was. Forget fancy discs and water-cooled brakes, back then we had four-wheel drums and a set of balls.

The brakes were hopeless, the effect of which was like planting your foot on the wheel and praying for the car to stop. You didn't know what was going to happen when you planted your foot to the floor. The brakes could pull you to the left, right or straight into a wall. I was going in hot and was sure I was about to slam into something. Thankfully, the only thing I hit was the apex.

Aside from stopping, my biggest problem was the rubber on my wheels. I'd spent all my cash on making the car go fast so I couldn't afford the best tyres. The guns of the day were the Dunlop Road Speed RS5 tyres, but they were well out of my reach. So instead, I'd gone for a set of Michelin boots. They were horrible in the wet, OK in the dry, but they lasted longer than anything else. I think they'd cost me two months' pay. Sitting in second, with a race to be won and my previous experience at the Carousel, I was doubting their grip.

I edged closer to Kevin Johns and his all-conquering Cortina. Without any fear, I took the Carousel. Tyres squealing and threatening to give way, I put in my all at Hungry Corner. Johns was in my sights and I was ready to have a go. My moment came on the second-last lap. I was on his bumper and thought: *It's now or never.*

I'd been watching on for the past couple of laps, studying every sway and kick of his car. He was strong in some sections and weak in others, and it was his vulnerability I attacked. I felt that I had more power than him – after all, I had a Holden and he had a Ford! He was getting away through the tight technical stuff and I was on him in the high-speed sections. So, coming into the kink, I pushed all the study aside and just threw the FJ in.

Whoooosh!

The car screamed as the metal broke his aero-trail.

I thought we were going to hit. I grabbed the wheel and held on, ready to hold her straight should she buck. She didn't. I hit nothing. I had an almighty run on the straight and had nailed him. Clean and calculated. I was now clear in front.

Fuck, I thought. *What do I do now?*

Here I was, the kid, the rookie, on his first day of racing, leading a race. I was a lap away from my first race-win and it scared the crap out of me.

I'm going to fuck this up.

I thought about what I had to lose and it scared me. I had never been in this position before, not in life and certainly not in racing. I'd always been the carefree kid willing to give anything a go, but suddenly I had something that meant the world to me that could be taken away. So, I steadied myself.

Perfect, I thought. *Just be perfect.*

I had never been such a picture of concentration. Eyes fixed to the road, hands firm around the wheel, mind on the job, I went about being the best I could.

Johns came at me. I tried not to look but he was nearing at every bend. I didn't bother to block or try to stop his charge: this was about me, not him. I knew I could win this race if I didn't stuff up, so I kept my eyes ahead and tried to go as fast as I could. I hit every braking mark. Inch perfect, I put the foot down and pulled the FJ up just fine. Hands and eyes in sync with my feet, I also smacked each apex. I rolled off the wheel and feathered on the throttle, getting the power down without making the wheels spin or the car skew. And after one pressure cooker, get-me-the-hell-out-of-here lap, I had won.

'Yippeee!' I screamed to myself, not brave enough to make my emotion public.

I had a quiet tap on the wheel and felt like I was going to burst. It was just an unbelievable moment in my life, the greatest to that point, and it's still up there with my all-time highs. I didn't know any better back then, but seriously this was as good as any Bathurst win. It felt like Monaco, Monza and Le Mans, all rolled into one. I just couldn't believe that my first win had come on my first day of racing. Little was I to know that my next win wouldn't come for another five years.

Over and Out

I was spent. Done. After just one race meet, my career was over.

At least that's what I thought.

I took my race car apart and begrudgingly converted it back into the placid vehicle that would get me to and from work. I got rid of the good bits – the ones that made it go fast – and returned them to the people who I'd borrowed them from or packed them into boxes, thinking they'd never be used again.

I had no money. I'd blown it all on those three races and I didn't know how I could continue. So I retired from racing at the age of 18.

But it wasn't long till a light bulb went off.

Maybe I don't need money to race, I pondered. *It might take a while, but I could buy a shitbox and slowly work it up.*

I needed my road car and it was too expensive to keep on doing it up and pulling it apart. So I decided to build my first full-time race car. Dad came home one day and gave me the news.

'I think I have one for you, Richard,' he said. 'No one else wants it, but maybe you do.'

I went into the yard with Dad to inspect the car he'd found. It was a piece of shit. It was rusted out and had been clocked at least five times.

'It's an ex-taxi,' Dad said. 'Some bloke traded it in, but it's worthless to us. You can have it for 80 quid.'

I wasn't interested until I heard the price. I walked up to the car, an FJ, same model as mine but almost unrecognisable, and rubbed my hand along her side. The body was screwed, but I inspected further. The chassis was actually OK and all the bits and pieces on her were good too.

'I'll take it,' I declared. 'She'll be on the road in no time.'

It certainly wasn't going to be a small project, but I was willing to do the work.

First stop was the wreckers. I strolled into the yard, an old field of scrap delight, and almost fell over the thing. Among the rust and ruin was an almost-perfect FJ body shell. There was a big whack on the front right panel, and because of the ding I picked it up for a dime. I went home and pulled out the sledgehammer.

'Peter, hold the bloody thing there,' I commanded my younger brother.

I heaved the sledgehammer over my shoulder and brought it down as hard as I could.

Thud!

Instead of hearing a metal-on-metal clang, the sickening sound of metal-on-face shot into my ear. I smashed my poor brother right in the mouth. He went down like a bag of wheat. I thought I'd killed him. Eventually, no thanks to my shaking and panic, he got up, minus a few teeth and dripping with blood. I helped clean him up.

'Righto,' I said. 'Hold it again?'

He told me to piss off. So I went and got my other brother.

Slowly, steadily, the shitbox became a race car. I didn't have any money and knew I would have to borrow a lot of parts from my road car, and from mates if it were ever to race, but the foundations were being set. The car had a good early block, which was easy to bore out. I couldn't afford to take it to a shop and have it machined, so I bought a port and polish machine of my own. That was quite funny because I had no idea how to use it. It was utter trial and error.

I bought some old twin carbs and strapped them in, and made the manifold and the exhaust myself. I also got hold of some RVS150 Chevrolet valve springs and bolted them in with bigger inlet valves. That was unheard of. We stripped the whole car down and built it up from the ground. But when I was almost ready to race, I realised it looked shit.

'That won't do,' I said to my brother, who was there at the time. 'How can we race that?'

The car was a mishmash of colours. The roof and doors were blue, the mudguards black. Horrible. I didn't have the money to go and get it sprayed, so I did it myself. Well, tried to anyway . . .

I walked under the house looking for a two-pack bounty. I grabbed at the first can: a tin of blue.

'Na, only a couple of litres,' I said. 'Not enough.'

I tossed junk out of the way, looking for another can.

'Got one,' I said. 'A tin of red.'

I continued through the dark and found two more cans. One was white and the other beige.

I had a problem: I didn't have enough of any one colour to get the car done, so I decided to mix them all up. I grabbed a big bucket, slushed the dregs in and got a stick from the backyard and stirred the mixture together. I didn't really care what colour it was going to turn out, I was just happy knowing the car was going to be faster than what

I had. Then I grabbed my brush and slapped the paint on the car.

Lilac?

Yep, it was lilac. My first real race car was a pinky-purple. Nice.

6

BACK IN LILAC

Bathurst

Twelve hours of paddocks, plains and potholes ended when we edged over the rise. The world seemed to stop, if only for a moment. The rumbling engine of Keith Littlemore's GT Cortina fell silent and the endless chatter that had kept us occupied for 12 hours ceased. We were both in awe of what stood before us.

I had snuck a peek of Mount Panorama as we hurtled along the highway. I'd also seen pictures in magazines, watched old black-and-white footage on TV, and heard many a story from those that had been. But nothing could prepare me for Bathurst. Nothing. I needed to see it with my own eyes. Feel it in my bones. Smell and savour the sights and surroundings . . . the sounds.

Smoke rose from the endless campfires scattered across the Mountain, white puffs dancing up into the clean, crisp blue sky. The clouds above seemed low enough to touch. Cars and tents littered the earth, parked and pitched in the mud. I couldn't believe how many people were there: tens of thousands. But it was the track that blew my mind.

I'd heard that Bathurst was the place to be: tough, technical and enough to ruin even the best drivers in the world. I'd also heard about the elevation: the climb, the rollercoaster along the top, and the descent. But I had no idea just how steep the track really was.

'Wow,' I said to Keith. 'Look at the size of that thing. How can cars not launch into the air? Off the edge of the Mountain?'

His mouth was wide open, his eyes towards the sky, which now threatened to unleash rain onto the Cutting.

'Sometimes they do,' he said bluntly.

Keith, racing great Graham Littlemore's brother, and I decided to go to Bathurst in 1963 for the first running of the Armstrong 500. I had taken a keen interest in all the events around the country. Once a month, I would buy magazines like *Racing Car News* and *Auto Action*, which were both solid reads, very different to the crap that's put out today. I would walk down to the newsagent the day they would come out, buy them and read them cover to cover. Bathurst was at the top of my list. The endurance races that would make the place legendary hadn't begun yet, but Mount Panorama already had a rich and thrilling history. I used to circle the Easter weekend on my calendar with a big fat red pen, and count down the days.

Before the 500, they had a round of the Australian Touring

Car Championship at Bathurst in April. It was a tremendous event. The bikes would roar around Mount Panorama on Friday and Saturday – absolute two-wheeled madness. And then the cars, all sorts of wondrous beasts, would tear the place up on the Sunday and Monday. The Bathurst racetrack first started out as a dirt goat track. There were no fences, no facilities, just some markings on what barely passed for a road. Nobody knew about it then, but the story of how it came about is certainly worth retelling.

Martin Griffin, the mayor of Bathurst in the 1930s, was a mad motor racing fan, or a car enthusiast, as he would have put it. He was a Bathurst local and had grown up in the shadow of Mount Panorama. For one reason or another, he thought the Mountain would make a great racetrack. He must have been nuts. All rocks, boulders and sheer cliff face, it wasn't the type of place you would ever think of racing on. Racetracks were built on old runways: flat fields and wide open spaces. Not on bloody mountains. The Aborigines had used Mount Panorama as a lookout; on a clear day you could see to Lithgow. But Griffin was dead keen on turning it into a world-famous racetrack and went about convincing the rest of the council. Evidently, he wasn't stupid. Instead of telling the council they needed a racetrack, he told them they needed a scenic drive around the Mountain to bring in the tourists.

'What a view you'd have from up there,' he told them. 'Everyone would be able to see Bathurst and all its glory.'

With support from the New South Wales Light Car Club, Auto Cycle Union and the federal government, his vision become a reality. On St Patrick's Day in 1938, Mayor Griffin declared the Mount Panorama Scenic Drive open. He always knew that the road was going to be used for motor racing, even though he mostly sold it as a tourist drive.

Mount Panorama is really a one-off. There's nowhere in the world that you would get a racetrack on a piece of terrain like this. No crazy bugger would even suggest it, let alone make it his life's work. But Martin Griffin did and I thank him for it.

All the guys at the MG Car Club, everyone who owned a race car, had a lifetime ambition to race at Bathurst. They didn't care about winning or losing, they just wanted to cut a lap or two and tick it off their bucket list, which is why Keith and I jumped into his Cortina to go check it out. Back then we had no GPS, no iPhones, and no clue how to get there, but we were determined to figure it out.

I was having second thoughts as soon as the trip began. Keith was a wild driver, an absolute lunatic. We came down the Putty Road, all twists and turns, and Keith thought he was already blasting around Mount Panorama. He was flogging his GT, finding its limit and then asking for some more. I glanced over and snuck a peek at the speedometer: the crazy fucker was doing 180 k/h. I was shitting myself. I swore we were going to leave the road at some point and end up in one of the gigantic gum trees that were flashing on by, one after another, barely a blur. But I didn't dare object to his driving, or the stupid speeds we were doing. He might have thought that I was a skirt.

I'm not the best passenger at any time and I lucked upon a solution.

In the Cortina, the throttle linkage would come across under the dash and up through the firewall on the passenger side. I was stretching out and I stumbled across the throttle, which I could feel with my foot. I jammed the pad of my right foot in for a moment, pushing as hard as I could, and the speed slowly dropped. There is a God, and he wanted me to live.

'There's something wrong with this,' Keith suddenly said. 'It doesn't want to go.'

I shrugged, foot firmly jammed against the throttle under the dash. He was pushing it on, and I was shoving it back. That lasted for at least eight hours.

I couldn't believe how dangerous the track was when I finally got over the shock of its extraordinary size and elevation. There were no fences around the track, not even at the top, just a massive drop that could kill.

I remember watching John Roxburgh tumble down there in his Datsun. He rolled and rolled, picking up speed with each metal-bending thud. He seemed to launch higher into the air following each sickening smash into the rocks, like a crazy kid on a trampoline. He must have dropped 500 metres before finally coming to a stop, in a world of hurt.

I vividly remember the Dipper, which was a sheer, dangerous drop. It thrilled me to my core, and I'd never seen the likes of it before. I had no idea how you could get down without launching into the air. It dropped more than a metre than what it does today. They filled it in at some point. The actual surface was pretty good for the time, though certainly not what it is today. Because the Dipper was a tourist drive and wasn't used day in day out, it was spared from the trucks and the traffic, which make a mess of most roads.

There were very few facilities in Mount Panorama to speak of – I couldn't even find a toilet back then! Forget any type of barrier; the only thing between the racetrack and the pits was a painted line that would wash off in the wet. The garages were little more than a big tin roof, held up by wooden poles, all creak, sway and not to be trusted. The bays, where the men would work on their cars, were separated not by walls, but by bits of different-sized bark. Some had bulky redwood chips on their floor, others had finely chopped pine, while the lucky ones had pebbles.

There were no kerbs at all on the track. The road would quickly break away into dirt and then dry brown grass, the type you didn't want near a cigarette on a hot day. The only fencing was provided by the farmers – pieces of saggy wire strung through wood posts – separating them from the high horsepower and annual racing madness.

Keith and I drove straight up to the top of the Mountain. That's where we needed to be, so we parked the GT just near Skyline. There were people everywhere, but compared to today, it was very tame. The atmosphere was electric, although there were no burnouts, pissed mutes or flaming toilet rolls. We took a peek at the track and figured the best view would be from McPhillamy: it was an awesome piece of road and we just knew that there was going to be plenty of action. But once we were there we walked up and down looking for a better view and couldn't find one.

We jumped back into the car, strapped in, and drove back down to Bathurst for the worst night of sleep in my life. We hadn't arranged accommodation, so Keith found a nice bit of green in a park, right near a bridge. He pulled up the handbrake and said 'goodnight'. I nestled into the bucket seat, utterly exhausted. With the hamburger I had just devoured from the local takeaway still lingering in my mouth and hanging heavy in my guts, I passed out.

It didn't last long.

About an hour later I woke up shivering. The temperature had plummeted. I swear it was below zero. Almost blue, frozen to the core, I reached into my bag and grabbed every piece of clothing I had, dumping it all over my body: a makeshift blanket. I drifted off again and then woke up with a pain in my arse. Literally. I'd tried to stretch out and now had the Cortina's shifter jammed in my cracker. Seriously, cars are not designed for sleep. We persevered and made it to sunlight.

It pissed down on the Saturday, before qualifying, and the place became a mudbath. I had never seen anything like it. There was no drainage anywhere and the place was full of bogged cars and drenched bones. But we were right about McPhillamy: the view was awesome. The cars sped through the bend, flat on the throttle, edging cautiously to the right, tyres screaming and bodies pinned down by gravity. I'm not sure what happened in qualifying; I don't think I even asked. I was just happy watching all the cars hurtle on by, regardless of their subsequent times.

1963 was a special year; in 2012 we would celebrate the 50th anniversary of that very race. Manufacturers and sponsors were beginning to understand the importance of motor racing, and this event was the one they wanted to be involved with.

The slogan of 'win today, sell tomorrow' is firmly rooted in this era. The first of the 'Bathurst Specials' was unleashed in 1963. It was the Holden EH S4, which was a powerful machine and I wanted one as soon as it was released. It had a 179ci engine and a 3.36:1 diff. Six were entered that year, but they were no match for the Ford GT Cortina 1500 of Bob Jane and Harry Firth. I was gutted but Keith was happy. I thought I would be with Holden until the day I died. If only I knew . . .

Bathurst was special. Even back then, I was sure it was going to become something big. International drivers had already begun coming over, and for them to make such a massive trip, it had to be something good. The race was quite well promoted, and although the footage didn't look flash, it got at least a couple of hours on TV and that broadened the appeal. It had whet the appetite of fans and would-be racers like me.

I was only 18, but my aim was to race there one day. I had to go and have a crack. I didn't really dream of winning it, just doing a lap. This place was brutal, brilliant and only for the brave. I wasn't scared one bit, but getting a car that would make the distance seemed a mission impossible. I certainly didn't dream that I would one day become a Bathurst legend. Not then, not ever.

Purple Rain

The lilac machine was ready. Well, it definitely looked the part – with two-pack house paint slapped on – but I needed a few bits and pieces to actually make it move before I raced. I ripped off whatever I could from my road car: wheels, wipers etc., but I was still missing half an engine. Kerry Horgan, a member of the MG Car Club and a race enthusiast, liked what I had done.

'Mate,' he said. 'I'll lend you whatever you need. You can whack it in, use it, as long as you let me have at least one race.'

I agreed.

It was a good deal because I wouldn't get to race in it without an engine. I had circled a date in my calendar a few months before. There was a local meet coming up at Lowood Raceway and that's where I was planning on making my comeback. I knew Lowood well. Along with Lakeside, it was the other big track in Queensland and I'd been there many times before; it was the same track where I had witnessed John Hough's tragic death. I didn't even think of that incident, not for a second, when I filled out my entry form. I was more worried about the lilac machine.

Kerry brought over the bits I needed. He heaved them from the back of a truck and onto the grease-stained floor. It didn't take me long to turn my Holden into a full-blown racing beast – now with a complete engine. I was ready, the car was ready . . . what a feeling. I was about to come out of retirement and resume my short but spectacular racing career.

I was happy with the car. I'd built it from scratch and I knew it was going to be as good as anything out there. I didn't have the money, but the love that had gone into this thing was worth more than cash. And though it lacked in certain areas, it had its strong points too. I'd been pretty innovative, and my access to all the latest and best parts from the spare parts house would ensure this lilac machine would be a flyer.

I thought I would never race again a year ago, and I'd honestly thought I was done. So to be entered into another race, this time with my own dedicated race car, not a road car I couldn't afford to pull apart, was something special. And I had built her myself: it had cost me 80 quid at first and my brother his teeth.

I had no expectations about how I would do. I didn't care if I won or came last. Actually, that's not true – I didn't want to finish last. But really I wasn't thinking results when I strapped in; I was just happy to be going racing again.

The sun burnt off the last of the dark. The early morning birds laughed while the fresh scent of grass and green hovered in the air. There is nothing like a racetrack at sunrise. Endless paddocks to the left, cows and sheep to the right, the sounds of nature interrupted only by the thunderous crack of car engines.

I think I qualified fifth in the local meet-up. I can't remember much, except being pretty stoked with my car. She was a beauty. I wasn't sure what I had, given testing had been limited to illegal runs on the highway, but after qualifying I knew I had a race car that could raise hell. Her strength didn't lie in the engine, rather it was the handling that made all the difference. I had all sorts of wondrous bits and pieces in her, many highly experimental, and they worked a treat.

Kerry Horgan thought the same.

'This is the best handling car I have ever been in,' he said, after his stint. 'Just brilliant. You have a future, mate. A bright one. Now let's see if you can race.'

And that I did. I finished towards the front; certainly not a win. But that didn't matter, because I was back. But then–

Boom!

Again my world was rocked and I was forced to retire. This time it was a genuine bombshell.

7

SPIT AND POLISH

We Have a Live One

Kempy, a hell of a nice guy but a bloke who had obviously spent his whole life behind a desk, grabbed the grenade and pulled the pin. We were standing in the bunker, a brick structure, all walls but no roof. I looked over to Kempy: he was skinny but had a stomach that somehow managed to overlap his belt. He wasn't the sort of bloke you would expect to see in the army, definitely not the type that should have any sort of explosive in his hand. But here we were, at the Australian Armed Forces base in Wagga Wagga, freezing our butts off in the middle of winter . . . watching Kempy about to toss a grenade.

A war in Vietnam was raging. People were dying and it was getting worse every day. Not that we cared, not really anyway. My number came up in 1965. It was the first draft and the third thing in my life I had won.

A couple of years before I had won a chook. I took it home, put it in the fridge and it went off. Inedible. Next I won a record, but I didn't have a record player. Great. I improvised and made it a frisbee.

And then in 1965, I won a ticket to war.

We'd been taught how to throw a grenade, and it wasn't that difficult. There was a target about 30 metres away from the bunker. It had been blown up by every recruit before Kempy and had been replaced.

We played with real hand grenades. *Live ones.* Kempy was supposed to throw it as hard as he could. He didn't. Poor Kempy should have been behind a desk, maybe compiling a tax return. He wasn't. He grabbed the grenade, all straight arm like we'd been taught, but as he brought his arm back to fling it away, he dropped it. The live grenade landed a metre from my foot. There were a bunch of us in the bunker, surrounded by brick walls with limited escape.

'Move!' someone shouted. 'Moooove! Live grenade!'

I bolted for my life. I pushed at blokes, pulled at khaki fabric and found the narrow exit to the chamber of death we were now trapped in. I dived, hitting hard compacted dirt, grazing my elbows, knees and palms.

BOOM!

Deadly metal shards ripped chunks from the clay bricks, leaving strange splatter holes and puffing out red dust. I could feel blood flowing from my grazes and dripping down my limbs as I looked to the bunker.

All were out, no bodies, no death. I then looked to where Kempy was before he unleashed hell. He was there too, hunched over with his hands pressed against his ears, knees to his chest. He slowly rose and looked to the destroyed bunker, red with embarrassment.

Thank fuck Kempy didn't kill anyone. We cleared the bunker, and aside from a few cuts and abrasions, we were fine.

Welcome to the army.

The Razor's Edge

Things weren't looking good in 1965. Australia had been brought into the war to fight against communism because the greatest army in the world had found resistance against a jungle mob they thought they could crush in weeks.

When my number came up, I faced the prospect of going to Vietnam. But I didn't care. I was fearless and for me everything, even a war, meant a new adventure. There was every chance I would wind up in a stinking hot jungle shooting a gun, but back then, before the horrors were known, it sounded pretty cool.

My letter came in the mail. It told me I had been selected to serve in the Australian Armed Forces, pending medical approval. I was instructed to go down to the local post office.

When I finally got there it was busy. There were kids everywhere being shoved into rooms, looked up and down and given the green light, sometimes the red. I was ushered into a room where a doctor waited. He asked me to strip down to my undies, made me poke my tongue out and say ah. He also inspected the glands underneath my arms and asked me questions like do you suffer vertigo, have epilepsy or get allergies? I said no and he sent me on my way.

A week or so later another letter came, this time telling me I'd been accepted to do two years of national service in the armed forces.

My parents shoved me in the back of the family sedan and trucked me off to Kelvin Grove. It was a quiet ride, not much was said. I think Mum was upset, but she didn't show too much; she wasn't keen on me doing conscripted national service. Dad was Dad, and just wished me the best.

I jumped out of the car, slammed the door, excited for my next adventure. I lined up with a bunch of misfits: short, tall, skinny and fat. An army dude, dressed in all his gear, herded us on to a bus headed to the airport. There were no security checks, no bag drop, not even a ticket. A plane was waiting for us: a DC-9, and it was chock-full. Everyone was jovial, playing jokes and larking around – what else could you do? One of the air hostesses was a good sort. A bloke a couple of seats up from me called out.

'Miss, I feel sick,' he shouted. 'Can you bring me a bag?'

She came over, bent down, and held a spew bag to his face. From his lap he pulled the fruit salad he had saved from lunch and held it next to his mouth before throwing it into the bag.

There was no point in fretting about what lay ahead, but no doubt some kids were shitting themselves deep down; some probably would have thrown up for real. Many on that flight would end up in Vietnam . . . some would never come back.

We flew down to Sydney, where we boarded another bus and ended up in Wagga. From there we travelled over to Kapooka, where the first three months of basic training began.

When I arrived, I had to go to the store to pick my gear.

Nothing in the previous world mattered, and it was all khaki and slouch hat from here. I was fitted out with everything: shorts, shirts, pants and shoes. And when I say shoes, I'm talking about nothing like you see today. They were as stiff as hell. Blisters in the making. I think they made them that hard on purpose to show us what pain was and how we could conquer it. I eventually broke the shoes in.

I was also given ceremonial gear – dress jacket, shirt, tie, trousers and shoes – which we were ordered to keep immaculate. I'm sure you've seen military parade shoes, all reflection and shine, but maybe you don't know how much effort it actually takes to make the sun reflect in them. When they say 'spit' polish, they really mean it. I can't tell you how many hours I spent hocking on my shoes and rubbing it till my wrists were numb. My shoes were sparkling by the end, though.

We got a rifle too, complete with bayonet and bullets. Firearms weren't too uncommon back in my day, and I'd shot a gun before. Prior to the draft I'd been in the Citizen Military Forces (CMF), and we would go to camps and military bases and play war. In the CMF, I'd fired a 303, as well as fired plenty of shots from a slug gun and a .22.

The booming voice of the corporal woke up everyone in our platoon. All sixteen of us packed into a tin hut.

'Up and at 'em,' he screamed.

It was fucking freezing and the tin hut was more like an igloo. It was below zero outside, and throwing off our warm, cosy blankets to face the chill and the corporal was a chore. Shivering, we steeled ourselves for the first dawn inspection.

'What's this?' the corporal asked as he brushed his hand

across a recruit's face. He rubbed a little harder, his callous fingers pricked by the two-day growth. 'We shave in the army, boy,' he yelled.

The recruit looked like he was going to shit a brick. The corporal pulled a razor from his pocket, the blade catching the first of the day's sun, before leaning down and grabbing a rock. Then he stared at the recruit and began slapping the piece of steel on the rock, sharpening it an inch away from the boy's face. He must have pissed himself, surely! Again, the corporal grabbed at the recruit's face, this time locking the boy's chin with his left hand and dry-shaving him with his right.

The rest of the platoon made sure they shaved after that. For me it wasn't a problem. I only had bum fluff and couldn't have grown a beard if I tried.

That's not to say army life was easy.

Frozen Feet

I begrudgingly threw the blanket from my body and stepped out of bed.

I screamed as I fell straight to the icy floor, sharp pain shooting up from both feet. I put my hands on the ground and attempted to push myself up.

'Argh!'

More pain, this time in my wrists.

I looked down and my hands were the size of the Incredible Hulk's, but not green. They were red. My feet were even bigger.

Kapooka was absolutely freezing and I went off to the medical centre and was diagnosed with chilblain. I didn't know what that was, just knew I was in severe pain. My arms and legs worked fine, but the things attached to them were frozen chunks of meat. Someone told me that pissing on them would help, so I walked down to the toilet block, whipped out the old fella and had a go. Nothing. No relief, just stinking piss all over my hands and feet. Training was going to be agony.

There were two groups of guys in the army. The first were the regular blokes, who'd volunteered and did a minimum of three years' service. The next group were the lotto fellas, who did two.

The regular blokes used to look down on us, and I guess I don't blame them because we were pretty green. Seriously, they couldn't have picked a more diverse bunch of people with us lotto fellas. Sure there were some fit blokes, 6-foot tall and dripping with muscle, but mostly they were fat and would struggle to do a single push-up, or bone-skinny nerds likely to be blown over by a stiff breeze. I'm not being disrespectful, but they weren't particularly athletic, and a lot of them had come from desk jobs and school desks. These blokes were from everywhere: Charters Towers, Longreach, Townsville and Brisbane – there was no discrimination.

There was a lot of running, monkey bars and sit-ups. I will never forget that on the chin-up bar, dead set, some of these poor blokes couldn't even lift their body weight. Not once. I wasn't a body builder, but I was quite active and used to swim, so I had no problem lifting my weight.

The only problem I had was with the chilblain. Woken

at 6 am, I was dreading what lay ahead. I couldn't even feel my feet, and I knew that was going to be an issue with the 25-kilometre march coming up. My feet ended up being OK in the end, though. I soldiered through the pain until everything went numb. But early into the march, one foot after another, I felt a jab in my leg.

'Ouch,' I muttered under my breath, not game to make a scene.

I knew something was wrong. I continued to march, back straight, shoulders out, but my leg hurt like hell. Then I realised a piece of bone had snapped from my knee. I was just walking along and bang. It just went. The pain eased off and I continued.

Bang!

It went again. The bone fragment was loose, and every now and again it would jam up in my knee.

Whack!

I went down like a bucket of wheat. There was no warning when it went, and I didn't even know what had caused the initial break, but it kept on jamming in the joint, and it was 20-odd kilometres of pure pain. I didn't dare stop, or tell anyone I was hurt.

Then we had to run a mile in five minutes, backpack, gun and all. And if you didn't make the mile in that time, they would make you do it again. There were no exceptions. I was never a runner – my feet are as flat as a pool table – so I was in extreme agony. Click, clack, the bone kept on locking up in my knee. I felt like giving up, lying down and crying in pain. But that wasn't me.

It wasn't all pain and punishment, though. There were

plenty of good moments, and there was one trip I will never forget.

I had never ever seen snow. Sure, Queensland got cold, but all you had to do was put a pair of pants on. But there it was, like a scene from a black-and-white movie.

We had the day off and they'd bussed us out to Falls Creek. I knew that snow existed, of course, but I struggled to believe I was standing there in a sea of white. And it was nothing like I'd expected. I thought snow would be soft, like cottonwool, but it was hard, crushed-up ice. I was absolutely amazed. I picked it up in my hands, screwed it up into a ball, and threw it at some bloke's face. As I said, I thought it was soft. Ouch.

I knew from the moment I was drafted that I wasn't going to be able to race, but I used it to my benefit. I was broke anyway, and didn't have the cash to get my car on the track, so I thought being conscripted would be a great opportunity for me to save. I wasn't paying board at home and the only expenses I had were personal ones, which for me was almost zero. I didn't drink or smoke, nor did I do much else. Like it or lump it, I was here, and I thought saving to go race was the best I could do. You wouldn't believe it, but there was a bloke just two huts down from me thinking the same thing. His name was Peter Brock.

RAEME

I graduated from basic training with a passing out parade. It was the moment I became a solider. I remember it because I was able to put the coat of arms on my slouch hat, and I have to admit, I was strangely proud. I have always been a patriot and I was happy to be doing what I could for my country, and was ready to do whatever was asked.

The interview was next. I sat down in a makeshift office and my destiny, my future, would come down to what I said next. An old army bloke looked through my papers.

'What are you thinking, son?' he asked. 'What do you want to do? Infantry? Special forces?'

'I want to race cars,' I fired, grinning from ear to ear.

He had obviously noted my mechanical background in my files, because he suggested the Royal Australian Electrical and Mechanical Engineers (RAEME). I smiled. That was my first choice; my second was transport because I wanted to drive trucks.

I was selected to go to RAEME and I could have ended up anywhere in the country: there were bases all over Australia. One of the biggest was in Bulimba, a suburb in Brisbane. And I was lucky enough to be sent there. Not only was I about to be removed from the cold shit weather, I was also going to be within striking distance of home-cooked food and my car!

I loved it when I arrived – I got to work on my car and could also take all my dirty laundry back home. Army life wasn't so bad!

They had two sectors at Bulimba, which, to this day, is still a really big army base. One was at Peel Street, on the edge of the city, and that's where I ended up first, working on the international trucks and the Land Rovers. I spent a number of months there. Because of my training, I eventually became an instructor to the younger blokes and I was able to work out their skills.

The other sector was Bulimba itself, where all the serious stuff was based: the trucks, the tanks and machines that went bang! I was moved there after a while and I was required to get several licences before I could begin work. Forget the CAMS test, I had to get the paperwork to drive a tank. A civilian licence meant nothing, and eventually I had licences to drive virtually every terrestrial machine in the army.

Driving a tank was cool. We used to run the APC (Armoured Personnel Carrier), and they went like a cut cat. They had a 6V72 in them, which was a two-stroke GM diesel. The Bulimba yard was massive – imagine 20 football fields stacked together – and we used to rip around at 80 k/h.

But the best thing about Bulimba sector wasn't the vehicles, or the proximity to Mum's washing services: it was the machinery. In the workshop, where I spent most of my time, we had lathes, presses and other heavy-duty shit that I'd never even seen, let alone been able to use.

I never lost my desire to race, and it was always in the back of my mind. I was saving as much as I could, and when I saw the machines I knew my dream of becoming a professional driver could still become a reality. I had a new FJ and I wanted to work it up to go racing. The machines gave me a workshop that could help make that happen.

Having access to the machinery meant I could do all the work I wanted on my FJ without having to go and pay for it. I was given a job sheet every day, and once I got through that I was allowed to work on my car. The time that I was given to service a vehicle was very generous. I got there at eight o'clock in the morning and could blast through a day's work by 11 am. After that you could jump up on the back of a truck, pull the tarp over and have a nap, or you could jump back on the machines and build whatever you wanted, as long as you got the OK from the boss. I was sweet because I serviced their cars, so I had no problem working on my own stuff.

The first lieutenant was a great guy. I used to work on his car all the time. He turned a blind eye to pretty much everything else I did. Of course, you had to do all your work, and do the right thing, but he didn't mind me working on my own car when I was done for the day.

I could take my car in and do pretty much whatever I liked. I machine-drummed the brakes, worked on the suspension, and made bushes for the springs. Basic stuff, but jobs I would have had to pay for if it weren't for working in the machinery.

Canoes and Cartons

At the barracks we had two canteens: a dry one and a wet one. The dry canteen was where you ate your food, which was served on steel trays and consisted mostly of mash and meat. You would chow down and then head back to bed. The wet canteen was the one that served grog. I didn't drink but I still used to spend a bit of time there. I would go up with the guys and chat with them around the bar. It was a good opportunity to kill time and watch them do some funny shit, beer under their belts.

Some of the blokes used to absolutely hammer themselves. One of them actually set off the fire alarm.

'OK, who did it?' shouted the corporal as the angry fireman looked on.

Nobody gave the cheeky bastard up, so as punishment

they closed the camp. That meant nobody in, nobody out, but more importantly, for most on base, it meant a dry bar. No grog.

The blokes got real toey. It was a Saturday night and they were itching for a drink. They were effectively prisoners. They couldn't go out or have anyone come in, and they couldn't have a drink. There was a guard at the gate and huge fences, so there really was no escape except for the river out the back. I was with a bunch of blokes, all bored and raring to go. They spotted the dinghy and a light bulb went off.

'Right, let's go and get some grog,' one of them steamed.

Everyone else nodded.

The Hamilton Hotel seemed a stone's throw away from the camp, and was just across the Brisbane River. You could almost smell the girls' perfume wafting across the brown water, almost taste the beer. The dinghy proved too much of a temptation.

'Let's row across,' the same bloke shouted.

Again everyone nodded.

They went round and collected cash before jumping in. It wasn't a big boat, but plenty large enough for a couple of slabs. So they pissed off into the dark, shoved their oars into the water and disappeared. They reappeared about 30 minutes later, equipped with grog. The remaining mob on shore cheered as they came into view. I wasn't interested in the booze, more so the river, which was running like a fox terrier being chased by a bulldog. The river was in full roar and the dinghy began to shudder and shake. One of the blokes, egged on by the thirsty cheers, stood up and saluted the crowd.

That's when it all went wrong.

The current grabbed the boat and almost tossed the bloke over. He went white as the angry water took hold of them and hurled them downstream. The men grabbed their oars and gave it the heave-ho. They did well, but not well enough. A ferry had come from nowhere, shooting up a tsunami-like wave, and about 15 metres from shore, with the entire barracks screaming them on, they went over. The weight of the booze toppled the dinghy upside down and the bloody thing sank. The blokes in the boat headed straight for shore, the blokes on the shore headed right for the boat.

'The beer!' they screamed.

It was hilarious. Fully clothed men were diving in left, right and centre trying to retrieve the loose beer bottles streaming down the river. One, two, they shoved them in their pants, threw others back to the shore. Shit, it was funny. I don't think they lost a single bottle.

Off the Hook

I don't remember what day it was, barely the year, but I remember the conversation. Me and my mate Allan Pickering were called into the office. The sergeant major smiled.

'I have selected both of you,' he said. 'We've been asked to send two guys over to Vietnam, and we think you are the best. You'll need to do a medical, and we'll organise the paperwork.'

The war was bad. People were being sent, and they weren't coming home. I knew that, but I still didn't care. I was young, carefree, and willing to walk whatever path was sent my way. I was ready to go.

But it turned out my body wasn't. I was sent to the army

hospital, where they pulled out my file. My dodgy knee had been recorded back down at Kapooka.

'That's no good,' the doctor said, shaking his head. 'No good at all. You need an operation.'

Allan went to Vietnam and I didn't. Thank God he came home. I ended up having my 21st birthday in the army, sitting down doing nothing. Just another birthday for me.

I got discharged in 1967. The army taught me many things. Most of all, I knew that if I was to get anywhere in racing, I would need to do it on my own; I couldn't work for others. I needed to be self-employed and earn the money myself. I have no regrets about the time I'd spent there. To be honest, I think it was a good thing. The army was all about discipline, and from what I see today, a hell of a lot of young blokes lack it. A stint in the barracks would sort them out.

8

SEVEN DOLLARS TO WATCH,
TEN TO TOUCH

Civil Again

Dad steamed down and stood in front of me, fuming.

'That's it,' he said, slippers walking over the grease and grime, dressing-gown shielding him from the cool night air. 'I've had enough. It's time you boys find somewhere else to work. I can't stand it anymore.'

It was 2 am and Dad had just been rudely awoken by the sound of a chain grinding through a block and tackle as Barry and I hoisted another engine into the air. The crude rig was hooked up using a beam located right under his bed. No wonder he was pissed.

Once I got out of the army, I decided I would never work for anyone else. I didn't want to have to answer to another boss and wanted to be my own man. I also had my heart set on racing again. My two-year forced absence had made me more desperate than ever to get behind the wheel of a high-powered machine and to throttle the life out of an engine. I knew that would never happen if I had to work for someone else. Not only would I not have the money to build and maintain a car, I also wouldn't have the time working to someone else's schedule. I decided the only way I would be able to race was to work for myself. So that's what I did.

I started my first business with Barry Covington. Barry was a good guy and we'd become close during my time in the army. He lived in my neighbourhood and shared my passion for cars. He was a handy mechanic too, with a good job at the Caltex Service Station in Holland Park. Through a common interest in motorsport and mechanics, we joined forces.

Barry and I started working under Dad's bedroom, probably not the best idea but our only option. We quickly gained a reputation and things began to pick up. We became popular with the younger guys because we were prepared to do things that no one else would dare do. Barry and I were into our hot rods and would have a go at anything, no matter how absurd it seemed

And then we got chucked out.

Not surprisingly, Dad couldn't bear the noise any longer. We were banging and bashing at all hours, not to mention making a mess, spilling grease and oil everywhere. So we had to find an alternative workshop. We hadn't been looking long when we stumbled across a little place in South Brisbane, just near the site of the future Brisbane Expo. It wasn't big, more shed than factory, but it only cost eight bucks a week. We were in. I met this little Greek bloke named Ike, who didn't care what we did to the place, or in it, as long as we paid our rent. He also didn't care how late we worked!

By this time I had a new car. While I was in the army, a newer model Holden caught my eye. I loved the FJ, but it was old hat compared to the EH. Chalk and cheese. It was all hot rod and hell on wheels. I remember seeing the red engine for the first time and knowing I just had to have one. Despite two years of solid saving in the army, I still couldn't afford a new race car. I looked around and eventually found one in my price range: $1300. I knew there had to be something wrong with it.

The car was covered in every type of animal shit you could imagine. Sheep shit: yep. Dog shit: of course. Horse shit: heaps of it. The car was a secondhand ex-McTaggart's traveller, a real farm car that had seen plenty of work and even more poo. But that was fine, I was willing to clean it up; besides, it ran great and the engine was clean.

I did a bit of work on the EH while still in the army. First thing to do was blast her with a high-pressured hose, after that I went about turning her into a race car. Graham Littlemore approached me one day.

'Want to build me a race car?' he asked. 'From the ground up?'

Of course I did. By this point, I'd modified a lot of road cars, but I'd never attempted to build a car from scratch. A real race car. I put my own car on hold to help Littlemore build his rocket. Graham worked for British Leyland and raced a road-going version of the Mini Cooper S. He wanted another Cooper S, but this time built from a body shell with all the specialised racing bits inside. It took more than seven months to complete the car and it was a real goer. Graham was very impressed, and truth be told, so was I. The car went on to become a real record-breaker with Graham behind the wheel. He was a wild man, and an absolute crazy driver. I was quite surprised that he didn't wreck it in his first race.

I built a load of other stuff when I was in the army with access to all the big machines. Now that I was out, I had plenty of time for new projects. I also had time to chase some skirt.

Dick and Jillie

The phone rang.

'Julianne, it's your boyfriend,' her mother said. 'He wants to talk to you.'

Jillie fumed. 'Tell him I'm not home.'

'But he insists,' she said, demanding her daughter come and grab the handset planted firmly in her palm.

Jillie took her hand from my leg, pushed herself off the couch, and steamed to the phone.

'No, he's not here,' she barked down the receiver. 'And anyway, you and I are done. It's over.'

Jillie stopped for a minute, listened and then laughed. Her boyfriend had just threatened to kill himself. She later told me what he'd said: 'I know he's there. His car's out the front. If he's not gone in five minutes, I'm going to drive myself into a tree.'

Jillie slammed the phone down, thinking it was nothing more than a desperate attempt to keep her by his side. It wasn't.

Vroom! Screech! Bang!

Exactly five minutes later a horrifying noise shook the house.

The silly bugger had actually done what he'd promised. We didn't dare go out there – that was left to Jillie's dad. He bolted out and found a smouldering wreck at the base of a nearby gum tree, which only seemed mildly disturbed by the 80 k/h-hit.

Jillie's boyfriend was in a bad way. The impact had smashed the entire front of his car, sending the steering wheel to the roof. His legs were broken, his face bloodied and bruised, but he was alive.

An ambulance was called and Jillie and I got out of there. We didn't even dare look as we jumped in my car and took off. I knew the bloke too, and I felt a bit sorry for him, but it was just bad luck. Jillie was mine and I wasn't giving her up. Not then, not ever.

I first met Jillie at my family home. She sat on the wall watching me as I pulled apart her boyfriend's EH. She had dark brown hair, long and silky. Her face was like a fine portrait: soft and put together with a delicate brush. And her body . . . oh man, it was something else. Needless to say, I noticed her straightaway. Maybe I kept on booking in her boyfriend's car just to see her again. I knew she would come.

I'm not sure who spoke first, but I suspect it wasn't me because I was pretty shy. I was immediately comfortable with Jillie; she made me feel at ease. I suggested she bring her own car down to my makeshift garage one day, knowing I'd have more time to chitchat if her boyfriend wasn't around. Soon after she did, watching me as I pulled apart her Mini.

'So, you want to go to the disco?' I asked, filthy overalls and all.

'Sure,' she said.

'OK then, I'll see you there.'

There was only one disco in town and it was a corker: the Rumbling Tum at the Glenn Hotel. It was early days as far as that scene was concerned and the place was a sight to behold. I didn't want to pay the entry fee to get her in – it cost an arm and a leg – so I told her to meet me there. One of my mates was pumped about going. He was on a mission to pick up, and was more than excited when he saw the women bopping away on the dancefloor. Problem for him was the one he liked wasn't exactly a woman.

'What do you think?' he said proudly.

We'd just gotten in and I was yet to find Jillie. We knew there was something not quite right with the so-called bird he was grinding away with, but we didn't want to spoil his fun.

'You lucky bugger,' I said. 'You better do the business, at least get her number.'

Our suspicions were confirmed. The girl ended up being a guy. She was a transsexual. I won't tell you how he found out, but I will tell you we took the absolute piss out of him later. It was hilarious.

I eventually met Jillie. She looked stunning, and I should have felt awkward but I didn't. I wasn't much of a ladies' man – they might've liked me but I was more interested in cars. I'd had one girlfriend before, a German bird who wanted to get married. She was OK until she mentioned house, kids, and rest of your life, so I got out. Bolted. Jillie was different. We just got on, and ended up dancing the night away. I'd like to tell you what the DJ played, but I can't. I was totally captivated by Jillie . . . and the trannies!

The Quarter Mile

The 472 Chevrolet shook the little Triumph to its very core. With each rev the wheels threatened to spin, the body shuddered, the earth moved. Then the Triumph fell silent, only for a moment, before bursting to life as the start lights went out. Rubber spewed into the air and the deadly machine was doing 100 k/h in just a matter of seconds.

And then feathers started flying from the window.

The 'Chicken Man' was a real joker. Aside from taking his hands from the steering wheel at dangerously high speeds and hurling feathers out his window, he also made chicken noises and did the chicken dance.

Welcome to drag racing in the 1960s, a place of feathers, flying and fearsome speed. I first heard about the likes of Chicken Man when Barry Covington asked me to work on his car. It was a Renault R4, the first in Australia, and we bolted a Holden engine to its belly. I was still in Bulimba when he approached me.

'Can you make this thing go as fast as it can?' he asked. 'From zero to flat in the blink of an eye. And don't worry about making it turn. All I need is straight-line speed.'

'Why the hell would you want a car that doesn't turn?' I said. 'That's ridiculous.'

'There are no corners on a drag strip, my friend. It's all about big horsepower and getting it to the ground.'

I was intrigued. 'I'm in,' I said. 'And after I finish I'll race you in my EH.'

My EH was a road car, but it was still very hot rod. It was lowered, had all the shoes, gear and horsepower. I thought she would go great down the quarter mile, but after hearing of the Chicken Man, I thought she needed some cosmetic work before I raced.

I called my mate Dennis Glindemann, an apprentice sign-writer, and asked him if he could help. Dennis came round the night before I was due to drive down to the Surfers Paradise Raceway to see how fast my EH could go. He was slightly surprised that I wanted to have my road car signed up.

He had a solution.

'Watercolours,' he said. 'They'll wash right off once you're done.'

The car looked a treat. He signed it up with numbers and the name of my business. I was proud as Punch as I rolled out the driveway but consumed by dread as the clouds gathered overhead.

'It will wash right off,' I said, repeating Dennis's words from the night before. I waited for the heavens to open up, to see his hours of work dribble away.

Thankfully it stayed dry.

Surfers Paradise Raceway was top-notch, real state-of-the-art in its day. And I went OK. I struggle to recall the details, but I certainly held my own. I even competed against the dedicated drag cars and didn't get left behind. The road cars were actually a pretty good match for them big bangers in those early days. Sure, they would get the jump on us, but eventually we would mow them down.

We ended up finishing Barry's car and it was a real rocket. He won plenty of races in it, and flogged the car to its very core. I kept up with the drag racing, but it was more a hobby than anything. My real passion was on the track, and it didn't take me long to get back.

I poured all of my money into my EH *again*, and turned it into a decent race machine. I was tempted to grab the paintbrush and go for lilac once more, but this time I had a bit more money and went for something a little bit more professional. We painted this racing EH a brilliant red.

I wasn't one bit nervous when I returned to Lakeside for my latest comeback. To be honest, I was just glad to return to the track. I couldn't help but notice how many EHs there were when I arrived; every man and his dog seemed to have one. There was one bloke from Sydney at Lakeside that day, who came with a reputation.

'He's the man when it comes to EHs,' someone said. 'He will have you.'

His car was immaculate and he certainly looked the part. His name was Graham Ryan and I wanted to give him a hiding.

And I did.

I absolutely blew Graham and his reputation apart. My EH was a little red rocket, and no match for any of the Holdens there. I didn't win, but I had the fastest EH, and that was a big thing, considering I'd built it myself and beaten the supposed best. My car was bloody brilliant.

I think I finished sixth all up. Six months earlier I was in the army, racing a forgotten dream. And now, a couple of years since my last race, I was back on track with a very decent car. At this point of time, I would still say it was more a hobby. I had no idea where it was going to lead; I had no serious ambition or intention to be the best.

Of course, all that would change.

Woolloongabba Dabba Doo

Cocky, confident, I walked straight up to Bob Glindemann, brother of my sign-writing pal Dennis.

'Mate,' I said to the Shell man who had quickly established himself as a real player on the motorsport scene. 'I want my own servo. Do you have any pull at that joint?'

He nodded, smiled and then glanced at one of his mates standing in the Shell tent at Lakeside, as if to say 'Who the hell does this bloke think he is?' He looked back.

'I think we can work something out if you have the goods.'

Bob was an area manager for Shell, and there was no way in the world I would have fronted him if I hadn't already known his brother. But fate is a funny cross-dressing lady, and mostly she is kind to Dick Johnson.

I was already using Shell fuel at this point for my race car, and I figured he knew who I was. I could have been using Castrol, they were big, but I liked my Shell and knew Bob's brother, so I was plenty confident he would help me out.

'We'll talk some more,' he said.

It was a moment of bravado and balls that would forever change my life, leading to a relationship that still exists to this very day. Shell and Dick Johnson: fits well, hey?

I had outgrown my garage. I only had three spaces in my workshop and needed more, requiring the help of a company like Shell. But let's back up, because not long before fronting Bob, I almost went broke.

Soon after moving into my garage, my partner Barry left. He was working full-time and he just couldn't handle the long nights and non-existent pay. It wasn't a messy divorce.

The only thing we owned together was a debt to the Greek, a spanner or two, and a shitty old jack. He let me keep the lot.

I kept all my old work and picked up some more, but with the added responsibility of rent, it just wasn't enough. I wouldn't say that I was about to go bust, though I was certainly struggling.

Enter Dad.

Knowing that I was doing it a bit tough, maybe fearing I would return to his house with rattling midnight chains, he found work for me. Ever the salesman, and more so a caring father, he went out to countless car yards and told them about his son, the mechanic, who could fix their cars.

I don't know exactly what he said, or how cheap he told them I was, but he found a bloke who was willing to give me a go.

'OK,' Murray Simpson from Woolloongabba told Dad. 'Let's see what your boy has.'

I didn't disappoint. I took in everything Murray had and sent it back crystal clean, in perfect order and ready to roar, no matter how rusty or wrecked it had been when it arrived. Murray was impressed, and he kept on sending damaged cars my way. At first it was only a few, but eventually they came in thick and fast. Murray was a lovely bloke, an absolute gentleman, and we made a great team.

His business tided me over when things were really slow. In fact, things boomed after a while and got so good that I had to put a couple of blokes on. I'm not sure how I found them, word of mouth, I guess, but one of the blokes I hired was brilliant – we called him Charcoal; he could pull an engine out of a Cooper S and do the gearbox in eight hours. It would take anyone else two days.

Hiring my own staff was a big deal. I had to think hard about it before I put someone on. I really didn't know if I was going to be able to part with $60 a week to pay a wage – I wasn't even earning that much myself and I didn't think I could afford it, but I did. And I got some winners. After hiring Charcoal, I found another gun, Barry Turner, and he was so good that I eventually had to let him go. He got an offer of $95 a week, which I couldn't compete with. But it was all part of learning to be a boss. I could never have dreamed I would reach that point, not that I thought too much about where I was.

I was 22 and a business owner with a couple of employees. Just four years before I was trucking around spare parts and cursing my boss. I took it all in my stride. Seriously, I didn't stop and reflect. I certainly didn't worry about where I was or what might be. All I was focused on was being able to make enough coin to go racing.

And so business was great and I had outgrown my three-car backstreet workshop, largely thanks to Murray, and I needed something more. That's why I approached Bob. He came back to me not long after I'd asked him.

'I think we might be able to work something out,' he said, no doubt pushed along by his brother, who I had nagged. 'But you'll have to enrol in Shell school first.'

What? School. No. I hated that crap the first time round. But a good six years after clearing that place I was being asked to go back again. Lucky it was only for two weeks.

'No problems,' I said. 'Whatever it takes.'

So I slammed the rollers shut and closed my business. I hated the fact I wasn't going to be able to work on a car for a fortnight, but I knew it was something I had to do. The Shell school was in Spring Hill, at the back of one of the franchises owned directly by the company, all shiny and new.

By this time Jillie and I were going strong. Beyond boyfriend and girlfriend, if you know what I mean, and we were considering our future together. We used to lie around at night and talk about what could be. She was never pushy, only supportive, but she thought linking up with Shell and getting my own franchise was a good idea. We even talked about her being a part of the business, and although she was already working full-time, she agreed to come to the school a couple of times to see what it was all about.

I had my eye on a service station before I knew I even wanted one. I used to pass it every other day. It was owned by the Addams family (yeah I know, bad name), and it was apparently run much like that very same gothic bunch. I liked it because it was close to the city, on a major artery that fed straight to its heart. The servo also had a huge workshop, big enough for four cars, but I had no idea when it was about to become available.

'How about that servo at Woolloongabba?' I asked Shell's Bob Glindemann. 'I would love that.'

Sure enough I was told it was being reacquired by Shell, and soon it became mine. I was thrilled, well, until I actually walked in there, a proud new owner.

Swoosh!

I was barely a step into the workshop when my arse flew

into the air, my back crashing to the ground. Ouch. My feet were no match for the slippery crap the previous owners left caked on the ground, which was sloshed with grease an inch high. I kid you not, it almost came up to my ankles. I'd never seen such a mess.

So I pulled myself from the shit, aches and all, and launched into it with shovels. It was so bad that I eventually had to find mattocks, such was the neglect and abandon. I scraped, dug and tore, before letting four litres of toxic commercial degreaser do its work so that the floor was clean enough to paint.

No workshop of mine was going to be covered in filth.

The service station, called the 'Westbound' by Shell, wasn't much like the type you see these days. It wasn't a supermarket with butter, eggs, barbecue-flavoured Shapes and condoms; in the shop we just had chocolate bars, soft drinks and smokes. The income also didn't come from fuel. Back in those days, the markets were even more regulated than what they are today, so there was hardly any margin at all. The money was to be made from the service centre, the workshop, and I was fine with that because that's why I bought the place.

But still, like today, we gouged on what we had. The soft drink was overpriced, the chocolate too. But as I said, there wasn't much of that; the shop was more spark plugs, batteries, points and fanbelts than Mars bars, Paddle Pops and chocolate Mooves.

I only had two double pumps: one fuel gun on each side of the machine. We sold super and standard. Diesel did exist, but if you wanted that stuff you had to go far and wide. LPG wasn't even a thought; there was too much of the other stuff to worry about that. And because it wasn't self-operated like it is now, at times I had to pump fuel for the customer, smile and all.

Bing. Bing.

The bell would go off – that's the way we'd set it up. Before we could even hear the screech of brakes, or the slow death of a rumbling engine, the car would run over a piece of rubber hose and push air all the way along to the end where a bell was rung by the passing gush.

Bing. Bing.

The bell used to give me the shits. Sure, it meant there was a customer, but it used to drag me, or one of my staff, away from the real work of tinkering with cars.

Bing. Bing.

The boys looked at me.

'Yeah, OK,' I said. 'I'll get it.'

I was closest and that was the rule. I came up with a system, where whoever was closest to the incoming car got the job of pumping fuel. I tried to be smart and stay away from the pumps, but sometimes you just got caught.

Truth be told, it wasn't that bad. I got a lot of business out of pumping fuel.

'Hey, buddy,' I'd say. 'That thing isn't running too good. Maybe you should bring it back on Monday. I'm pretty busy, but I can book it in. Give you a real good deal, too.'

It worked a treat. Come Monday the car would be there. If you were nice enough, you'd get their business. And I was plenty nice. But at the end of the day, it was more than that. Once we got them, we looked after them. As a mechanic, I always took care of my customers, giving them the best quality and offering them the cheapest price.

Bing. Bing.

Off it went again. We turned and looked. The customer wasn't at the fuel pump, he was off to the side, and we wondered what was going on.

Bing. Bing.

He yanked open his bonnet, and stood and stared. He peered inside, looking for at least two minutes before hastily removing the radiator cap rather than gently screwing it off. Steam poured from his engine. A cloud of mist and crap spewed out.

Bing. Bing.

The bloody bell rang again, but not because he was walking or driving over it. He grabbed the hose connected to the bell, and shoved it in his radiator.

Bing. Bing.

We pissed ourselves. You should have seen the look on his face when he walked around to turn on the tap. He followed the hose all the way to where we were standing and then saw that it was attached to a bell. Needless to say, this cheap repair ended up costing him a fortune. Sucker. Some things that happened at the Westbound were just plain hilarious.

I had work coming out of my ears. The garage was big, but not big enough for the jobs I was taking on. Rain used to fuck me over and set me back for weeks. I could never knock down a gig, so we would work on cars outside as well as in the shop. At least until it rained. We could fit four cars inside, plus one on the hoist and one in front. It was always a big shuffle: manoeuvring them in, and then sliding them out. We kept only the things we needed inside the garage and did the rest of the job outside. I'd employed three mechanics by this time, and we were all flat out. We were booked out weeks ahead.

Some customers used to give me the shits. Especially with the cars we worked on. I couldn't stand seagulls, the people who just wanted to watch. I still can't. They used to come in and stand around and watch you work and ask dumb questions like 'What's that?'

Then I found a sign.

'We charge five dollars an hour,' it read. 'Seven dollars if you watch. Ten dollars if you help.'

That did the trick. But seriously, that's what we charged – five dollars an hour. A bloke wouldn't even put fuel in your car for that price now, let alone pull out your engine.

9

HOLDENS AND HEARTBREAK

Going For Choke

Ian Palmer, whose brother Ross owned a little company called Palmer Tube Mills, looked to his left as the hot Holden stopped right beside him, begging to be beaten.

Brrrrr! Brrrrrr!

The Holden shuddered and shimmied as its young driver revved the engine, staring down Ian and my brother.

'Let's have him,' Ian said menacingly.

Dyno knew what Ian's Ford could do. He had helped me turn it into a thunderous thrashing machine. We'd put Triple SUs on the two-door beast, thrown in a four-speed racing gearbox and worked the engine till it could take no more.

'But what about the accelerator cable?' my brother asked.

'We don't have one.'

Dyno and Ian had been hooning around earlier and the

accelerator cable came loose, fell onto the exhaust and burnt through. Gone.

'Can you fix it?' Ian asked.

'I'll have a look,' my brother replied. He got out, lifted the hood and went about attaching the choke cable to the accelerator.

'That'll do the job,' Dyno said. 'Just pull on the choke to accelerate.'

'Sweet,' Ian said. 'I'll work the throttle, you take the gears. Let's smoke him and his Holden.'

They squared off, Ian holding the choke on the dash with one hand, the other firmly on the steering wheel.

'This bloke is toast,' he said.

He glanced towards the Holden hot rod, snarled at the driver before looking back to the lights. Once they turned green he dumped his left foot.

Ppppt. Pppp. Ppp. Pp. P.

The car slowly stalled . . . *dead.*

Ian screamed, not in defeat but in agonising pain.

'Ouuuuch!' He slapped and swiped at himself. A burst of light flew from his lap and clunked onto the floor.

Dyno looked down and saw the blazing cigarette lighter on the ground. 'I think you pulled that instead of the choke,' he said. 'Dickhead.'

The Holden blazed off into the night.

The loss wasn't my fault because I'd turned that Ford into a mean machine in my new garage. It was one of many performance cars I was working on at the time and business was good. I wasn't loaded by any stretch, but I had enough money to pay my bills and some left over to think about racing. I had the servicing department, fuel accounts with local businesses, and I was doing a decent trade in the shop. I kept myself busy. Sometimes too busy.

Ring. Ring.

The bell rang and I bolted. I was always frantic in the workshop with a million things to do, so I took off like a bull at a gate. Suddenly I was floored four strides in. My elbow smashed against the cold hard floor. But it wasn't my arm I was worried about. I looked down to my leg.

'Ouch,' I muttered, too tough to scream in front of my staff.

A pool of viscous red blood was gathering on the concrete, quickly expanding into a river and flowing across the ground. I grabbed myself just below the hip in an attempt to stop the crimson gush.

A thick piece of metal, still connected to an EH, was jammed through my leg, in one side and out the other. The chrome strip on the EH's mudguard had come loose and had pierced straight through just above my knee.

I couldn't move. Finally I yelled for help.

'Bring some cutters,' I shouted, trying not to sound panicked. 'Now!'

I was in agony. I can't remember who brought me the snips, but I snatched them right off him and clipped the piece of metal between my leg and the guard, freeing myself from the car. I now had a 30 centimetre-long piece of metal poking through me. I tried pulling at it.

'Fuuuuuck,' I said, and I rarely swear. Especially not back then.

That's when I asked to be taken to hospital. The boys dropped me off.

'Just get it out,' I said.

So the doctor grabbed his tools and went to work. I was so relieved that I paid no attention to what the nurse did next. She cleaned the wound, and then jabbed me full of penicillin. Not good.

'I'm allergic to that,' I said in the aftermath, my body blowing up like an angry puffer fish.

I had another week of pain, maybe worse than the wound. Just like the chilblain in the army, I couldn't stand up for a week. But I would recover – nothing was going to stop me from racing. Not again.

ESP

Jillie became a very important part of my life – not only because she towed my EH, but also because I fell in love with her.

Jillie and I did everything together. We went to clubs; I didn't dance but we watched people do the 'Hanky Panky', and the 'Camel Walk' to Tommy James and James Brown, while petticoats swirled to tunes like 'I'm a Believer' and 'To Sir with Love'. With the soundtrack of the 1960s ringing in our ears, we watched movies at the drive-in, classics like *The Graduate*, *Midnight Cowboys* and *Yellow Submarine*, walked the Brisbane Foreshore and cuddled on her parents' lounge. Life was good.

And then things changed.

We were coming home from the speedway at the

Exhibition Centre in Brisbane, another night of bonding under the stars, high octane adding to the occasion. Jillie looked at me.

'I feel weird,' she said. 'Kind of cold and giddy.'

I looked at my arm. The hairs were standing up, an ice-cold shiver shocking my spine. 'Me too,' I said. 'Something's wrong. But what?'

'I don't know,' Jillie said. 'But I have a horrible feeling.'

We drove back to Jillie's house, an eerie silence engulfing the car.

There was no mobile phone back then, of course, no way to be told if there was anything wrong. But we suspected there was. Call it ESP, if you believe in that kind of thing.

We slowly rolled round the corner and into Jillie's street. All was dark, except for the burning glow of the lights flickering from her home. Unusual but expected.

'This isn't good,' she said. 'Something is *really* wrong.'

We pulled up in the driveway and got out of the car. There didn't seem to be any movement coming from inside the house. Uneasy, Jillie grasped tightly onto my arm. We edged towards the front door, and she turned the key.

Our worst suspicions were confirmed when we saw Jillie's mum sitting on the lounge like a zombie. They both began to bawl.

Jillie's father had gone to the bowling club that afternoon and had never come home. A Saturday afternoon ritual for the hard worker and all round good bloke, he'd finished up with his mates, jumped in the car and was on his way home to spend the rest of the evening with his adoring wife. A corner away from his house, however, with one turn to negotiate, he had had a heart attack, lost control of the car and smashed into a pole. He was dead on impact. The lights in his family home, all of his street, went off for a moment such was the hit. And like Jillie and me, his wife immediately knew something wasn't right.

It was one of those dreadful moments when you fear something is wrong and you soon find out there really is. I'm sure it's happened to all of us at some point in our lives. To this day, Jillie and I still can't explain what we had really felt that night.

With Jillie and her mother both grief-stricken, I moved out of home for the first time to help them where I could. I suppose it was a blessing in disguise, the worst bringing out the best. I had been with Jillie for almost a year, maybe more, by then and now we were living together. I guess it's fair to say that her father's death brought us closer together.

I don't remember clearly who popped the question, but we were soon engaged. I suspect it was Jillie, because it was something that had never really been on my radar.

'Don't you think it'd be a good idea if we got married?' she said, or at least I think that's the way it went.

I nodded. 'Sounds good to me. Never even thought about it, but yeah, why not?'

I didn't think it was a big deal. Jillie can't even recall the specifics, but we both know we got it right. We were engaged in November 1968 and I had no hesitations about marriage. The soon-to-be union was already paying off. Jillie had already quit her job and was working for me; she did the accounts and also served petrol. Hell, she would have pulled out an engine and given it a rebuild if we'd let her. She was just an outstanding worker, and an equally outstanding woman. No wonder the ex drove himself into a tree.

The Game-Changer

I was back at Lakeside, heart thumping, engine roaring. Gordon Clough was to my right; Evan Thomas and John Humphries behind. I floored my EH off the line, tyres smoking and steering wheel shuddering as the rubber gripped and sent my open-faced helmet smashing into the back of my seat.

I had been plodding around in my Holden for a while now. I had the cash to take my EH to all the local meets, ten a year, but certainly not to anything interstate. I hadn't won a race, not since my first-ever outing, but I was doing OK. I didn't expect to win – sure, I wanted to – but as I said, the old EH could be up against anything on the day: mixed classes, cars and formats. The Mustangs were killing me.

Although I wasn't winning the races, I was collecting an award at nearly every meet. They had a thing called the Kaiser Stuhl 'Man of the Meet', and inevitably, it ended up in the back of my EH. The award wasn't about who had the fastest car, but who put up the bravest fight. And I am proud to say that was mostly me.

I was pretty flamboyant with my driving style and I think that helped. I always seemed to be getting my EH up on one wheel. Going under the bridge at Lakeside, there were bumps aplenty. I would hit them as hard as I could and send the EH flying into the air. You had to be really brave, and I was. There are a lot of photos to prove it!

I watched Norm Beechey, a legend of our sport, smash the Lakeside lap record in 1965. He blasted his way to a time of 1.07.02. In July 1968, I beat it. Smashed it with a time of 1.05.40.

It was around this time that I was starting to get some press in the racing publications. Mostly, I think that was because my good mate Des White was a contributor for *Racing Car News*. I still wasn't winning races.

But on this day, racing against Clough, Thomas and Humphries, I got a little bit more than I'd expected – I won!

I should know how, but I don't. All I know is that it was my last-ever race in the EH, and I sent her out a winner. I was about to upgrade – something else had caught my eye – and the EH had already been sold to my brother. It was pretty surreal to get my second race win under those circumstances. I was over the moon, but not too upset about kissing my EH goodbye. I suspected I was about to strap down into a game-changer.

The 1969 Torana LC GTR I fell in love with was a dark iridescent green. Not your average racing green, but a weird bright green and absolutely beautiful. I stared at the strange colour as I rubbed my hand along its aggressively styled body. It had a longer nose than the standard LC, which had only just been released, and a bigger snout to accommodate a larger engine.

The Torana LC first appeared at the beginning of 1969 and came with either a four- or six-cylinder engine, depending on your budget and persuasion. The in-line six had a capacity of 138 inches cubed, with the option of a three- or four-speed manual gearbox, or a Trimatic automatic transmission.

The LC had already caught my eye; it was the *Wheels Magazine* Car of the Year. It was a bit like an EH, only smaller, slighter and much more nimble. But this GTR was something else altogether. Mostly it was about the engine – definitely not the tan upholstery that smacked me right in the face as I peered through the window. The GTR had a 161ci, 2.6-litre engine, with a two-barrel Stromberg VW carburettor pumping fuel to its fiery heart. It had a bit of guts to go with its wiry frame.

I'd predicted the Torana was going to be the next big thing. We knew damn well it was to replace the HT 350 and eventually race at Bathurst. I had heard on the grapevine that Harry Firth, the premier race car builder of the time and a rally champion in a Cortina, was about to switch from Ford to Holden. He was to become General Motors' main man with the Holden Dealer Team (HDT) and it was the Torana he had earmarked to take it to the beastly Ford Falcon GT-HO. Norm Beechey had just started out in a GTS 327 Monaro, which was a real big banger and expensive to both buy and maintain. With a price tag edging towards $5000, it was out of the racer's reach.

As I continued to study the LC's lines and the potential power of this fleet-footed machine, I was interrupted by Ron Schwartz, the sales manager at Eager's Holden, who used to work under my dad, and is now retired.

'It's the first one, Richard,' he said. 'The first damn one in the world.'

I knew I had to have it, there and then. The *first*!

'How about we do a deal?' I said to Ron. 'I know you already sponsor the tower at Lakeside – why don't you expand

and put some cash into a car? I'm a GM man through and through. Raced them my whole life.'

Ron knew that; I was forging a reasonable name.

'I'll get my mate Dennis Glindemann to paint her up with "Eager's Holden". She'll sparkle. What do you think?' I continued.

He smiled. 'Sure, Richard,' he said. 'We'll sell you the car at a reasonable price.'

It was my first big deal. I think he took a couple of hundred bucks off the original price and I snared the car for $1800. I bought it on a hire-purchase, and I can tell you it was a better deal than what my brother got. I ripped all the good shit out of the EH before I slung him the keys. The good parts were destined for the LC.

10

WEDDINGS, FUNERALS
AND THE MOUNTAIN

Still Chipping Away

My eyes lit up.

'Fifty bucks a win?' I beamed.

'Yep.' Bob Glindemann nodded. 'And $30 for a second and $20 for a third. We'll also provide you with racing fuel and, of course, oil.'

Shell had just made me a part of their racing team and it was a ripping deal. Some blokes today get $20,000 a win, on top of contracts worth up to $1 million a year, but back then $50 was big money to go racing. So I proudly stripped the new GTR, did away with the green I liked so much and turned it into a Shell machine: yellow and red, much like Norm Beechey's Monaro.

Glindemann, the racing boss at Shell had made me a part of the company's Queensland racing team. They sponsored a sports car, a racing car, a production car, and I was their improved production man. I couldn't have been happier. But I had some concerns about the new GTR.

I had a lot of work to do to turn this new car into a thrashing machine. I'd spent years getting the EH right. Progressively, I'd gotten that car right where it needed to be and it was maybe the best of its kind in the country. The new Torana was a different proposition.

Immediately, I was concerned about the power. I planned to race it in the improved production class and the rules stated that I had to keep it at 161. That was a bit of a step down from the EH, and the straight-line speed was going to be less. But we did what we could.

We had all the good parts I'd taken from the EH. The carburettors went straight in. We made a new exhaust system, made a gun set of headers. We had to use standard pistons and con rods, but we put in an oil cooler and a bigger radiator because the standard one just wasn't good enough. We also put in a camshaft, port and polished the head, and whacked on bigger valves along with some new springs.

We didn't touch the interior – that wasn't allowed. We had to leave all the upholstery the way it was because that was the rule. The only thing we could do was put in a roll cage, if you could call it that. It was nothing more than an aluminium hoop, a half-cage going from the B-pillar to the rear window. I don't think it would have done much in a shunt.

Nothing changed with the gear we wore; it was still prehistoric. I used to have my race suit, which was a cotton suit, tailored at a local shop. It looked like something Stirling Moss would have kicked around in. It wasn't fireproof, not by a long shot, and it did nothing in the way of safety – there was no special underwear, socks or cool suits, and the footwear was something more appropriate for a day on a yacht. They were called driving shoes, and were actually fairly comfortable because they were made of flexible material. We had standard pedals in all the cars, and you needed a big foot to even attempt a heel-toe. Not easy.

The GTR had the opal gearbox, and it wasn't that strong to be honest. The ratios weren't flash either. It was a four-speed, but you only ever used the third and fourth gears. And slicks weren't out then and not part of the motor racing scene anywhere, so we all ran on threaded tyres. The gun tyre was the Firestone, which would have been terrible in the wet because of the fine grooves cut into them, but surprisingly good in the dry.

The only two circuits we were now racing at were Lakeside and Surfers, and I felt the car was better than the EH when we rolled it out. But not by much.

We had years to perfect the EH and we had a lot of work in front of us to unlock the Torana's full potential. One of the major problems was that the engine would overheat. The temperature would creep up, probably because it was only a 161 and we were asking a bit too much from it. We weren't allowed to give the Torana anymore because it had to be the same capacity as the production model. It was down on horsepower to the EH, but it was a lot lighter and far more nimble.

But the car must have been OK because I ended up taking out the Queensland Touring Car Championship in 1970. To me, racing was never about winning titles because

I was just out there to have fun, and to win something like that was just a bonus. In all honesty, I probably got it for the fact that I turned up to every meet and collected points, whereas others only competed in a few select events. Being my own boss, I didn't have to ask anyone for time off work. We were running against some pretty good cars and I only ever tried to do my best, race by race. I think we were more consistent than anything else, finishing every race in that year.

I also collected my first-ever point in the Australian Touring Car Championship in 1970. One of the rounds was held at Lakeside and I managed to do quite well, all local knowledge and 'not on my turf, boys'.

There was another important development in July with Holden bringing out the XU-1. It took us to a 186 engine, which was a big upgrade in power. I didn't go out and buy a new car because the GTR was essentially the same and only needed some slight modifications. I put the XU-1 spoiler on the boot and did work on the engine. The only way you would have known it wasn't an XU-1 was by looking at the chassis number. Everything else complied. I still have the logbooks for that car sitting in my drawer at work.

The extra power gave us a lot more straight-line speed, which we desperately needed. The XU-1 still only had standard brakes, but they were pretty effective for the time. The car was good, but I think we saw a lot of improvement, simply because the drivers in that era were pushing themselves and finding an extra ounce of brave.

Married Man

Jillie organised the wedding. I had absolutely nothing to do with it, except for picking the date.

'Do whatever you want, Jillie,' I said. 'Pick the church, the reception place – hell, you can even pick my mates – but whatever you do, make sure it doesn't interfere with a race.'

That was my one request. I didn't want to miss a race, not even to get married. But sure enough I missed one. It wasn't Jillie's fault, though. She made sure to look at the calendar and booked us in on a weekend with no meets, but fate obviously wanted to give the other blokes a chance because the Lakeside round was postponed due to wet weather and moved to the day of my wedding. Bastard.

Des White was my best man and he wasn't happy. He had to bolt straight to the wedding after his commentary duties, whack his suit on and dash in for the service. He made it by the skin of his teeth.

We got married at St Andrew's Church of England in South Brisbane. I wore the bag of fruit with the bow tie, and Jillie looked stunning in her traditional white gown. I didn't take much notice of that sort of stuff, but I wasn't about to run out the back door when I saw her, put it that way.

Jillie's uncle gave her away, and I remember being upset that her father wasn't around to hand her over. It was a very special service. Not lengthy or overly religious, but very good.

We went straight from the service to the hospital to see Dad, who was in a bad way. Years of smoking had given him emphysema. He loved his unfiltered Cravens and would smoke at least one pack a day, even refusing to give up when he was diagnosed with the horrible lung disease. Dad was once a big, strong man, but on the hospital bed he was all skeleton covered in skin.

It would be the last time I would see him alive.

Dad was doped up to the eyeballs and wasn't doing well. I'd been to see him a couple of times before the wedding and he hadn't even acknowledged my presence. But on this occasion, he opened his eyes and recognised me. I will never forget that. I told him about the service, told him I wished he was there, gave him a kiss and said goodbye.

He died two days later.

Dad was quite old when he had me, but really, he couldn't have been a better father. I can remember jumping on his shoulders in summer, him heaving us down to the beach, a kid in each arm. We used to swim in the morning then he would go home and fix us breakfast, all smiles and love.

Dad taught me that I should never lie. That's the biggest lesson I learned from the old bloke.

'Tell the truth, son,' he would say. 'And you won't have to remember a thing.'

I really took that to heart. Even today I try to avoid interviews and I refuse to get on social media like Twitter because I have real trouble not telling the truth. I'm a bloke who tells it how it is, and it always gets me into shit. I can't help but speak my mind and it often rubs people the wrong way or lands me in some type of strife. But that's me, like it or lump it.

Dad was always a very hands-on person and no doubt he gave me my foundation in mechanics. Working on cars, boats and bikes kickstarted my career with engines. He would let me drive, even though I was far too young.

Earlier at the wedding ceremony, as I was waiting for my stunning bride, I couldn't help but think of Dad. He wasn't that religious, but Mum was, and standing there at the end of the aisle reminded me of a moment in my youth. Mum had demanded he take us boys to church.

It was a Sunday morning, rain belting down on the tin roof. Mum dressed us in our Sunday best and waved as Dad pulled out of the driveway. The sun came out just as Dad stopped in front of the chapel.

'Too good of a day to be listening to that crap if you ask me,' he said. 'Do you blokes really want to go?'

My brothers and I shook our heads. I looked across to the field and saw hundreds of mushrooms pushing up from the ground.

'I'd rather pick those mushrooms,' I said.

Dad turned towards the field. 'Well, mushrooms it is. That should kill enough time to keep your mother happy.'

Jillie and I drove to Sydney for our honeymoon. A race meeting was coming up at Oran Park in New South Wales and I thought we could fit in some sightseeing too. We had a couple of weeks off, and it was the first time either Jillie or I had left the business. My mum promised to go down and keep things in check while we were away.

Sydney was everything I thought it would be. I was absolutely floored by its size and scared shitless by the traffic. Our hotel was in Chatswood, but we ended up in George Street, bumper to bumper, trailer pulling a race car. We overshot the runway a bit there.

Jillie had a great idea.

'Let's go to Kings Cross and see *Les Girls*,' she said.

Les Girls was a new show that had just opened, and was said to be a risqué burlesque-type deal.

'I hear it's good,' she continued. 'You might even see some tits.'

Well, it was a good show. That's if you like seeing a bunch of poofters running around naked! Wow. What an eye-opener. We also saw *Hair*, which also featured some nudes. We were certainly coming of age.

While in Sydney I saw the Harbour Bridge and the Opera House for the first time. Jillie and I walked around The Rocks and took in sunsets and ate snapper. We also travelled to Canberra, Thredbo and Melbourne, before returning to Sydney. Overall, the honeymoon was nice, but I had something else on my mind because I was really there to race. Sorry, Jillie.

I knew a lot about Oran Park before I got there. I'd read about the place in all the racing magazines. The pictures always showed these whopping crowds: race fans out in their thousands, cheering and screaming as the cars tackled the small but demanding circuit. It was a big deal, a huge event. To get down there and bomb was a real kick in the arse.

Oran Park was my first proper interstate meet and it didn't go so well. In fact, the car was a piece of shit and I was a turd. Allan Horsley, who was the promoter, did a tremendous job. It was one of those tracks that you just had to have a crack at.

I wanted to test myself on a new track against different people and Oran Park presented the perfect opportunity. I'd been really hoping to do well there and thought I would do OK, but that didn't happen. Everyone tried to make excuses for me, saying it was because I was on my honeymoon and not focused, but that's bullshit. I just couldn't come to grips with the track and my car was nowhere near where it needed to be.

I was there a couple of years later, still in the Torana, and I managed to finish fourth in the race. Allan Moffat invited me into his Coca-Cola tent. He looked at me and smiled.

'You ought to keep this up, boy,' he said in his thick Canadian drawl. 'Because one day, you never know, you could just make it.'

I will never forget those words. I needed the encouragement. And I won't forget what happened afterwards either.

I was on my way to Calder Park, car packed, trailer loaded. Rain was belting down and the ground was all slop and slosh. I touched the brake and the car took off, wheels locked, hurtling down the hill. I couldn't turn, bracing myself because I was about to smash into a parked EH right in front. The parked car had no hope and began to slide, right into a dam. I got out and waited around for the owner.

'Where's my car?' he asked, when he finally arrived.

'Well, about that,' I said, pointing at the deep brown water, 'you might need to get a new one.'

Mountain Mishap

Again I edged over the rise, full of hope and wonder. My heart fluttered, just as it had the first time, and maybe even stopped for a second as Mount Panorama again revealed itself, as though reaching for the clouds. But this time I wasn't here to watch. I was here to race. And I couldn't wait.

Bathurst had a big meet in Easter. They had the cars and the bikes, a two-by-four meeting. It wasn't an endurance event, not the big one, but that mattered little – I was about to have my first taste of the Cutting, McPhillamy and Conrod.

I came packing a GTR, and that concerned me because of its lack of power. I'd already struggled on the straights at Lakeside and Surfers, and the prospect of going down Conrod against the big bangers was giving me nightmares. I tried to mask the problem by putting a huge camshaft into the GTR to give it some balls.

My first lap at Bathurst wasn't about the track but about my car. I wanted to be all head down, studying lines, braking points and acceleration marks, but I couldn't. My car was spluttering and banging. I got it around Hell Corner. That was easy. But then the car spewed and spluttered again so much and I almost didn't make it up the hill. 'Shit,' I cried. 'Why? Why now?'

I thumped the wheel in frustration. Here I was at the Mountain, a lifelong dream come true, and my car was an absolute dog. Whatever I did to the engine didn't work. It was frustrating to cart the thing all the way down there, to be so excited about firing around the best track in the world, and then to find out your car was crap. I knew I was in for a long weekend, but sometimes Bathurst can be cruel.

I wasn't about to give up. The first day was a write-off, practice was horrible and qualifying was poor. All fart and fluff, I put the car back on the trailer and drove down to Kelso, where I found a couple of quiet streets. The team fiddled with the engine and floored it down the road, but the car still popped and banged. There was nothing we could do and we went to bed full of fear and fright.

I was pretty nervous the next day, trying to get the car off the line. I thought it would stall. I was really shitting myself, but I was at the back of the field, which made it better, less nerve-racking, and I ended up starting off OK and passing a few blokes. The car actually went pretty well down the hill, at around 190 k/h. I slipstreamed Bob Jane's Mustang, but it was the ascent that was a terrible problem. Embarrassing.

I had to keep telling myself that it was a dream just to be there. I was at Mount Panorama as a hobbyist more than anything else, and to be driving at Bathurst was a thrill. Instead of worrying about the car, I learned as much as I could about the famed stretch of road. Lines and apexes were tough at Bathurst back then because there were no kerbs to give you a guide. You had to figure it out for yourself, and it took a few laps to even have a clue. The best thing about the track was the big tree before the top of the Mountain. The shadow it cast gave you a reference point, one of the few markers on the track. I am still shitty they chopped it down.

Through McPhillamy Park there was no fence on the left-hand side. You would touch the dirt, gravel spewing off the cliff, car threatening to go the same way. You could sort of see where the lines were because of the rubber that had been laid down by the faster guys who had left an impression on the road for the rest of us to try to follow. Their marks would be left on the edge of the grass and the bitumen, and that's how you knew where you needed to be. You could also watch them, where they dropped an edge of a wheel off the road, how close they went to a fence, and how far they were out of the corner when you would see their rear ends shake, rocking with flat-footed power to the floor.

All that was great, but where you made time at Bathurst was under brakes. Coming down the Mountain and into Skyline was what it was all about. There were no concrete walls, just banks, and you had to be bloody brave. A mistake could send you rolling down the side of the hill. And it was a massive hill.

Over the years I would change my lines. It wasn't easy figuring out the quickest way, but it's a matter of exploring. I found that the fastest route for me was a lot different to those of other drivers. Even today, watching the likes of Craig Lowndes hurtling over it, I'm astounded by the way race car drivers approach Skyline. It's really strange because they hang right out to the left, whereas I always stayed mid-road.

I enjoyed my first outing at Bathurst, even though I was disappointed that my car was a piece of shit. I was there, and that was an achievement in itself for the bloke who almost gave up on his dream when he was broke after his first race.

Trucking Along

I racked up three Queensland Touring Car Championships in my Torana, the Holden turning out to be the good car that we'd expected. With Firth at the helm, and Brock and Bond the stars, the HDT team had made real progress and we followed suit. I went back to Bathurst in 1973, desperate to make up for my horror debut. I was hoping it would be easier. It wasn't.

'I'll tell you what,' Bob Forbes said after we agreed to team up, 'I'll send the car up and all you have to do is build the engine. I'll do all the work and then send two of my guys over to help you drop the engine in and get it back down to the Mountain.'

It sounded like a sweet deal to me. It wasn't.

On the day, I had the engine built and ready to go when the chassis arrived.

'What the fuck?' I screamed; I normally didn't get angry. 'This isn't a car. It's a shell.'

The only thing they'd done to it was put in a roll cage. That was it.

'Christ,' I swore. 'What the hell I am I going to do with this?'

There were only four days left until Bathurst – the race I'd been waiting for since I first jammed my right foot into an accelerator. The ghosts of GTR still haunted me; I could feel another disaster was looming. I got on the phone and tore into Forbes, who I called a few names before calming down and getting to work.

The car was a shell, which essentially meant we had to build it from scratch. Suspension, gearbox, brakes, body and bars – they all had to be done. We worked day and night, flogged ourselves and put every job on hold at the servo. Our business stalled, but what could we do? This was Bathurst.

In the end, we got it done. Well, almost.

We couldn't finish the exhaust because we had no tubing. But there was absolutely no time left. We had to hit the road.

On the Friday afternoon, less than 16 hours before practice, dog-tired and with no midnight oil left to burn, we headed off. Three of us left my service station in Brisbane, and we piled into the front, junk stacked in the back. We whacked the car on the trailer and went south, the dilemma of the exhaust still unresolved. We were fucked.

After an hour of driving we came up with a plan because the fatigue from the past few days had really started to set in.

'I'm rooted,' I said. 'Can't keep my eyes open. We're going to have to do shifts.'

So we agreed on a system. It would be 100 kilometres of tar and bugs smashing against the windscreen before a driver change. Then the guy on the far left in the passenger seat would get out, run around the car twice to wake himself up, and replace the driver, while the rest of us shuffled over. The former driver would shift to the middle, entering dreamland in an instant.

I was never a big sleeper and that worked to my advantage. Meanwhile, the guys were so spent and knackered they would pass into a deep sleep as soon as they shifted from the wheel. Instead of the 100 kilometres each driver was supposed to do, I would drive only ten and then stop.

'Wow, I'm screwed,' I said. 'What a big stint. You boys look fresh.'

I would then shift over, and they'd be none the wiser. Sneaky Dick.

We got to the Shell service station at Orange and finished the exhaust. The car felt OK in practice, anything would after my previous bomb, and I eventually qualified. I have no idea where I finished, but I damn well know I was ten seconds a lap faster than my co-driver Bob Forbes.

Then the race officially started.

Off we went. Again the Torana struggled for power ascending the hill, but it made up for its weakness across the top. It was a totally different feeling knowing the car was going smoothly. Rather than stressing about things beyond my control, I was able to worry about the race. Grice passed me by along the top of the Mountain.

I can't be going fast enough, I thought. *Have a go, you mug.*

Bathurst was a different game in 1973. It wasn't like today, where it's flat-out every lap, a sprint race. It was about survival. While guys whine about having to conserve fuel in the V8s now, back then we had to conserve the entire car. Seriously, we had a little bit more to do than flick the fuel trim back or roll off the throttle. We were managing brakes, tyres, steering, gearbox, the lot. Anything could go in a heartbeat if you pushed too hard. It was like running a marathon. If you sprinted at any point, you lived with the fear of breaking down later, but you also drove with the fear that you weren't doing enough. So when you were passed, you were tempted to floor it, and get back in front. It was a dangerous game. So I got Grice back.

Physically, it wasn't a problem. Bathurst was the longest race I had ever done, and we didn't have power steering, cool suits or power gels, but I was fine. All I thought about was what lay ahead, loving every moment and feeling an electric buzz. I felt totally alive, in my element. For me, it was about putting your head down and reeling off laps; being comfortable and conserving not just the car's energy, but your own. You had to be in tune with your car and know what it was doing in order to get the best from it. They weren't bulletproof like the cars today. You had to make it last.

You couldn't rush the gear changes; you had to be gentle with them. You couldn't abuse the clutch; you had to let it out easy, even at the start. You couldn't hold it flat; you had to cool the valves down, because the XU-1s were dropping them everywhere. To finish the race was an achievement. To finish it with a result was outstanding, especially against the factory teams.

We came fifth.

Still, I was unknown. I don't remember if I even signed an autograph, but shit, have I made up for it since. I was reasonably well known in Queensland, but here, in Bathurst, I was a nobody. On the other hand, Norm Beechey, my idol, the bloke who I wanted to be, was an absolute rockstar. He sat up on the roof of his car and signed autographs for an hour after the meeting.

As soon as I got back in the road car, I thought something was wrong. I was sure there was a problem with my speedometer. It said I was doing 110 k/h, but it felt more like 20. I sped up a little and began passing everyone.

Turned out, nothing was up with the car, but with me. I was absolutely blown away. After flogging down the Mountain at 260 k/h, life was now in slow motion. I'd never felt anything like it before – or since.

I had another good result in the Torana on a separate interstate trip. We decided to pack up and go to Adelaide the following year. It was a double-header, a hill climb and a race at Mallala. The hill climb wasn't great, but we won the feature race of the day, and it was my first major victory. Overall, the trip cost me $3000, but it was worth every cent to get that interstate win against some very good cars.

I have to thank the BDA Escort that blew up in front of me with a couple of laps left to go. Otherwise, it most certainly would have been a second.

Pigeon Pair

Jillie looked at me, a serious frown hardening her face.

'Dick,' she said quietly. 'I've got something to tell you.'

I was immediately worried.

Does she want to quit the servo? I thought. *Go back to working at the menswear store? I can't afford to lose her. Maybe she fancies another bloke?*

'Dick,' she said again, distracting me from my paranoid thoughts. 'I'm pregnant.'

'You beauty!' I replied.

What a ripper.

It was a planned operation. I had been hard on the tools for a couple of months, and so the result wasn't too unexpected. I sat back and thought about becoming a parent as the news sunk in.

Would it change the way I raced? I thought. *Change my dream?*

Not on your life. Sure, I would have an extra responsibility with this bundle of joy, but I decided there and then it wouldn't change anything else.

There's an old myth that race car drivers don't know fear until they have a child. Some guys won't have children because they think they'll become scared of risking their lives. That's absolute bullshit. Having a child shouldn't make you fear death – you should be freaked out about it, anyway.

As a racer you need to have confidence in your own ability, and losing that is the only thing you should fear.

Jillie began feeling unwell about seven months into the pregnancy. She'd gotten through all the normal fouls, morning sickness and sickly cravings, but now she was feeling dizzy and breathless. She came home from the doctor and put it in a language I could understand.

'Dick, I have high oil pressure,' she said. 'They want me to come in and stay.'

Jillie ended up in hospital for almost four weeks and it was bloody brutal. Not that she was in danger or anything, but because I was left without my star bookkeeper. I was a mess, absolutely hopeless at accounting, so I would lob up to the hospital every afternoon with a stack of paperwork under my arm.

'No, Richard,' the nurse scolded. 'You are not taking that in with you.'

I would smuggle it in anyway and when I returned the next day, with a pile of fresh receipts and wage tickets, the previous day's accounts would be done.

It wasn't only the bookwork that got to me. I was living at Jillie's mum's place at the time and she was over in Adelaide because her other daughter was also about to give birth. Being the only man in the house was tough – I didn't know how to cook. I ended up making do with steak and onion sandwiches from the takeaway down the road and cans of fried rice from the market.

Kelly Johnson was born on 11 September 1973.

I don't think I'd ever cried in my life up until that moment when I laid my eyes on her for the first time.

My wife handed me the perfect baby wrapped in a blanket. Kelly looked up at me silently with her big blue eyes and I was overwhelmed with joy. It was the best day of my life. Jillie came home with Kel a couple of days after the birth. I was stoked, but Jillie wasn't so happy. We were driving past the Mater Hospital in Brisbane a short while later.

'Never again,' she said, pointing at her belly. 'Never.'

She didn't know that she was already five months pregnant with our next child, Steven.

Jillie was fuming when she found out she was having another.

'What's wrong with you?' I asked. 'You look like you have the shits.'

'You bastard,' she screamed at me. 'I'm pregnant again.'

I laughed.

Steven Johnson was born in 1974, another healthy bundle of joy, and this time without the first-up complications. Kel and Steven are both the same age for a week, with Steve born on 6 September. And boy, are those two close together!

I was over the moon when I found out I was going to have another child. I never cared for what I got; I wasn't one of those fathers desperate to have a boy, but Jillie and I were thrilled to have a pigeon pair. We knew so many people that had tried and tried, only to end up with four boys or four girls. We pulled it off in the space of a year. Jillie decided it had to stop there.

'Either you keep your hands off me forever,' she said, 'or I'll get fixed up.'

She went with the latter.

I bought our first house shortly before Steve arrived.

I was at a hill climb at Mount Cotton when one of the blokes told me about a new development.

'My brother has just bought a new joint up at Daisy Hill,' he said. 'It's fantastic. You ought to check it out. There are a number of blocks up there, six or seven.'

So one day I took Jillie over to Daisy Hill. It was on a dirt road and didn't look like much from the street.

'Big deal,' I said. 'A big block of dirt on a hill.'

But then I got out of the car, and walked to the top of the hill filled with shrubs and boulders. Sweaty from the climb and not overly impressed, I turned around and was smacked in the face by a stunning view. I could see the Gold Coast to the left, Mount Warning to the right: it was a sparkling vista fit for a king and his queen. Magnificent. I decided to buy the block of land there and then. I offered the owner $4000; it ended up costing me $6000.

We now had a one-acre block of land and no house. Des White, the best man at my wedding, agreed to design my new home and a bloke I raced against signed on to build it. Happy days.

It was a truly beautiful house once complete. Split levels, double garages and stunning views. A dream come true. Our home was a four-bedroom deal with all the trimmings. Everything I could have ever hoped for. It was better than my parents' house and Jillie's mum's place, but I was very sad to have left her. Jillie's mother was an absolute gem. One of the kindest ladies I have ever met. From the day I met her to the day she died, I never saw her angry. Not once.

11

BEATEN BLUE

Passion Pop

Harry Firth peered across the grassy plain, his fiery eyes sending my temperature rising. I clung to the wheel, foot flat, daring myself to brake as late as I could. His stare was cutting right through me. I nailed the corner as he loomed large in my windscreen, squinty and scared, before I left him in the dust. I continued relentlessly as I launched through the air, such was my speed over the bump after Dunlop Bridge. I was giving it all I had.

I thought my big break had come when Harry invited me to do a test in his HDT Torana at Lakeside. Peter Brock and Colin Bond were his men, but on occasions he struggled to get them both to Queensland. An event at Surfers Paradise was coming up, and Bond was off doing a rally. He needed a driver and I wanted to be his man.

'How was that?' I asked, as I emerged from the car.

Harry, a surly bloke, cunning and sometimes cruel, nodded. 'OK.'

I was given the green light to race Harry's HDT car on the Gold Coast. I thought that this was the break I'd been waiting for. For years I'd been toiling away, stubbornly doing my best with free oil and fuel. I knew I couldn't compete with the big guys on my budget, so if I wanted to get anywhere I needed support. And they didn't come any bigger than HDT. They were Holden's top team. They were factory. French and Moffat were Ford, bashing everyone around in the thunderous Falcons, and Firth, Brock and Bond had them firmly in their sights. GM funded their operation and I knew they had a decent plan. Brock was already a superstar and the Torana was coming along in leaps and bounds.

I knew a fair bit about Harry. He was a determined man with a ferocious plan. Harry had serious clout behind him and he was after three things: race wins, championships and Bathurst titles. Zupps, a Queensland-based car dealer with weight, had become involved with Firth. They did the team's engines and I already had a deal with the company, local boy and all.

I first met Larry Perkins the day before the race. He was young, bold and brash. We were at Lockhart Motors in Southport; he was told to put the stickers on the car and I watched him slap them on.

'That'll do,' he said, bubbles marking the sticker's surface. 'They're only stickers. Who cares?'

Harry did. He was fuming.

I strapped down in the HDT Torana at Surfers. Brock was in the more powerful SLR and I knew I'd have my work cut out, but I was out to impress. This was my chance. I knew the Surfers track better than anyone, and the HDT car was supposed to be the shit.

But it wasn't. The team obviously didn't care about the old-hat car and had put all the resources into Brock's new SLR.

The HDT's clutch was horrible; it kept on slipping, but I wasn't about to quit. I ragged the car for all it was worth, gritted my teeth and gunned the thing beyond its limits. I passed cars, held others off, all block and bolt, and managed to come second. It was a one-two for HDT and the turning point of my career.

Or so I thought. Harry said little after the race.

I marched through the bottle shop, even though I didn't drink. I peered at the bottles; they could have been in Chinese, for all I knew. I grabbed one, wrapped it up and took it to Harry. I'd been told he was into his wine and I was desperate to impress.

Again he said little.

I hunted down his address and continued with the grog. Maybe he liked champagne? Still I heard nothing. Maybe it was because I knew squat about alcohol. He was probably into Moët and I'd given him a Passion Pop. I kept on sending him bottles, but my phone stayed quiet. Even though I had the support of Zupps, I feared I didn't have a chance. And I was right.

I was just a backwater Queenslander. Queenslanders were second-class citizens because all the racing took place in Sydney or Melbourne, where the factories were based and where all the teams came from. You might as well have been from Bali as far as racing was concerned; Queensland was just so far away from everything. And the cost of transporting a guy that lived there to all the southern meets was also a factor to be considered. I wasn't prepared to move.

I wanted in but Harry already had his two guys, Brock and Bond. He obviously didn't want me and I can't lie, it hurt. He would later overlook me for a bloke named Charlie O'Brien and that really cut because I thought I was a much better driver.

I had nothing against Brock, who I first raced against in 1970. It's hard to compare drivers, taking into account the different cars involved, but I honestly thought I was every bit as good as him; Bond too, given what I had and what I was up against. Brock was a good bloke. We got on from day one. I think I first met him and Harry at a Zupps function in Queensland. He was a guy doing his thing, and I was doing mine. Still, I was slightly green about what he had, compared to me.

Behind Enemy Lines

I strapped on my belt and turned the ignition before the thunder and lightning struck.

Rrooooom!

The V8 engine of the Ford Falcon burst to life, a sonic boom punching my ear and rattling my brain. I had never been in a Ford, let alone a V8, and the engine sitting to my left, shook me to my very core. I was sitting in a XA two-door Falcon, about to race at Lakeside. It was a tough-looking car. A furious mean machine with fat wheels, flared arches and a devilish hump on the bonnet. Big and bad.

The 351 Cleveland engine had been moved back, firewall ripped apart to turn it into a sports sedan. I revved again and this time my teeth chattered.

I had a moment.

What am I doing? I thought. *Why am I here? In a V8? In a Ford?*

That moment only lasted a second. I was here because Bryan Byrt had called me at exactly the right time.

'Why don't you come drive my Falcon?' he'd asked. 'Frenchy has been suspended for some shit in another car and I need someone to drive my sports sedan. What do you think?'

I thought fast – this was going to be a life-changer.

'No problems,' I fired. 'When and where?'

My switch to Ford happened in an instant. I dumped my beloved Holden over the phone. But it was coming and I had had enough.

Zupps pulled out of HDT when they moved to the SLR 5000 and I was left without backing. I sold my GTR – the XU-1 clone – and again I was a man staring into darkness. It hurt because I really thought I was on the verge of scoring a factory drive, my test at Lakeside, and my feats at Surfers ringing in my ear.

Sitting in my servo, with nothing but a helmet and a pair of driving shoes, I thought about giving it all away. But I just couldn't resist, given another race at Lakeside was coming up. I knew Barry Nixon Smith had a car and I asked him if I could rent it.

'What do you think?' I asked, of the ex-HDT car. 'It's just sitting there doing nothing.'

He agreed for me to take it on.

The car was a mess. Barry, alongside Dennis Geary, had driven it at Bathurst and had trashed it after the ex-HDT had rolled coming out of Forrest's Elbow. The car had been partly repaired before I picked it up and brought it back to the garage on the Tuesday.

'Project, Dick?' someone asked. It obviously needed some work.

'No, I'm going to race it on Saturday,' I said.

I worked like a madman, 24-7. I rebuilt the entire car and rolled it out on the Saturday, no idea what I was going to get. We had no time to test it and it was a complete lottery. But the machine was a ripper, the best I'd ever had.

'Barry, that car is a shitbox,' I said. 'I'll give you $2500 for it, though I think I'm going mad.'

Barry sold me the car and that's what kept me in racing. I had no support – well, some from Shell – and I also really enjoyed driving the thing. I can vividly remember flogging all the new SLRs with that car at Lakeside, but I was treading water and had no hope with Holden – which is when Byrt called.

It was 1974 when Byrty offered me a drive at Lakeside. I didn't know if it would lead to anything, certainly not to a lifelong association with Ford, but I was desperate and willing to give anything a go.

I didn't give a shit about Holden. I just needed someone's support to race, to the point where I couldn't have given a rat's arse if they'd offered me a Lada. If someone else was willing to pay the bill, I was going to drive. I still had the ex-HDT XU-1 and was doing well. Even though I got a bit of a name beating guys in an inferior car, it meant little when getting someone to back you. In fact, it was devastating. I'd put my heart and soul into trying to get noticed and scoring a deal with a factory team, and did everything I could. I spoke to all the right people, sold myself, sent bottles of wine, but I was a Queenslander and I think that killed off any hope.

I never thought I would end up in a Ford. Never. My heart was all Holden and I was firmly focused on getting a gig with them, to be part of the Holden team. And don't think switching teams wasn't a big deal back then. The Holden–Ford rivalry was stronger than it is today, and I didn't have my doubts when I made the move. It was just the way it was. When somebody asks you to drive their car and offers to spend their own money, it's a no-brainer. I had to jump. I would have even been happy to drive a Hyundai Excel.

My first drive in a Ford was at Lakeside, in the old green and purple car they had raced at Bathurst. It was the first time I was in a V8 and it was a bloody challenge. Sure, the machine had grunt, but with that came some nasty, dirty backbreakers. Stopping the car was a nightmare and cornering it was just hell. I was used to the light, nimble Torana and this thing was an elephant.

Tyres were a massive issue. You could thrash the hell out of the XU-1 and not worry about the rubber or brakes, but the big Falcon was a different deal altogether. Its tyres were tender to say the least, and the heat the car generated was unbearable. The engine – the big V8 with the injection and the intake, all thunder and lightning – was right beside me and I was constantly soaked in sweat. The noise was deafening too. We didn't have earplugs back then and it amazes me that the huge noise didn't send me deaf.

Meanwhile, passing with straight-line speed was an eye-opener.

So this is how they do it, I thought.

You couldn't do this in a Torana, unless you got it to follow a perfect exit in a precise spot. It'd be tough work for a Torana, but in this thing it was easy. Foot down, you would eat them up.

It wasn't until a few laps later that the beast got the best of me. The suspension cracked going through the kink and I almost ended up in the lake. Despite this, Byrty was happy with what I had done; I'm not sure why.

'We're going to get a brand-new Falcon and we want you to run at Bathurst,' he said. 'What do you think?'

You know I said yes.

You Fucking Drive

The new Falcon wasn't ready – wouldn't be until 1977 – and after missing out on 1974, I decided to take on the Mountain in an Alfa, teaming up with John French.

What a mistake.

Halfway through the race, after a fuel stop, I was zooming over the top of the Mountain when I moved onto the brakes to go down Skyline, and started shuffling the gears.

Crack!

The rear of the car screamed and jumped, threatening to send me toppling down the hill. An explosion had ripped through the exhaust pipe and the car backfired. It was a tremendous thud that shook me to my core. A spark had been ignited at the back of the car, the fuel exploding and sending flames into the air as I launched through the Dipper.

I thought I was going to die.

I charged to the pits, door open, in a desperate attempt to escape the fire and fumes. I hung one foot out of the car as I pulled into the pit-lane, undid my belt and fell out as some guy with a fire-extinguisher charged towards me. He put the fiery hell out and I got back in the car and strapped down again. I flicked the switch and sent fuel pumping through the Alfa's veins. And I was away, problem solved.

Bang!

The car went off again in pretty much the same spot. Fuel and fire swirled, the heat scorching my bones. I returned to the pits, where they put out the fire, refuelled the Alfa and sent me on my way once more.

Boom!

The car went out, this time louder and with more force.

'Fuck,' I screamed. 'Fuck this. I'm out.'

Instead of rolling out of the flaming car, I steamed out, just as hot as the smouldering piece of shit I had been driving, and strode over to Frenchy and stuck my finger into his chest.

'Listen, mate,' I yelled. 'I'm not here to die. That's three times the car's gone out like that. Fuck it. Why don't you jump in this fucking thing and have a go? See what an explosion feels like.'

By this time, the brake light inside the boot had sent a spark that set the tank alight.

'You jump in,' I insisted.

'No, no,' he said. 'Not a chance.'

Frenchy retired the car. That was the year Kevin Bartlett won with Goss.

Thank God I moved to Ford.

Number 17

We might as well cover two things here: where I got the number 17 from and how I became known as Dick.

First to the 17.

When I first started running the EH, I wanted to be in team Littlemore. I was preparing Graham's car and, to be honest, I idolised the bloke. I had it in my head that he and I would be a bit of a team. His Mini was bright orange with lashings of red, and I did my car up the same way: I slapped on identical markings, grabbed some house paint and slapped on the orange and red too.

My mate George had a flatbed truck to cart Graham's car around. I also had him make up a trailer so he could tow my car behind too. It looked pretty neat, almost like a convoy, kind of like we were a big deal.

Graham's race car number was 71. I thought I should get 70 or 72 just to seal the deal, so I applied for both those numbers and was knocked back. They weren't available, not that I had ever seen them race, and I was stumped. Then someone, maybe Graham, suggested I reverse it.

Seventeen, I thought. *That sounds OK. I could live with that.*

And that's how I got the number that would help define my life. In truth, it was more that once I officially secured it, I was never bothered to come up with something different.

It was me who decided to change my name from Richard to Dick. My mother hated anyone calling me Dick, and she called me Richard right up until the day she died, but I was left with no choice, much to her disgust. The reason for the name change was simple: I went to write my name on top of the windscreen in the old EH and realised Richard Johnson was just too hard to fit. I would've needed a double-decker bus! So Richard became Dick, which fits better on the windscreen.

12

BANG ON

Vern who?

I threw my hip across the seat and plunged my foot into the throttle, the furious power of the 351 Cleveland engine instantly sending the scenery – trees, faces in the crowd, sponsor signage – into a dizzying blur. Reds, greens and blues melded into a gushing brown, the raw power making minced meat of everything but the road.

Shit, I thought, as I hurtled down the straight at the first race of the 1977 season held at Symmons Plains, Tasmania, *this has some go.*

My competition gradually vanished into dots in my rearview mirror.

This is going to be easy, I thought, tasting pure straight-line power for the first time.

But the right kink knocked my confidence clean from my gut as the car squeaked and squirmed under brakes.

The car didn't want to stop, let alone turn. I'm not sure where I finished but it was far from first. I clearly had some work to do.

The all-new XB-GT Falcon built from the ground up by Byrty left the old Torana for dead when it came to power, but not for handling and finesse, thanks to the car's massive, heavy frame. And that meant trouble – we'll get into that later.

The GT Falcon was brand spanking new and I entered the 1977 season full of hope and confidence. I was convinced that this was going to be my breakthrough year, even though I'd failed to make an impression in the first race.

Byrty's sparkling blue beast, rather plain with its white writing but strangely striking at the same time, was born to win. I had seen Byrty's passion long before he offered me my first fully paid drive and another chance at racing.

'Dinner and drinks are on the line,' he said, throwing down the gauntlet to John Zupps at a Surfers Paradise meet when I was racing in the Torana. 'I'll shout your whole crew if you win; you mine if you lose.'

Zupps agreed.

That type of shit went on at every Queensland meet because Byrty had a staunch rivalry with Zupps going back a while. I reckon that's probably what got him into racing. Both Byrty and Zupps were the biggest and the best dealers in Brisbane – Byrty for Ford, Zupps for Holden – in a time when race wins meant sales. Byrty began his car-dealing career in Wollongong. In a period of booming sales and whopping margins, he made the most of the market and quickly expanded into Brisbane, becoming the top Ford man in the state. He also made a lot of money, putting his cash into racing and his heart into beating Zupps.

No doubt ego was involved. Both men wanted to be top dog, victor taking all the spoils. But while Zupps had the assistance of Holden and Firth, Byrty did it all on his own — it was his cash, his knowledge and his name alone on the line.

Byrty was paying the whole ten yards with me driving his GT Falcon, and back then, that sort of stuff was unthinkable. He was footing the bill for me to go and live my dream, and that was all I could have asked for. I would have been drowning in the sea of ex-racers had he not offered me a deal.

This is what I'd always wanted and I was determined to make a name for myself, and for the first time in my life I knew I had a backer that could get me there. But I didn't set unrealistic expectations, and neither did Byrty. Not once did he stare me down and demand results, nor did he set me KPIs or anything as ridiculous. He just asked me to do my best. The reality was, despite the competition, our team was never going to be top dog because no one could really usurp the factory teams. Zupps and HDT had the best of Holden, in terms of factory support, cash and fanbase. Moffat and his dealer team had the same sort of backing from Ford, and although we knew we couldn't match it with either Zupps or Moffat, we were determined to be the best and maybe knock them out with a sly uppercut here and there.

I didn't have too much to do with the development of the car, which was all left to Ian Noble and Roy McDonald, pioneers of their time. They originally began building the car in the garages of Byrty's city dealership, but it became a massive and unproductive distraction for his staff, so he rented a shed right near my workshop.

I had built almost every car I had ever raced up to this point, and it was strange not to be planning and producing each component of this machine, but it wasn't entirely bad. I used to lend Ian and Roy a hand when I could, given my mechanical expertise, but my brief now was just to drive. Most drivers today have absolutely nothing to do with the car. Sure, they provide information and feedback, but you'll never see them with a tool in their hand. They rock up with their helmets, their attitudes and not much more.

I was OK stepping back because really all I wanted to do was drive. I also had my own business that needed attention, so not having to worry about building and maintaining my own race car allowed me to try to make some money, or at least keep my head above water.

Byrty confirmed his pursuit for excellence – not that he needed to – when he sent me and Peter Molloy to the US on a fact-finding mission. Moffat was the Ford gun and he used his Canadian heritage to source parts and knowledge from the company's founders in North America. Byrty figured if he wanted to beat the best, he needed to know what they had and how they did it, so Molloy and I went over to America, and unearthed some of his secrets (but probably found more hangovers and headaches than anything else).

By this time I was drinking, and though it wasn't much, it was enough to get me into trouble. I had my first drink back in the EH days, and getting drunk for me involved just two stubbies. I was never really interested in going out and boozing up because I was too busy trying to make a name for myself, but I relaxed my stance as the years went on.

The first time I got drunk was sometime in the 1970s. I was up the North Coast with some mates and we went to a pub. One of the guys had his old man there, and he was buying the beers. I tried to go one for one with him, I suppose, just trying to prove I was a man, but that didn't work out so well. After an hour or so I had to stop. I ended up outside, throwing my guts up everywhere, in a world of hurt.

There wasn't really a boozy culture in the sport. After the races, a lot of the industry guys would have a few in the Shell tent, and that was it. It never got out of control, not in the early days anyway. Drivers weren't rockstars in the 1970s. We didn't have grid girls and women didn't throw themselves at us.

Back to the GT.

I slowly came to grips with the car. It wasn't a machine you could all out thrash; you had to massage her for much of the race or things would go bang! I taught myself how to ease her gigantic frame around corners, how to delicately caress her brakes. I looked after the tyres and asked the engine for no more than I needed.

We weren't winning yet, but we had plenty of good results. We were always strong on home turf and we had a cracking round in Calder, narrowly missing out on a win. But this car was built for Bathurst and that's where we went to make our name.

I had been in the GT Capri with Graham Moore in 1976 while the XB was being built. Byrty always had a presence at Bathurst and decided to sponsor the Moore car with me and him behind the wheel. We came third in our class that year and were now hoping to match that result, or go better, against the big boys.

Byrty signed Vern Schuppan to race with me, and I have to admit, I was a touch nervous being alongside such a big name. Vern had driven everything; from Indy cars to Le Mans, he was a star with an unrivalled résumé back in Australia. He had finished second in the 1977 24 Hours of Le Mans, and I was expecting him to teach me a lesson or two. But he ended up being the student and I the master.

It was the moment that gave me the confidence to be a star.

I was quicker than Vern the moment I got into the car, even though I didn't expect to be.

Geez, I thought. *This bloke's a superstar, and I've got him. Maybe I can give it all a shake.*

Vern struggled with the car because it was difficult. I'd learned how to handle the beast, how to conserve energy yet stay fast. He had no idea.

We didn't finish the race, another retirement, but I think that's the moment my career really took a turn. Not due to the result, of course, but because I had outclassed and outdriven a renowned star. It turned heads and finally put my name up in lights. Not that anyone expected what was to follow when it came to my career. How could they?

We finished the season on another high, my name continuing to glow. Byrty was absolutely pumped about the last race of the season, which was held at Lakeside. Not only was it the final fling of a good year, but it was also a race on home soil against the best of the best. Brock was there,

Moffat too, and this was our chance to show the blokes from the south what a couple of Queensland backwater-battlers could do.

Things started well. We came hurtling out of the blocks and smashed our way to pole. Brock's HDT SLR had nothing against our privateer Ford, the same went for Moffat and his manufacturer-backed XB. We were in a whole other class. With just seven laps to go I was leading, a fair distance in front. Things were perfect.

This is it, I thought. *You're going to beat the big guys. Where to now?*

Bang!

The car exploded. Something fired, then clunked and I was out, no power at all. I got out of the car and walked back to the pits, beaten and feeling deflated. Byrty slapped me on the back.

'How good was that?' he said. 'We had them on toast. I can't believe we showed them up. We had the quickest car by miles, and that's some achievement. Don't worry about the result. They know we are here and they know we should be feared.'

I smiled because he was right. The future was bright.

Byrty organised a little trip to celebrate. He decided we needed some relaxation time, so he booked us all a trip to Hayman Island. The place wasn't much back then, still untouched and only partially developed. Keith Williams and Byrty had also just bought Hamilton Island. (That's right, they *bought* the island that would then go on to become one of the world's most sought-after holiday destinations.) Byrty took us there in his helicopter.

I suppose it was the first time I had met blokes with serious money. Equipped with helicopters, launch pads and race teams, these guys were way out of my league. But I wasn't jealous and I didn't want what they had. Well, not entirely true . . . I wanted Byrty's boat. I was keen on boats, and he had a corker. A big, powerful machine that could take me to the type of idyllic places found on postcards. But I was a battler, struggling to pay off my house and car, earning no more than 50 bucks a week. It was nice having access to the islands and helicopters, but I knew it would never be me. I was a driver, not a millionaire, and I was content with the life I had.

While we were at Hayman Island, we decided to go for a run after a night of drinking cocktails (we were pretty conscious of our fitness back then). We ran maybe four kilometres, nothing too extreme, and my poor mate David Harding, a promoter for Surfers Raceway, was fucked. He was puffing, panting and sweating up a storm. So we decided to head straight for the pool.

'Na, boys,' he said. 'I need to go and have a shower and clean up.'

We watched him walk up the stairs and turn into the corridor of the first floor.

'Isn't his room on level two?' I asked. The boys nodded.

He came down about five minutes later. 'You wouldn't believe it,' he said. 'I walked into my room, stripped nude and turned the light on. I went to jump in the shower and heard a noise. I turned around and there was a couple, lying in bed, staring straight at my cock. I'd walked into the wrong room!'

I'm glad David didn't walk into my room.

Twisted Metal

Without warning, the seemingly endless blue above disappeared and was replaced with a thick black menace.

'Oh shit,' I said, thundering towards the Oran Park flip-flop at over 200 k/h. 'This isn't good.'

I was right.

The sun that was streaming into my face just moments before, forcing me to squint as I hunted down Brock's Torana, had vanished. Now I could no longer make out the deep-red Marlboro sign splashed across the back of his car.

Everything was grey.

A moment later I was hurtling from the road, rain thrashing down on the track and turning my car into a grass-plough. I moved straight into third gear as the rain continued to belt down, the ground a slushy mess.

I was on slicks and I instantly knew I was fucked.

I rocketed onto the grass, my four wheels digging up the ground as my car destroyed all in its path.

Don't hit that, I thought, glancing at the blur of concrete and steel in front of me.

I grabbed the wheel and heaved. Nothing. I mashed at the break. Nothing. I yanked the handbrake. Nothing.

I became a passenger as my vehicle spun out of control and there was absolutely nothing I could do except brace for the impact to come.

Bang!

I hit the track's observation tower at over 110 k/h. My body rocked back and then forth, like a ragdoll shaken by a giant. My arms were firmly clenched against the wheel, my feet jammed against the firewall. My elbows and knees, makeshift shock absorbers, weakened the blow, but still it hurt like hell.

This was my first massive shunt: a real balltearer at Oran Park in 1977. I have no idea how I wasn't injured. I sat back for a moment, my brain trying to comprehend why I wasn't dead, before I frantically grabbed at the buckle that was keeping me strapped in.

Get out, I thought. *Get out and check out how bad this thing is. Byrty will be fuming.*

I sprang from the car and examined the wreck. I shook my head.

This isn't gonna race for a while, I thought. *It's fucked.*

The accident at Oran Park was a moment of sheer terror and metal-on-wall madness. I could lie and say it wasn't scary but it was, and straight up I decided that I wouldn't think of it again; it wouldn't change the way I raced.

Crashing, and the prospect of injury or worse, is something that comes with the job. I knew that before I'd signed on for my membership at the MG Car Club. I had a front-row seat to a fiery kill at Lakeside when I was just a boy. I knew I would one day hit a wall, come across something dangerous, but that was a risk I was willing to take.

I'll take a moment here to tell you everything about my experiences with crashes and carnage.

The first thing to do when you leave the road, spew off the track beyond control, is try to hit nothing. I know it's not rocket science, but this is an important factor to remember. You have to forget about your machine and study your surroundings. You need to know where and what your biggest threat is. Once you identify that, usually hurtling towards you at you at a warped speed, you have to work out whether or not there is anything you can do to avoid it. Most times there isn't and you become a helpless 'passenger'. Wet grass, broken brakes, bent steering, all you can do is brace.

Other times you have limited control over your machinery. If your car is still working, and you have some sort of traction, you can either brake to slow down, turn to get out of the way, or accelerate, as stupid as it might sound, to send grip back to the rear wheels to avoid the hazard. You only have a split second to make this decision, but it should come as natural instinct. Race car drivers have spent years behind the wheel, testing themselves to their limits and finetuning their skills in car control. They know when to hit the pedal, which one and by how much, and what to do with the wheel. And believe it or not, a spilt second can feel like an hour when you make such a calculated choice.

As clichéd and as ironic as it sounds, moments really do slow down at a crisis point. Your life doesn't necessarily flash before your eyes, but you certainly have time to weigh up the threats and choose a course of action.

I am one that prepares myself for a crash. Accidents are going to happen and you have to be ready. But, of course, you don't always see them coming. Bang. That's it. You've hit a wall, thanks to some talentless cock behind you. There's nothing you can do about those, and the result is luck of the draw. When you see a hit coming, the obvious response is to prepare yourself.

Some say that you should go limp. I've heard stories of hikers claiming they'd survived a fall from a cliff because they'd made sure to relax their muscles. In the end they didn't break any bones because there was no taut object to provide resistance.

That's absolute bullshit. You have to prepare your body for impact. Run at a brick wall and what do you do? You tighten your body, clench everything and make yourself as hard as possible. You don't go limp and slam straight into the thing like it wasn't there. That's your body physiologically reacting as part of your survival instinct. The same goes for a crash, and that's what I think has kept me alive through some pretty serious shunts.

I hang on for dear life. I push my feet as hard as I can into the floor, sending the force to my back, jamming it against the seat. I also push for all against the steering wheel, pinning my shoulders to the back of the seat. I tense my neck as hard as possible, tucking my chin on my chest. I don't want my body to be flung around an inch more than it should. Ultimately, it depends on what you hit and how hard, but I believe this method has saved my life. I've never been thrown around, and that's because I've commanded my body to stay still.

The sideways collisions are the worst. You can't really prepare for those. Your back and neck have no say about where they're going to be thrown and the worst injuries occur in a T-bone.

With collisions, there is no time to be afraid; you worry about your injuries later. After a crash your first concern should be your car. You assess the damage to your race machine before yourself.

And you can't stew on them. If you are afraid or concerned, your career is over. Racing is about the millimetres and fractions of a moment – if you worry about your own safety, you can't push yourself, and that'll be the end of you.

The thing about crashes is you have to be honest. You've got to ask yourself whether it was your fault or not. If it wasn't, you shrug it off and put it down to bad luck: the conditions that presented themselves or a rival. If it was your fault, you need to reassess your own abilities. Maybe you aren't as good as what you thought.

13

BREAK AND MAKE

Gone Again

The sun gleamed and the water sparkled. It was another perfect day in the Whitsundays. Bryan Byrt grabbed his new toy, ripped on the throttle and thrashed the brilliant blue sea into a frenzy of white. A wave suddenly reared up in front as he hurtled along on his jet ski, and he slammed into the water.

He pulled himself back onto his jet ski and returned to the shore. He was OK, but his arm hurt like hell. The ocean had slapped him with the force of a spurned woman swinging at his face. Even after a couple of days, the pain hadn't subsided. Byrty went to hospital to have it checked out, expecting to be told he had torn a muscle.

Instead they told him he had a year to live.

Byrty was diagnosed with cancer at the beginning of 1978. He had a tumour under his arm. Obviously at this point he forgot about racing, and focused all his energy on saving his own life. Byrty wasn't about to give up after being told of his hopeless situation. He travelled to the US to seek experimental treatment and did everything he could to find a miracle cure.

There was nothing I could do except pray for him and race his car. The least I could do was try to win him a few races to give him some relief, however small. He loved racing above all and I knew I could make him smile with a good result.

The team only raced a couple of rounds in the 1978 Australian Touring Car Championship because of his condition, sticking to the local meets and a few others. The plan was to improve the car as best as possible and give the big boys a run at Bathurst. We did well in the meetings we went to, leading races and looking likely to win until problems caught us out.

At Lakeside we were in front when a hole in the radiator shot us down. At Surfers we ran out of tyres with only a couple of laps to go. We knew we had a good car heading into Bathurst, and we wanted to give it our all for our sick mate Byrty.

By this time Byrty was very unwell. He was in the US for further treatment when Bathurst rolled round and we feared he wouldn't make it home. Again I paired up with Vern – he, eager to improve; me, hoping the car would hold up better than the previous year. With Byrty's backing, we had confidence in the car and I went into Bathurst 1978 thinking it was my best shot.

With Byrty's plight our driving focus, we went hammer and tongs. We ate up the laps, pulled off good times and made it to the end. At one point I thought a podium was within our grasp, but our fortune faded and we held on for fifth. It was an incredible result, considering the dramatic backdrop, and my best to date. Byrty called from the US.

'Well done, Dick,' he said, his voice crackling under the strain of his illness. 'I am so proud. I couldn't have asked for more.'

I think I shed a tear or two, overwhelmed with a bizarre mix of pride and sadness.

Byrty died on 10 October 1978. He was on a plane, travelling from Los Angeles to Honolulu, when the horrible condition claimed his life. It was a black day. I thought only for my mate and his family when I heard the news, but my attention soon turned to racing.

This is the end, I thought. *Without Byrty I have nothing.*

My stop-start career was at another painful crossroads. Just when I thought I had turned a corner, when I had a full backer for the first time in my life, I returned to square one. My career was over. Again.

'I can't do this on my own,' I said to Jillie. 'I can't compete with these guys, I can't keep going without support. I just can't. I'm done.'

I knew I had the talent, but frustratingly, I didn't think I could do it without a backer.

Byrty's death caused a major shake-up in his business. His wife, Pat, ended up selling the dealership to a couple of guys that worked there. One was John Harris, a very astute sales manager, who hated motor racing with boundless passion. He was all about the bottom line and could not see the point in investing in something that didn't provide a monetary return. He'd nicknamed the race car 'the sponge'. He called me in shortly after buying the business. I thought I was gone.

'I'm going to run that damn business out of respect for Bryan,' he told me, reviving my career, if for but an instant. 'But it may only be for a year and then things are going to be different. *Very* different.'

The equipment, the workshop and the car were all owned by the business, so I guess it made sense to stick around for at least another year. For John, keeping the team going would also be helpful for local goodwill. I was glad that I would be driving again, but I knew it would never be the same.

And it wasn't. John committed to the local races and Bathurst only. Money was going to be tight and the team was to be run on fumes. I knew it was going to be a tough year, but those were the cards I was dealt.

Banana Bender

Whoosh!

A missile brushed past my ear as I stood on the start line of the 1979 Hardie-Ferodo 1000 about to be introduced.

What the fuck was that? I thought, hunching slightly after the near-miss.

Splat!

I looked to the ground a metre from my foot. A pineapple was splattered all over the road.

'Oh,' I said to one of the blokes in my team. 'This isn't good.'

Peanuts, pineapples and bananas rained from the sky, the heaving crowd directing a storm of primary produce our way. The shit came from everywhere, buzzing past my ear, bouncing off my car and thudding onto the road. I will never forget the start of that race. It was plain old crazy.

John Harris, though hailing from Sydney, was a proud Queenslander. We were living in the time of Sir Joh Bjelke-Petersen and Queenslanders loved themselves while the rest of Australia hated them. Harris thought it would be a good idea to celebrate our pride for our home state, and also make a buck or two out of it for Bathurst 1979. He based our whole campaign on Queensland and sold sponsorship and car space to Queensland companies like Kingaroy Peanuts. We had a bloke standing on the grid dressed as a giant pineapple while Queensland flags flew.

And the fans, who were mostly from NSW, didn't like it one bit. They threw shit everywhere, fruit and nuts piling up on the track. I was lucky not be smashed in the face with a pineapple. I think it was more about fun than anything else for the crowd. It certainly had nothing to do with hating me, because I was just a nobody. In 1979 I was a battler, a bloke who could walk through the crowd and still not be recognised.

Once in the race, I had Garry Scott by my side and we were going good, until I came to the Dipper.

Bang!

A shotgun-like explosion rang in my ear as I hurtled out of the right-hander at almost 90 k/h. I didn't have time to think, the dangerous left-hand kink already upon me. I heaved on the wheel, trying to send the car through the technical and challenging piece of road, but I was given nothing. The car didn't respond. A moment later I was in the concrete wall, arms reverberating and head bouncing backwards and forwards until I finally came to a slump on the steering wheel.

I was out. Again.

It was my first real crash at Bathurst and I was devastated. Even more so when I returned to the pits.

Everyone thought that the crash was my fault. I can still remember my skin burning from their deathly stares. I knew something was up as soon as I returned to the garage. It was a cold unwelcoming place.

'I didn't do a thing,' I said defiantly. 'The bloody car just went straight on.'

My team didn't believe me and it was an awful feeling to be thought of as a liar; it felt even worse than getting the crappy result. I would have truthfully admitted to it, had the crash been my fault, but it wasn't. I remember John Harris being particularly hard on me that day.

I left Mount Panorama with the shits. When I got home, I stormed back to my bed and slept it off. I woke the next morning to see a picture of my car in the local paper, on the front page no less, coming through the Dipper with a collapsed tyre. Shredded rubber on the rim. That was the shotgun I had heard and the reason I smashed into the wall. It was as clear as day.

As I said, I accept responsibility for things I've done wrong and I don't hide from them. You won't learn a thing if you pretend it didn't happen. If you make a mistake, you accept it and move on.

I am still shitty with the way some people reacted on that day. And even though I'm annoyed that John was adamant it was my fault, even after seeing the photo that had clearly vindicated me, he's still a pretty good bloke. For a man who hated motorsport, he gradually learned to love it. John ended up catching the bug and has now bought back all the cars the team had raced. He even has his own motorsport museum.

But for John, 1979 was the end. Any slight chance of continuing was ruined when CAMS changed the category again – they wanted the later model cars in, and a lot of the rules were adjusted to suit the arrival of the Holden Commodore. So John shifted all the racing gear to a container and pulled the plug on the team.

I had finished tenth in the 1978 Touring Car Championship, but it looked like I was going out with a twenty-ninth in 1979.

I was sure that was it. My career had seemingly ended in a wall at the top of Mount Panorama. Fitting. I was now another retired racer.

The Ultimatum

I smashed my hand into the TV in disgust, almost snapping the little pull/push button right off. Walking back and forth across my lounge room, fists clenched, I tried to come to terms with what I had just seen.

Garry Willmington, I thought. *You've got to be kidding me. Seriously, Garry?*

I'd spent the last 20 minutes or so watching Garry Willmington absolutely carve up the field in the first race of the 1980 season at Symmons Plains, Tasmania. He was driving a Falcon and looked like a world-beater.

I was in a world of hurt.

If Garry's doing that, what could I be doing? I thought.

The question would not leave my brain.

No offence to Garry, but he was no superstar. He was a good driver, but I knew I was much better than him; I could beat him. More than anything I was just shitty that I didn't have the chance. I thought I was OK with being retired, but right there, right then, I knew I was anything but content. I was absolutely furious.

'Honey,' I shouted.

It wasn't long until Jillie came round.

'You have two choices, Jillie,' I said. 'I can be a retired racer, work in the servo full-time and make decent money. We would be sweet paying the bills and we'd have a good life, but I'd be the crankiest bloke in the world. If you can put up with that, then that is what we'll do.

'Or you could let me risk it all and go back to race. We might go bust, but I'll do it with a smile on my face.'

She considered it for a moment before answering: 'You race, Dick,' she said. 'I can't stand in the way of your dream.'

I beamed. 'You know what? I think I can make a real good go of this. I reckon with the way the rules are, we can even win.'

'Mortgage the house,' she continued. 'Risk the lot. I don't want to live with a miserable prick.'

So that's what I did.

Bryan Byrt Ford still had all the race gear stowed away in a storage container; I needed to buy it but I didn't have the money. I also didn't have a car to race. I went to see John Harris, and although I didn't have the cash we agreed on a price. It was going to cost me $36,000 for the entire race gear and the car – a secondhand XD Falcon, a 302-automatic formerly used by the police as a highway patrol car.

'Jillie, were you serious when you said I could mortgage the house?' I asked my wife one day.

Turns out she was.

I went to the bank and did the deal. It had cost me $32,000 to buy the block and build our home, and the bank was happy to give me most of it back. Our place was now up for grabs, but I didn't consider the consequences for a second. I just wanted to race.

I handed over the cash and bought the car, spares, tools, and engines. I took them to our home – now the bank's property – and set up a makeshift workshop in my garage.

This was a massive job. If I wanted to be successful, and I needed to be with our house on the line, I couldn't be in this thing half-arse. So I quit the service station and employed my brother Dyno to run the business full-time. It was a big move leaving one baby behind to look after another – my dream. I knew that with Jillie at the servo and my brother there too, things would be OK.

I pretty much had no income and I was throwing my future into a race car, but I was OK with that. I hired Roy McDonald to come and work with me full-time and the two of us went about building the car that could make or break Dick Johnson.

Dyno and another mate would then turn up after their shifts at the servo and we would work until 11 pm. We would also work all weekend. We really had nothing: no truck, no manpower and no massive support. Just tools and the sweat on our brows. We practically had no time to put it all together, but we did it in the end. We bought our parts from Bryan Byrt Ford for cost, which helped. We also had some support from Shell. But mostly it was up to me, and damned if I was going to let anyone stand in my way.

The Interpreter

I thumbed through the CAMS homologation paper, a whopping document full of legal jargon and words that mostly remained unread. It was a new era in racing, and in order to stand a chance, I had to know the rules and regulations.

'Hold the phone,' I yelled, as I studied the text. 'What the hell is this?'

I looked again.

'The Falcon should be no lighter than 1265 kilograms,' the paper forcefully stated.

I beamed before turning to Jillie.

'Take a look at this,' I said. 'It says the car should be 1265 kilograms. Wow. You know the production car weighs at least 1500 kilograms?'

It was like being smacked in the arse with a rainbow. The production car was heavy and powerful, but here the rules were saying it could now be light and powerful. I knew I had a winner there and then. You didn't have to be Einstein to work out that a 1265-kg car packing 410 hp would go pretty well. In fact, it would be an absolute rocket.

Turns out that there had been a sleight of hand.

Before the 1980 season, Ford had pulled out of the racing, packed their bags and gone. They didn't want a thing to do with the sport. Senior management at the famous company didn't think there was any value in backing a car and pulled their funds. I don't know why, I suppose it could've been a case of having some bloke in charge who didn't like the sport. It goes in cycles; if the boss likes tennis, he will sponsor tennis. I've seen it on many occasions. You can forget all the research and studies – sporting sponsorship simply comes down to what the big guy likes.

And Ford's loss was my gain.

Without the company to rely on, CAMS looked to an old Ford battler to provide them with the information they needed. Murray Carter was a former Ford warrior, and as it turned out, a sneaky bugger too. When CAMS asked him to help, he happily obliged. He told them the weight of the new Falcon was 1265 kg – what he didn't mention was that this was based on the weight of the ute. What a legend.

So we went about stripping everything we could before building the car. We pulled out the floor, ripped through the soundproofing, even shaved off all the bolts. Anything we didn't need went. Soon we got it down to smack on the mark: 1265 kg.

There were no weigh bridges back then, so we borrowed four scales – the type used to weigh bags of wheat – from a farmer, and strapped one to each wheel.

Later, everyone would think we had 1000 hp, but that is utter crap. We just read the rules.

And then we went about building the car.

It was a huge task. Roy and I would work from 6 am till 6 pm, and then my brother would join us for more. We would work to 12 am every night, first stripping the car back to nothing and then adding layer upon layer of racing machine.

We sourced the best parts, designed new things and twisted, cut and bent pieces of metal before bolting them on.

Steve, my son, was a skinny little runt then. He was always around trying to help and he couldn't get enough of the car. He was with us as Roy was welding the fuel tank onto the machine, when I realised, after a while, that Steve had gone missing.

'Where's Steve, mate?' I asked.

Roy put out the flame on his torch and lifted his mask. 'Not sure,' he said, wiping the sweat from his brow. 'Haven't seen him for ages.'

We both got up and began searching.

'Steve,' we yelled. 'Where are you?'

We spent about ten minutes calling out his name before we heard a small voice.

'Dad, I'm here.'

We looked around but couldn't see him.

'Dad, over here,' Steve continued.

We traced the voice to the fuel tank. The little bugger had somehow crawled into the thing before Roy had welded it shut. We ripped the thing off and began again.

We had a few concerns when we first started work on the engine, which was supposed to be no good. The new model, a four-door Falcon, had changed its engine and we had to follow suit. The car didn't have the 4V heads of the previous model and was now a 2V, which essentially meant less power. Everyone thought that would kill us and we were worried, but we soon found out that the engine was in fact better. The ports in the 4V were far too big and the 2Vs worked a treat with the standard manifold. It was another godsend.

The engine was again a 351 Cleveland and we used a NASCAR block. They were strong and reliable, and we knew the engine would not be a concern. We also had the advantage of having the tooling for it in Geelong, Victoria – in the past, all the gear had been in America – and for the first time we had access to machines, which enabled us to make changes to suit our needs. Holden had always had that option and Brock was constantly at GM asking for modifications to his race car.

We were finally on a level playing field.

We chose blue for the car; we didn't see any need to change it. Dennis Glindemann advised us on the colours.

'If you want it to stand out on TV,' he said, 'keep it plain and use white decals.'

While putting the car together, I also had to think about cash. I was out on a limb and had to find financers to fund the dream. Although Byrt Ford gave us good deals on the car and its parts, and Shell offered us fuel and oil, they didn't back us financially. We had little bits and pieces here and there, but they were basically just leftover change from the previous year.

I was really struggling.

Not only did we have to build the car, we also had to build a new transporter. The back of the old flat tray truck was no longer suitable because it couldn't carry all the necessary spares and equipment now that we had become a decent-sized operation. So I bought an old trailer, a small semi, which was big enough to hold one car in the back and then some in its big aluminium box. We went about developing it into a race truck, and threw in tyre racks and even set up a couple of bunks in the front. Roy and I were going to attack the championship but we couldn't afford accommodation, so we made sure we could sleep in the thing as we drove around. We'd installed a mini kitchen complete with a stove and fridge. It was better than the fleabag motels we'd slept in anyway.

Our first race was in July and we almost didn't make the meet. We rushed and scrambled and had only just put the final bolts in on the morning of practice. We had no idea how it would run, but we were hopeful all the same.

We went out in practice and the car was horrible; we hadn't had time to set her up right. We'd literally worked until the last minute to get her going, and the boys were stuffed. I had a feeling that the car was good, and was convinced that a proper wheel alignment was all that was needed. Instead of dragging them through hell, I told the team to go and sleep – it was probably the first chance they'd had in the week – and come back in the morning to give it their all.

The next day, refreshed and awake, we gave the car a wheel alignment – and blitzed everyone in the race. The thing went like a jet! The Toranas didn't stand a chance, and we ended up winning the race by a huge margin.

We were absolutely surprised by how well the car had handled and stopped. We knew we had the power, but we didn't expect this at all. The Falcons I'd driven were heavy and hard to manoeuvre, but this thing was more like a Torana – nimble and light. It was pointy and precise while holding a huge power advantage over everything else.

Needless to say, we turned a lot of heads. People thought I was gone, but here I was, back and better than ever. In a little car that would come to be known as 'Tru-Blu'.

Who's cuter? Me (aged two) or the koala?

How I loved these outings to Caloundra Beach. Dad, my sisters, Diane and Robyn, and me.

When my sisters and I weren't at the beach we were in the pool. I spent every other morning at the Valley Baths.

I loved ripping into Dad's cars. Here I am playing mechanic on his FJ Holden.

A proud student at Coorparoo State High School. I was in year seven when this photo was taken.

Hanging out with my mate Bernie Keenan at Kapooka. Army life wasn't all bad . . .

What a sort . . . and I'm talking about Jillie, not me! Jillie and me with her parents, Dave and Muriel Walker (centre), at our engagement party.

My son, Steve, caught the racing bug early.

Steve and me a few years later. In the background is Tru-Blu being fixed after the rock incident. (Photo: News Ltd/Newspix)

I raced everywhere and anywhere. Here I am having a crack at a hill climb in an EH.

Celebrating at Lakeside after winning the Kaiser Stuhl 'Man of the Meet' award. Check out the racing shoes!

Racing for Bob Forbes at Bathurst in 1973.

In the XU-1 at Lakeside in 1974. I'm leading the race ahead of Peter Brock, Charlie O'Brien and Murray Carter.

Back at Lakeside in 1975. I just loved this place. I reckon I could still beat a few there.

Don't worry, it's a
Ford. I raced in a
Capri at Bathurst in
1976.

I got to race with
big-gun Vern Schuppan
at Bathurst in 1977.

What a motley crew. Have a go at the porn-star moustaches!
From left to right: Roy McDonald, my brother Dyno, John Duckett,
Vern Schuppan, Bryan Byrt, me, Ian Noble and Brian Michelmore.

Fair to say I'm a bit emotional here after crashing out of Bathurst in 1980.

I reckon I could give Daniel Craig a run! I'm all dressed up for a Channel 7 promotion. The letters I received after hitting the rock are in the shopping trolley.

This is what happens when your brakes fail – Surfers Paradise, 1981.

Winners are grinners. With John French at Bathurst in 1981.

Tru-Blu at the 1981 Bathurst. What a car and what a year!

Greens-Tuf at Surfers Paradise in 1983. That Falcon was one of my all-time favourites.

Lap one at Silverstone in 1988. I showed those Europeans a thing or two. See how far I'm leading?

I've had a few shunts in my driving career. This is a nasty one in a NASCAR race at Calder Park in 1988.

Talladega Nights . . . or maybe days. With my Redkote NASCAR in the US in 1990.

Me, Jillie and the kids, Kel and Steve, at Sears Point Raceway, California.

My third and final Bathurst win. Celebrating with John Bowe in 1994.

Decked out in my racing gear as I have a crack in an RX-7 at Eastern Creek in 1995.

With my good mate Peter Brock before a father-and-son challenge at the Australian Grand Prix. Steve and I took on Brock and his son, James. The Brocks were no match for us! (Photo: Gary Merrin/ Newspix)

Chatting with Will Davison, the kid who broke DJR's seven-year drought, after his win at Winton Raceway. (Photo: Robert Cianflone/Getty Images)

James Courtney and me looking serious. James led DJR to victory in the 2010 Sydney 500. (Photo: Robert Cianflone/Getty Images)

400 starts for Dick Johnson Racing. Steve and me posing away. (Photo: Ian Hitchcock/Getty Images)

Steve with his wife, Bree, and my grandkids, Lacy and Jett.

The workshop in the early days.

The racing museum out the front of my workshop.

14

READY TO ROCK

Chipping Away at the Old Brock

Peter Brock looked at me and smiled. Sweat dripping from his hair, race suit stained with champagne, he extended his arm and shook my hand.

'Keep it up, mate,' he said. 'You almost had me. Let's get this thing on.'

I had Brock spooked – well, maybe more excited. For the first time in three years, he was forced to push and puff all the way to the end. His trademark red HDT Commodore was a smouldering hunk of burnt rubber and bent panels after we went to war.

Until now Brock was untouchable. Coming off back-to-back Bathurst wins, and a Touring Car title, he was a man in complete control. He had the backing, the balls and the brilliance to assert himself as the most dominant driver in the history of the sport.

And now . . . he was bored.

With Ford pulling the plug on their motorsport program, Brock had no enemy. No rival. No Moffat. He was a superhero without a villain, like Superman without his Lex Luther. And at Amaroo in 1980, he marked me as his man.

'You're it,' he said. 'The Ford guy to take it to us.'

Up to this point, I'd pretty much come from nowhere. Earlier I had showed my hand at Lakeside, but most people had put it down to the fact that it was my home track. Some even called it a fluke.

I didn't have a big budget, but I had a good car and I went to the Amaroo CRC 300 to prepare for Bathurst. I couldn't afford to run at Sandown, the traditional lead up for the big 1000-kilometre race, so Amaroo, a 1,9-kilometre racetrack in Western Sydney, was my chance to test my machine and see where I was at.

I left happy.

Practice and qualifying went superbly. My car was a rocket, and despite not being overly familiar with the track, I lit up the timesheets with a series of blistering laps. I wasn't expecting much, but on Saturday I almost put the new car on pole. I was within a whisker of Brock, and ended up sitting next to him on the front row for the race on Sunday.

I grabbed the steering wheel, all clenched fists and ready to go, and glanced over at Brock. He was so relaxed he looked almost asleep. My heart was racing. For him it was probably just another meet, another win, but for me everything was on the line. I had mortgaged our house to get this deal and if the car was no good here, I was fucked. What chance did I stand at Bathurst if I couldn't mount a challenge here?

The flag came down and I gunned the 351 Cleveland. The 2V heads shook the tarmac as they sent rubber thundering across the ground. I accounted for Brock and his new Commodore, reducing the famous red-and-white livery to a four-inch square in my rearview mirror.

The car was a killer. With power to burn, it launched out of the turns, ate up the straights and mowed down the backmarkers that stood before me. But I expected that. Thanks to the reduced weight, the blue beast turned on a dime and broke for it when asked.

Brock was flogging his car beyond its limits just to hold on. I seemed certain for a win, but late in the race my tyres went. In a matter of a couple of laps, my car turned from grippy gun to slippery snake. I'd worn out the rubber, and that was a problem because these tyres were all I had. One of my biggest expenses were tyres, and I couldn't afford to bring in multiple sets like the rich teams could. Back then I had to sacrifice rubber, and that's just the way it was. So I was forced to back off and Brock eventually hunted me down. But deep down he knew I had him beat.

'Wow, that was good,' added Tim Pemberton, the V8 media stalwart in charge of PR for Holden and Brock. 'You're the first bloke to take it to him like that for a while, you know that? I reckon I should do some PR for you. I really think people are losing interest in Brock and you'd be doing us both a favour if we could make something of you.'

Nicknamed 'Plastic', Pemberton could see how beneficial it would be for Brock to have a Ford up there fighting against his Holden. Due to Brock's domination, the category really was losing interest and they needed to reinvigorate it.

PR meant nothing to me back then, and to be honest, I still don't understand the media today. My view on publicity has always been to do something good and the newspapers will take notice. I didn't know that you had to suck up to them in order to get coverage; I prefer not to do that even today. I wasn't interested in talking the talk, just walking the walk, but a bloke called John Bowe would later school me on that. He was the biggest kiss-arse I'd ever seen.

The 1980 Amaroo race was a big turning point. I went from a hopeless battler to a man who became Brock's biggest threat. All rhetoric aside, I thought that I'd earned it with two good showings. Hell, I really believed that I could beat him, and Bathurst was where I planned to make my stand.

Ready to Roll

We rolled the crisp blue Falcon, all shiny and sharp, out of my Daisy Hill garage and jammed it into the back of the truck. Then we gathered round, slapped skin, and congratulated ourselves on getting the car that we genuinely believed could win us the Bathurst 1000.

We were stuffed. It had been a remarkable campaign to get to this point after deciding to form a team during the first round of the championship while others were already out on the track. As they zoomed around at meets, tested and trained their cars, we were frantically building a machine borne of dream and dedication.

We finished the car a week before Bathurst, and we didn't have a lot to do in the final hours. We didn't really make any further modifications to the Falcon after Amaroo, because we didn't need to. After the race, we knew we had a car that could challenge the best, so there was no panic or overhaul. It was simply a matter of finetuning, washing and putting the car on the truck.

Back then there wasn't a lot you could do to prepare your car for quite possibly the most demanding 1000 kilometres anywhere in the racing world. Come Saturday night, you'd stick a new engine in to make sure the car was going to survive. The gearbox was always a concern; leading into the race, many would throw a new one in too, hoping it would ensure no clunks or carnage. (It didn't.) The diff was never a problem; it was bulletproof. But the brakes were always an issue. All you could do was change the pads before the race.

Cars were such delicate things and I found it was best to use a tried-and-tested method because you knew what you were going to get. Better the devil you know.

Basically, you had to make sure everything worked before slapping the car on your truck. If you didn't have it right by now, you were certain to end the race on the back of a flatbed truck.

Ready early, and in no particular rush, the boys and I decided to have a few days of rest and recreation on the way over. Looking to refresh and unwind, we stopped off at a resort in Beaudesert for beers, jokes and sleep before heading to the Mountain. It was the best possible preparation.

We unloaded the car in the dusty Mount Panorama paddock and wheeled it to the pit-lane, full of hope and promise. We thought we had a winner; our first outing did nothing to say otherwise. With power to burn, I floored up the Mountain, eating each bend and rise with the fully blown 351 Cleveland. I floated smoothly over the top, the car getting in and out of the deathly bends without a scare. Coming down was simply exhilarating – she was fast, furious and on the limit.

'She's beaut,' I said, rolling her back into the garage a content man. 'The best I've ever had.'

Despite a history of failure, I was now a seasoned Mountain man. It felt as though I had been there forever, and the car was a real winner.

Set-up was pretty low-tech back then, and there was nothing much you could do except grab your steering wheel and squeeze it to an inch of its life. We could adjust the shocks, set the sway bars and springs, but that was about it. We wanted to make the car as low and as close to the ground as possible, which was tough because we had to drive clear over a 10-centimetre bar to be deemed legal. But that's a load of crap, because the only reason they wanted us off the ground was so we didn't ruin their track.

There were no computers, no data – hell, we didn't even have lap times. A bunch of officials in the control booth marked you off every time you passed the pits. That was our tracking system back then, and the only way they knew if you'd completed a lap.

We used to keep our own lapsheets of the entire top-running cars, including the major teams. Sometimes the official sheets were wrong, and if you lost a lap you were buggered, so making sure you had your own lap charts was important. A pain in the arse but a necessity.

Jillie used to do ours. She'd keep tabs on all the cars, and time the top dozen on every single lap, noting down the results on a board in the garage. If there was ever a dispute, the top team's lap charts would be called on to solve it. There was a lot of honesty involved, and you'd hate to think someone won Bathurst by being given an extra lap when they shouldn't have. It may have happened, I don't know.

A Bee's Dick from 10K

I floored my way over the line, the crowd cheering on and stopwatches blazing. It was a near-perfect lap, my best at Bathurst so far. I eased off the throttle and waited to hear my time.

'You have a 2.21.17, Dick,' the message came. '0.3 up on Brock. You are on provisional pole.'

I had to pinch myself.

That's at least a front-row start, I thought. *A front-row start at Bathurst. Wow. Who would've ever thought?*

There was also $10,000 on the line for pole, an astronomical sum, the likes of which I'd never seen.

I pulled into the dusty old pit-lane, and Kevin Bartlett was flying across the top of the Mountain in a monstrous blue-and-yellow Channel 9 Camaro. He was the only man who could steal it from me. His car was a real flyer and a mean machine: all horsepower, flared arches and American muscle. We had both dominated the earlier practice and qualifying sessions, Brock struggling to hold on in his new Commodore. KB and I had both set the equal fastest time in qualifying and couldn't be separated, but now I was standing in the lane, fingers crossed he would stumble.

He didn't.

KB blasted his way to a 2.20.97 and snared the glory and the cash. I was pretty bummed. Shattered, to be honest. For a moment I was the king of the world, sitting at the top of the pile and ready to be celebrated as a Saturday hero. After what I'd been through, it would have been a huge boost and validation for putting it all on the line. And we could have really used the $10,000. Instead we got a big fat nothing.

But our despair didn't last for long because we knew we had a ripper of a car and a great shot at winning the big prize – the Bathurst 1000. We went about analysing the competition and working out a game plan. Kevin Bartlett's Camaro was the gun. He had everyone, for raw pace and power. Meanwhile Brock's car, the 308 Commodore, was a little underdone when it came to horsepower, and he knew it. For the big long straights and frightening climbs, the Commodore just wasn't up to it. But the Camaro had power to burn. It was bloody quick up the hill and was even faster coming down. The Achilles heel to that car, however, was the brakes, which often struggled against the Camaro's heavy frame, and we knew KB had been complaining about the brakes all through practice and qualifying. We had the power too with our 351 Cleveland, maybe not as much as him, but thanks to a sneaky punch from Murray Carter, we didn't have nearly half the car to stop.

That night I sat down with Roy, a cold beer in my hand and a warm meal on the table.

'The car's strong and reliable,' I said. 'We'll make it to the end without a problem. We just have to make sure we nurse the thing and not overdo it.'

We studied our opposition.

'KB's the big threat,' he said. 'But he's got a massive problem with his brakes. The way he drives, he'll be out before he reaches halfway. Maybe sooner.'

'What about Brock?' I said.

'He doesn't have the horsepower,' Roy replied. 'He'll be there until the end, but he won't stand a chance if we can nurse the car and the tyres. This is ours, mate. You just have to keep your head down and your bum up. And maybe pray for some luck.'

We left dinner quietly confident. You never know what's going to happen at Bathurst, and I'd been racing there long enough to know it as well as anyone else. There's always apprehension and fear of the unknown, but we figured we had done all we could and had a better shot than anyone. Our plan was to go out hard, build a lead, and then nurse the thing home. I was going to run at about seven-eighths during the first stint and hand it over to John French, who would be in a position to cruise around and watch the others fall.

I awoke on Sunday morning to be greeted by a series of newspaper reports that said I was the mystery man who could take it to Brock. I'd been racing for a long time to this point – hell, I was almost 35 – but I'd mostly gone unnoticed. After my past couple of races and a near miss on Saturday, I was billed as the dark horse that could end Brock's perfect reign. Brock had won the past four races, and I think the media and the fans were hoping for a shock winner. I, for one, didn't have a problem with that at all.

I think Brock knew damn well that he was in trouble, that he didn't have the out-and-out pace of my Ford. And the one thing about Brock was that he was honest. As race car drivers, myself included, we play mind games to try to land mental blows on our rivals. Brock didn't do much of that. He called a spade a spade and I took him at his word.

I roared off the start line, leaving behind me the colourful spectacle of one of the world's most exciting sporting events. Fans cheered, engines roared, rubber burned, and I was able to keep my nerve to snare the lead. Starting at Bathurst is always a daunting experience. Sitting on the start line, the centrepiece of an event heaving with history, passion, dreams and nightmares, is the ultimate thrill. But shit-scary all the same. Starting from the front row was something else.

What if I stall? I thought. *Leave the car on the line and stuff up all my good work?*

The cameras were on me, beaming my image onto TVs all around the country. What pressure.

But I fanged around the first right, clear in front, and began my ascent towards victory.

Is this for real? I thought. *I can't believe it. This is Bathurst, the biggest race in the country, and I'm* leading.

Shit, I'm also on TV!

It was a wonderful feeling, and I really had to pinch myself and get on with the job. I had another 993 kilometres or so left to go. But things were looking good. Brock was wringing the neck of the Commodore, just trying to keep up with me. He was giving it everything, his car squealing and sliding all over the Mountain. Meanwhile KB, like we'd predicted, was not attempting to conserve and was flat-out on my tail. But I knew that wouldn't last and I was right.

I passed the start/finish line and KB was no longer in my mirror. Instead Brock was there, calling on all his talents just to hold on. I clocked off another lap and glanced to the pits as I went past. KB's brakes were on fire, his crew frantically putting them out.

It was now just me and Brock – in my eyes, anyway. I expected him to be there until the end, but I thought I could blow him away. Again I passed the pits, coming into lap 11, and Brock was no longer behind me. The four-time winner had clipped one of the slower cars coming across the top of the Mountain and was in for repair.

I remember going past pit-lane the next lap and seeing him sitting there, hands in the air.

Oh boy, I thought. *This is interesting. Two down.*

I ran hard for a couple of laps, doing my best to put Brock a lap down.

How good is this? I am one lucky guy.

All I had to do was cruise around, stay out of trouble and the race was mine. My childhood dream was about to come true; all that hard work and determination was about to pay off. All those naysayers were about to be proved wrong and our house was going to be safe.

I went into cruise control; my threats were gone. I fired up around BP corner, just like I had done throughout the race.

I saw a white flag waving in the air. You may know what happened next.

15

ROCK ON

Waving the White Flag

Whack!

My hands were forced from the steering wheel as what felt like a landmine exploded, the metal-on-metal frenzy launching my car violently into the air. I heard the rubber shred and the metal bend. My head slammed back into the seat and my body rattled. It was as if I'd just been hit with 2000 volts.

My 1.3-tonne piece of metal turned from race car to unguided missile in an instant, a concrete wall and a 200-metre drop firmly in its sights.

I thought I was going to die.

My 500 hp monster was completely out of control, heading towards the cliff edge at over 90 k/h. I tried to regroup; I grabbed at the wheel and mashed at the brake. But it was useless.

Bang!

The Falcon exploded into the barrier, the car's front end splatting and my body smashing against the back of my seat. I saw a marshal, dressed in white overalls, sheer terror spread across his face, throw his flag and dive for cover and roll down the hill. My car reared up on impact like a crazy horse bucking, and for an instant I thought I was gone. My arse firmly jammed into the seat, I felt sickened as the car bounced against concrete and launched towards the sky.

Time slowed down, as clichéd as it might sound, and I thought about what was to come. There was nothing but a sheer drop on the other side.

Thud!

My head smashed back into the seat, and I was spat back towards the track at the speed I had come. The tyres gripped onto the road, squealing, and my car spun.

I was alive but my dream was over.

I lent down on the steering wheel, only for a moment, and the anger rose.

What the fuck just happened? I thought, the frenzied pack of cars passing by me. Blood in the water.

I'm done. Out. Gone.

I kicked the door open and heaved myself from the car. I was mad.

Snap!

My head jerked again, back towards the car as my feet threatened to fall. I had forgotten to pull out my communication cable and could now add whiplash to my concerns. I stood for a moment and examined my car.

It was an absolute wreck. Engine smoking, tyres shredded, the entire front end was a mess of twisted metal. I took a deep breath and broke down.

This is it, I thought. *It's all over. I will never race again. Stuff me. Our house might be gone.*

I was facing a sea of debt and a shattered dream. I was another retired racer who would have to work the rest of his life to pay off this disaster. I walked over to the wall, slumped down and cried. My body shook and shuddered as the tears ran relentlessly down my face. I was inconsolable.

In a second I had gone from a Bathurst winner to a retiree. I was broken. Through the pain and hurt I tried to think about what had happened.

I had come up to the Cutting and seen the white flags waving. There was no yellow, and I'd edged off the throttle thinking a minor hazard was in front. White flags are quite ambiguous: they could mean a slow car, a service vehicle. So I'd slowed down as I came over the blind hill; I didn't want to lose time but I certainly didn't want to come unstuck on whatever was ahead.

I'd veered over the rise and first saw the truck, a tip tray with a wounded soul on its back. It had been parked to the *left* of the road, and hadn't represented a major concern. I'd immediately taken action to miss it, veering to the *right*, pretty much on the racing line. I'd thought I was fine.

And then, at the last moment, I saw the rock. It was huge, about the size of an overnight bag. I knew it would shred the underneath of my car and I'd tried to miss it. I'd heaved at the wheel and attempted to go up the bank. But it was too late.

The rock had shredded through my left wheel, before going on to mince the rest of that side. The front wheel and the back had exploded, my car becoming an uncontrollable heap. My hands couldn't handle the brunt, and had shot off the wheel. I was thrown around like a ragdoll as I headed straight for the wall.

There was no way I could have missed it, and I've replayed the situation over a million times in my mind. The track at that point wasn't wide – maybe about 7 metres. The truck was hanging to the *left* and measured at least 2.7 metres from side to side. My car was 1.8 metres wide and the car was about 1 metre away from the truck. When you add that all up, and factor in speed and surprise, there was nothing I could do aside from stop, and I didn't have time to bring my heavy horsepowered machine to a halt. Not with a blind descent.

In the split second I saw the rock, I knew it would end me. There was no room between it and the truck, so I went the other way. It was really a hopeless situation.

I had no control once I hit it. Nothing. I clenched my fists on the wheel and braced for impact. That was all I could do. I had a moment to think, my eyes firmly pointed on the concrete. It didn't look that big and I was convinced I was going to go straight over the top.

And I almost did.

With tears continuing to stream down my face, the bitter taste of salt water and defeat seeping into the corners of my mouth, I thought about my future.

It was the end for Dick Johnson.

I had put everything we had into this. Everything. I didn't have a cent left. I was leading the race, on my way to winning it, and a second later it was all gone. My motor racing career was over, and on top of that, I was in danger of losing our house.

I jumped on the back of the tow truck, feeling absolutely cold, and was still a blubbering mess when I got off. Ivan Stibbard, the Bathurst promoter, was the first to greet me.

'I'm so sorry for you, Dick,' he said.

I didn't respond.

'We will do whatever we can.'

I was sure he was more worried about me suing him than he was about my welfare. He also asked me if I was injured; I wasn't. Physically, anyway.

'Here's the culprit,' he said, pointing at the rock, which someone had heaved down from the Mountain.

It was the first time I had seen it with more than an instant to spare. The size of two footballs, it was diamond hard. While my car was an absolute wreck, the rock didn't even have a chip. I looked at the rock. I hated it.

Jillie found me and I was still shaking as she ushered me into the truck. Frenchy and his wife were sitting there, stone cold. Jillie hugged me as tears rolled down her face. She knew what we had put in, and the effort I had gone to and the sacrifices I had made to get to this point. It was just heartbreaking. I tried to summon the courage to comfort her, but I couldn't. I had nothing to say and felt like a complete failure.

To have a dream finish like that, within a second, was just gut-wrenching.

We pulled ourselves together by trying to pack things up. Like zombies, we walked around, moving bits and pieces, throwing stuff into the truck.

Then the stories started. The painful, hurtful stories that made a bad situation worse. I went from sad to mad.

'Someone threw that rock, Dick,' a passer-by said. 'We heard it was a Holden fan. He was shitty that Brock was going to lose and wanted to end you.'

It was around about that time I was called to the commentary box, to do a live interview on TV. I was still numb and can't recall much of what happened. I didn't have my head in a good space at all.

But here's what was said in a conversation with Channel 7's Chris Economaki.

CE: I am sitting here with a gentleman who's had perhaps one of the more unfortunate experiences in motor racing. First of all, Dick, are you all right, physically?

DJ: Yeah, well, thanks to the safety equipment that's in the car, there's no physical injury whatsoever.

CE: Leading the race and things going your way, and the story is, that someone decided to throw a boulder over the track and in your path. Is that a correct report?

DJ: Well, it was just as you crest the hill, coming out of the Cutting, there was a rock the size of an overnight bag. It was right on line and you cannot see it until you crest the hill. I tried to avoid the rock, but because of these complete utter irresponsible morons . . .

CE: I agree with you totally.

DJ: I can honestly say that I will never ever race at Bathurst again until such time they have a 20-foot-high wire fence, and the entire spectator areas are completely wired off from the track because that is just so dangerous. I just couldn't believe my bloody eyes with these galoots out there that just throw boulders. Like, it was enormous.

CE: It probably took more than one person to pick it up.

DJ: Well, I hit it with the left-front tyre, and the left-rear tyre, and it just shattered the wheels, the tyres, the lot.

CE: Terrible thing. Dick, the operation, we have been told, is a private operation. What did that crash cost you in dollars and cents?

DJ: Well, unless I can get $40,000 to rebuild the car, you've lost me. Because I've just had a gutful of the whole bloody operation – it is just so bad. And the spectators here get paralytically drunk before ten o'clock in the morning, and it just ruins the whole race. We went out there and I ran the race for as long as I was in it, to a plan where I would run 22s, which we ran for the first ten laps or so, and then we sort of buttoned off the pace – we broke the opposition, absolutely demoralised them and we could have run around at 25s so easily, the car was doing it so easy, everything was magnificent. And I owe a hell of a lot to the boys in the crew, to all our sponsors, from Palmer Tube Mills and Kill Rust paints, Bryan Byrt Ford and the Bank of Queensland, and all those people in Queensland who support us. I really thank *them very much, but believe me, I feel very, very disappointed for them.*

I was absolutely shattered, but, as you can tell, furious too. I was told the rock had been thrown by a spectator, and that made my blood boil. I can hardly remember the interview, but I knew I was raging mad. I didn't ever think I would go back to Bathurst and didn't want to if an animal had thrown that rock. Peter Brock always said I wore my heart on my sleeve, and judging by this, I guess he was right. I just couldn't hold back after something like that.

It was then that Channel 7 commentator Mike Raymond interrupted.

MR: Dick Johnson. Dick, just if I could interrupt? It's Mike Raymond from the commentary panel. Dick, the switchboards at all the [Channel] 7 stations across Australia are jammed with people who are so upset with what has happened. They, believe it or not, are ringing and just genuinely pledging money to help you. Now this has happened in the last half hour. Everyone knows what has happened to you, and we want you to understand that everyone admires what you've done so far in your qualifying efforts yesterday, and also this morning in leading the race, and we'll keep you informed. I know the viewers across Australia are absolutely shattered by what has happened, the same as you are shattered. It probably wasn't a motor racing supporter who threw that, probably some idiot that just came in to cause a disturbance, so, take time out and we will keep you informed on what happens, Dick.

CE: Dick, I have just one more question for you. You've been in motor racing a long time. Have you ever been so emotionally let down [as you are now]? I saw you get out of the truck there, and I could see you were touched right to the core. It had to be more an emotional shock more than a physical one. Has anything like that ever happened to you in racing before?

DJ: Never. Because, you know, this was our big shot. We had stuck every single bob into this.

CE: How long do you think it will take you to get over this? The rest of your life, I would imagine.

DJ: Oh, believe me, I'll be back. But, by Jesus, I won't be back here until they get that fence up, I tell you.

I was in tears by the end of the interview, bawling on national TV. When Mike Raymond told me that viewers were donating money, I just lost it. I was completely overwhelmed, but really I didn't think much of it at the time. I was too upset and too distracted with the fact that I needed at least $40,000 to give me hope.

I went back to the garage, hugged Jillie again and continued to pack up. *For the last time*, I thought. Not long after, Mike Raymond walked up to me.

'Dick, I told you I'd keep you informed, right?' he said.

I nodded.

'Well, Edsel Ford II has just called in and offered to match every dollar that the public raise.'

Edsel was the vice-president of Ford Australia and the great grandson of Henry Ford, the company's founder.

I gave Mike a false smile. I was too distraught to care and I really thought it meant nothing. I was done. Over and out. I packed my gear, my bags and left Bathurst for the last time.

Or so I thought.

Notes, Coins and Letters

Ring. Ring.

I walked into our house, totally stuffed after a 14-hour drive and the phone was going off. I wasn't in the mood to answer it. I had left Bathurst at the break of dawn with Ross Palmer, my mate and my sponsor, by my side, who had cancelled his flight home to take the trip with me.

'Ross, I am done,' I'd told him, my most recent memory of Bathurst still awash with darkness. 'There's no way I can continue. I just have to forget about myself and make sure I can pay the debts off and raise my kids. I'm over.'

Ross had just nodded because he'd known too it was a hopeless situation.

Ring. Ring.

'Leave me alone,' I screamed.

After all the highs and lows, I was emotionally spent. I felt like I needed to sleep for days.

Ring. Ring.

'OK,' I yelled to no one in particular. 'I'm coming.'

I reached the phone and picked it up.

'What? What do you want?' I belted into the receiver.

'Sorry,' said the voice. 'Have I reached Dick Johnson?'

'Yes.'

'Dick, it's the ABC calling. We're wondering if you'd be available for an interview regarding Bathurst?'

'Why?'

'Peter Brock won the thing. Why don't you speak to him?'

The guy went on to ask me if I'd read the papers. I hadn't. I slammed the phone down and grabbed the local rag.

I couldn't believe it. Here we were in the middle of a federal election, and my ugly mug was smack-bang on the front page.

Ring. Ring.

'Dick, it's Channel 10,' the caller said. 'Can you talk?'

The story of this poor battler whose life's work had been knocked out by a rock was big news. I took calls from every major media outlet in the country. I did all the interviews, but still couldn't comprehend what was happening. Not until the mail started pouring in.

As people drove past my house, honking their horns, some stopping by to shake my hand, the mailman arrived. He reversed his truck to our door and poured the bags onto my porch.

Jillie and I spread the letters across the bed. We grabbed at the little envelopes and watched the coins and notes fall out onto the quilt. There were donations as little as five cents, while some envelopes had as much as $50 inside. We read every single letter and cried. Some were from kids who had emptied their piggy banks and sent me every coin.

'I know it isn't much, Mr Johnson,' one said. 'But it's all I have. And I want to give it to you so you can go back to Bathurst and win. That would mean more to me than my money.'

Others were from adults telling me I was a true Aussie battler. That I had touched their hearts and made them feel like I was one of them. One was from an American, who had been on holidays in Australia and had seen the Bathurst event unfold.

'I have never seen anything like that in my life,' he wrote. 'And the amount of support and kindness shown by the Australian people is just astounding. I have never seen such love from any people and it has given me a whole new outlook on life. I thank you, and I thank Australia.'

Most just told me they felt for me and wanted to help me get back on the road. In total, there was $78,000. We took it all to the Bank of Queensland and put it into its own account.

What I had to do was obvious. I had no choice but to go on.

We owed that to every man, woman and child who had sent in their money and well-wishes.

16

GOOD WILL HUNTING

Parts and Pressure

My suit clung to my sweaty skin as I walked into the hulking building of glass and steel. I had only worn the suit a couple of times, to weddings and funerals, and didn't ever think I would need it for such an occasion. I straightened my tie and nervously entered the executive meeting room, still wondering why the hell I was here.

But it could only be for the better. I had nothing to lose.

I looked at the five suits sitting around the table. I recognised them all, but only knew Edsel Ford II and Doug Jacobi by name. I was sure the rest of the intimidating faces sitting around the oak table were just as important as the president and the parts and service manager when it came to Ford.

There was no chitchat.

'Dick, we've brought you down to Melbourne because we want to sponsor you next year,' Edsel said.

'What happened to you at Bathurst was quite massive, and in light of who you are and what you've done over the years, we think we should help. Your story has touched not only the public but us, and it's only fitting that we should try and help you in your Ford.'

A smile erupted on my face. I didn't know that Ford wanted to sponsor me. They'd already matched the public donation, and I suspected they'd called me down to their headquarters in Broadmeadows, Victoria to ask for it back.

I'd known Doug Jacobi for a while. He looked after the parts division, which was then called Motorcraft. He was the one who'd initially made contact and invited me over to meet the Ford brass.

There was a fair bit of talk about the rock, and the events that came in its wake. There was also talk of the future and how they wanted me to win the 1981 Bathurst in a Ford. The company had been out of the sport for a couple of years, but this wasn't their attempt to get back into motor racing. They didn't want to put me in a factory team, just offer me some backdoor support.

It was news to my ears. I was offered an extremely generous price on parts, a new body shell and some cash. It was exactly what I needed to take the fight to Peter Brock and his all-conquering HDT.

My car wasn't an absolute ruin. I was able to save most of the components but the body shell was completely written off. The fact that Ford had offered to build a new one for me was a huge advantage. I was able to walk alongside the car on the production line and tell them what I did and didn't need. I told them to leave out the weight in the body, brackets, deadening, things like that. I also got them to cut off the overlap when they joined the panels together. It didn't sound like much, but all those things added up to a drastic reduction in weight. I was also able to direct them to make it the strongest body I had ever seen. Spot welds are usually placed about every 30 millimetres, but they placed these in every 5 millimetres, making the body light yet extremely strong.

For me, the biggest hindrance on my car was the springs. We were a couple of years away from getting coil springs on the back, but aside from that the car was good. Now I just had to make the most of it.

HDT and Brock were back behind the eight ball. They knew what they had to chase and went about hunting me down. But they were thrown an early curve ball – Brock had just released his production Brock Commodore and that was the car they were going to race. CAMS homologated it and ordered that the car have air-conditioning, just like the road-going version, so Brock ended up with a huge and useless air-conditioning unit right in front of the passenger seat. HDT were always going to lack the power of the Falcon but went into the season confidently all the same.

It was a wonderful feeling to have factory support, but I didn't really think about what it could mean for the fans. Brock had predicted that I'd become the Ford guy, and I guess now I was. I wasn't too worried about doing well for the thousands upon thousands of Ford fans out there, though – I was out there to repay a nation for the kindness and generosity it had showed me after the crash.

To be honest, following the events of that day, I felt that

I was being crushed under a mountain of expectation and pressure. It was really doing my head in. To this point I had been a carefree soul, easygoing and relaxed. Now I was a stressed-out fool, fearing I could not be the man Australia wanted me to be. Maybe that's what eventually turned my hair white!

Showtime

It was utter hysteria when I arrived in Tasmania for the first championship round of 1981. Before Bathurst I was a nobody privateer and now I was being mobbed by the media and fans, which was all a bit hard to take.

The first race of the year was at Symmons Plains and when I got to the track, I was greeted by hundreds of people, pens and posters in hand. I had signed a few autographs in my time, but mainly in Queensland, where I was a local boy. This was something new altogether. The media were also relentless. For the first time in a while, they realised they had a driver capable of taking it to Brock, and a backstory that was an editor's dream. Brock and I were front-page news and they didn't give the other drivers a chance. To be honest, the media were probably right. The rest of the field was way off the pace. No one in a Falcon could match it with me, and Brock was by far the best of the Holdens. It was going to be a two-man show.

I didn't really like the extra attention, but I figured it just came with the deal. Fame also had an upside. For years I'd been battling away in the mud, preparing my car in the worst possible facilities, usually at the track. But even before

I arrived in Tasmania, I got a call from a bloke who offered me his workshop for the week. It was a coup to land a proper facility before the race.

I unloaded my car at the garage owned by John Dixon and John Walker and went about preparing for the race there. I would end up being great mates with both men, and I still stay at Dixon's house whenever I'm in Tasmania.

I was nervous as hell when I rolled the car out to qualify, fearing I could not live up to the hype. All eyes were on me and I didn't want to let anyone down. For years I didn't have the backing or support, but I had both now and it was up to me. I told myself it was just another race and went and stuck the thing on pole.

I sat on the front row next to Brock. Of course. The small yet challenging track, set in a rugged rural terrain about 20 kilometres from Launceston, was heaving with spectators. The publicity of my clash with Brock had drawn in a record crowd, but I tried to forget all that and focused on my job at hand – getting off the line and taking the lead.

I thundered away and got to the first right-hander, a slight high-speed corner, in front. I then took the huge hairpin and powered down the straight. It was my race to lose and I knew the only way that would happen was if I fried my brakes because the hairpin was absolutely brutal after the flat-out section before. I went all out for a couple of laps until I knew exactly where Brock was, and felt that I had his measure. It wasn't that easy back then because we had limited radio communication and no big screens like they have today. But at Tassie, the hairpin was big enough so that you could look back and see the other cars entering as you exited. When I'd built up a sufficient lead – seeing Brock entering the hairpin as I left – I backed off, trying to maintain that gap.

I ended up surviving and knocking up the win. It was only my second win over Peter, and my first win in a Ford. I was stoked with the result given everything that had gone on. I thought I might be able to make all those people who'd put faith in me proud. I not only believed that I could now win Bathurst, but also the championship.

The season rolled on and I was never far off the pace. I don't think I ever finished off the podium and I also won my fair share, with wins at Adelaide and Perth. Brock and I were evenly matched and we exchanged blows, his car suiting some, mine others. All was perfect until we got to Calder Park, where the shit hit the fan.

'Dick,' Roy said, 'you better come with me. They're blowing up like you wouldn't believe.'

I had been at a promotion following practice, and I'd left the team with Roy. He was called in to scrutineering, where officials check over the cars to make sure there are no illegal modifications, when he realised he'd forgotten to do something beforehand – a little trick of the trade.

My car was 100 per cent legal, but I knew it was lighter than everyone else's and didn't want to tip authorities off. As a precaution, I always made sure the fuel tank was at its fullest whenever the car had to be checked out, so it was as heavy as it could be.

Bloody Roy had left it empty.

And this was the worst possible time to make this mistake because Calder was the only place in the country that actually had a weighbridge. Harry Firth, a Holden man and Brock supporter, was the chief scrutineer. His eyes lit up when they put my Falcon on the scales.

'1265 kilograms,' he stated, matter-of-factly. 'Interesting.'

The other drivers then blew up, one after another.

Strangely enough, it was mostly the Ford blokes who had the shits. Bob Morris, Murray Carter, Garry Willmington and Charlie O'Brien were all beside themselves because my car was so much lighter than theirs. The poor bastards had been scratching their heads for 18 months wondering why I was so quick.

Morris's Falcon weighed a whopping 1834 kg. Murray Carter's was the next lightest at 1533 kg.

That's when the penny dropped.

'Your car is too light,' someone said. 'What the hell have you done?'

'No, it isn't', I said. 'Check the papers. Check the rules.'

The other team owners couldn't argue with me. My car was smack-bang on the legal limit. Nothing could be done about it because the papers had been accepted and I was abiding by the letter of the law. It did, however, reveal my secret and gave the other teams a chance to lighten their loads and come after me. I wasn't so concerned about the other Fords because I was well in front of them when it came to the championship, though I was worried about Brock, because we were neck and neck. He immediately ordered a new car to be built.

Roy and I then jumped into our truck and quickly drove towards Oran Park away from the furore. We were almost there when . . .

'Dick,' Roy said. 'That copper just waved you down.'

'Oh boy,' I said. 'We're screwed.'

I was speeding. I had a Falcon in the truck, which almost went as well as my race car, when it got going anyway. But that wasn't what concerned me.

Neither Roy nor I had a truck licence.

I slammed on the brake, bringing the mammoth beast to a stop. The truck was huge and didn't stop in a hurry. We were 600 metres down the road when I finally brought the truck to a standstill.

We waited and waited. Nothing.

'Maybe he wasn't after us,' Roy said. 'It has been a while.'

'Yeah, must have been someone else,' I said, pushing on the accelerator and taking off.

Next minute we heard sirens blazing.

'Oh dear,' I said. 'This isn't good.'

I pulled the truck up again, sweat pouring down my face.

The copper stopped and got out of his car. I met him on the road.

'G'day, mate,' I said. 'Is everything OK?'

'No, it is not,' he barked. 'You just drove through a police stop.'

'No, I didn't,' I said. 'I stopped but no one came. I thought you guys were pulling someone else over.'

'No, damn it,' he said. 'We were waving at you. Do you know how fast you were going?'

I shrugged.

'Bloody 144 kays per hour,' he said. 'I need to get the sergeant up here. This is serious.'

I waited, shitting bricks. It was about ten minutes later when the burly boss appeared, grimacing and frowning. As he got closer towards us, a smile cracked across his rugged face.

'Bloody Dick Johnson,' he said. 'How the hell are you?'

'Not too great right now,' I said. 'I had no idea I was going so fast. I reckon I'm in the shit.'

'Do you know something, mate?' he asked. 'I sent you ten bucks after Bathurst last year.'

'Well, bloody don't take it off me now!' I fired straight back.

He laughed. 'No, mate,' he said. 'I wouldn't do that. Just remember that this is a hot area and you don't need to be speeding. Go on your merry way, but get your mate to drive. We all know you like to go fast.'

I grabbed a couple of shirts from the truck, signed them and threw them his way. I then looked at Roy.

'You're driving,' I said.

'But I don't have a licence,' he replied.

'Neither do bloody I,' I yelled. 'Just get in the fucking thing and drive.'

We both got our truck licences the next day.

Champion

I was about four kilometres away from Lakeside Raceway when my road car was forced to a deathly stop, the track within sight.

'We're going to miss warm-up,' I said to Jillie, the excruciating traffic adding to my nerves.

'Why are all these people here?' I continued. 'I've never seen anything like it.'

'They're here to see you,' she said. 'To see if you can beat Peter.'

The 1981 Touring Car Championship was to be decided on this day. Brock and I were separated by just one point going into the last race of the championship after eight heated affairs. I had won three, he had won three. Following a ferocious season-long battle, there was just no way of separating us. And I was nervous as hell as I edged closer towards the track, fearing I would miss the chance to sort out my car before the finale because of the traffic.

To make matters worse, Brock had just taken possession of a brand-new car. I was told it was an absolute gun, all the weight stripped back with power to burn.

Finally and fortunately, Jillie and I made it to practice, where Brock and I were neck and neck. It would come down to the race, maybe the start, the victor to take all.

It wasn't only Brock who was making me feel uneasy. This was my home track and thousands upon thousands of people were piling into the little circuit to see if the hometown hero could beat the legend. It was the first time a Queenslander had been in a position to win the championship, and the spectators came in their droves to see if I could do it.

There was also that small matter of the rock. I knew everyone's eyes were firmly planted on me and I was desperate to pay back all those people who had sent me their money and well-wishes. I felt it was my duty, my obligation, to get a result, and now I was close. It made my gut burn and my hands tremble.

I told myself it was OK; it was just another race. I knew this track better than anyone. Lakeside was hard on tyres and

I knew if I could look after mine, and find a way to keep Brock behind me, I would be all right. I was determined not to worry about it.

'If we win the championship, great,' I said to Jillie. 'If not, no big deal. I can handle second.'

That laissez-faire attitude went straight out the window after I took my place on the grid. I had landed pole position and looked over to Brock, an intense thousand-yard stare on his face. I had the urge to spew. Stomach knotted and heart racing, I dry-retched as I sat there waiting for the green light. I looked forward but that didn't help – there were thousands of people screaming and waving Dick Johnson flags.

I made my mind go blank for a minute to focus on the job at hand.

Now which gear? I thought. *First or second?*

But the panic worsened as I contemplated my start. Because of the gear ratios I had chosen for the race, I wasn't sure whether or not I should start in first or second. I feared choosing first might see Brock mow me down as I tried to find second. I also worried that I might bog down in second, or worse, stall.

I jammed the thing in second and let loose. The wheels spun as the cars were waved away by the crowd, the rubber eventually finding its grip and smashing me off the start-line. I pulled away from Brock, waited until I was a good car's length ahead, and then turned onto the racing line. I had it in the bag.

But three laps later –

Bang!

My front shuddered and a violent noise shot out.

I'd held my nerve up until that point, Brock refusing to go away. I was leading, just, and when I heard that explosion I thought it was all over. I didn't know what had happened. Nothing seemed wrong. And then I turned back.

The car did not want to follow my lead; it was like an oil tanker attempting a three-point turn. I quickly realised that I'd broken a sway bar. Sway bars give the car stability at corners, without them the vehicle becomes muddy with oversteer. I knew then that this was going to be a problem, but it wasn't critical.

I got a message informing me of the damage.

'Dick, your bar is hanging and flapping all over the place,' Roy said through the earpiece. 'They're thinking about giving you a black flag.'

A black flag is a death sentence: a call to return to the pits because a mechanical malfunction is posing a risk to other cars. This was a pure sprint race with no stops, and a black flag would have not only ended my chance of winning the race, but also the championship. A flag marshal sent a radio message to the chief steward telling him of his intention to issue me with the dreaded flag.

'Do that at your own peril,' said the chief steward at Lakeside, Ken West, who happened to be a mate. 'You understand that he's a Queenslander fighting for the championship, and we just happen to be in Queensland? If you value your life, I suggest you don't do it. It's your call.'

The flag marshal sensibly kept the flags tucked under his arm.

I was kept alive. With a crippled car I now found myself in the fight of my life. Brock was already threatening to make a pass before my misadventure, and he was now a complete menace. Smack-bang in my rearview mirror, he nudged my tail, darted left and right, looking for space. I hung on for dear life. Knowing he could spring a move at any moment, I used every inch of the road. I hung the thing out into the weeds, brought it back to the wall, sent rocks and dirt spewing into clouds behind me.

Brock's car was an utter mess. My debris had stripped all the red and white from the front of his machine. His windscreen was cracked and his tyres bare. Still, he was coming. I thought I was gone. I did all I could to hold him at bay, used every trick in the book, and by the grace of God, I was still in the lead coming into the final corner.

'One to go,' I said, Brock refusing to lie down.

I took the corner and floored my way across the finish line. The championship was mine.

I won it by just two-tenths of a second. It was a 36-lap war with the best in the business, and not only that, I'd taken out the 1981 Australian Touring Car title. I let out some emotion, a few screams of joy. I'd been chipping away at this thing for 15 years, and my perseverance had finally paid off.

I'd only just crossed the finish line when the crowd began pouring onto the track. Jumping fences and dashing across grass and gravel, more than a thousand people ran to meet me when I emerged from the car. They seemed happier than me, absolutely drunk on joy. A moment after my feet hit the asphalt, some bloke, a complete stranger, grabbed me and flung me onto his shoulders. He chaired me through the crowd, the new champion treated like a king.

I eventually escaped to spend a few quiet moments with my team and my wife. We hugged and cried, basking in our glory. Brock then walked over.

'Mate,' he said. 'I did everything I could to get you – not just in this race but all year. You absolutely deserve this. You have earned every inch. I can honestly say you were the better driver this year. Well done.'

Brock could have punted me off the road on several occasions during the breakneck finale, but he didn't, and that's the type of driver he was. If he couldn't win fair and square, he wouldn't. And this championship meant a lot to him, because he hadn't won many and was desperate to leave a bigger legacy than what he'd done in Bathurst. Brock was never a dirty driver, and was always a gracious loser. I guess that's why we all loved him so much.

I went back into my truck following the presentation and celebrated with my family and team. We walked out at about 7 pm, and to my astonishment, nobody had left. There were still thousands of people, waiting to get a piece of me. I jumped on my ute to avoid the crush. I signed autographs and hugged strangers into the night. It was just unreal.

17

THE ROCKSTAR

Mountain Glory

I slammed my foot into the pedal, the car screaming off the start line like a rabid animal smacked with a stick. The wheels of my Falcon were sent into a violent spin, the rubber gripping the road and launching me towards my seemingly impossible dream. I looked left – pole-sitter Kevin Bartlett was in my dust – and then back – Peter Brock was sucking on dirt.

Again I was leading Bathurst, but this time it was mine. No one would stop me.

I was greeted with absolute hysteria when I arrived in Bathurst 1981. *That* bloke who had been ruined by *that* rock had returned.

'From a Rockstar to a Mountain Man,' one sign read.

'Tru-Blu Aussie,' another screamed.

I was mobbed as soon as my feet hit the ground;

well-wishers telling me that this was my year and that I couldn't be beat.

Problem was I knew that I could.

Peter Brock and Kevin Bartlett had come along in leaps and bounds since the weight of my flyer had been revealed at Calder. They knew where all my speed had come from and had spent the past few months plotting to bring me down. And I was genuinely worried.

Both big guns had been on song at Sandown, the lead-up race to Bathurst, and I only managed to score a podium. Brock was coming to grips with his new and much-improved car and KB had found a few extra bits and pieces thanks to some lobbying with CAMS.

In my view, CAMS were biased towards the Melbourne drivers, and I'm pretty sure they showed him some favour before Bathurst 1981. KB seemed to get little resistance from the governing body when he asked for some small yet effective changes to be made to his car. KB was desperate to make up the gap, and CAMS were not interested in a one-horse race, approving a few modifications he suggested.

Among other things, KB was given the green light to strap disc brakes to the back of his car. I don't blame him or CAMS for doing it, because I was pissing all over everybody to that point. Everyone wanted to see close competition, and giving KB some small allowances would ensure a battle at the most important race of the year. I didn't complain, and why would I? I was just a backwater Queenslander; any objection I had would've fallen on deaf ears. I'm not that type of bloke, anyway.

My dream was to win Bathurst, it always had been, and

while winning the championship had been nice, it would only be a consolation prize if I couldn't win the big one. Despite my achievements during the year, I really felt they'd mean nothing if I couldn't win this race. Again I put myself under immense pressure, thinking of those thousands of kind souls that had given me their money after an incident at this very track. As their letters had said, these donations were so I could come back and win Bathurst, not the championship, and I took that to heart.

I feared my mind would collapse if I didn't win. Driving is very much a mental sport, and I really thought I would mentally fuck myself and end up in a chair with a blanket over my lap if something went wrong again. In fact, I told Jillie that if I failed this time round, I'd stuff all the money back into their envelopes and return them to the people who'd sent them.

Practice was a daunting experience. The car was good, as expected, but the level of support I had at the race didn't become apparent until I roared around Mount Panorama for the first time. Sitting back, checking my gear and trying to gauge the most brutal racetrack in the country, I couldn't help but be distracted by the spectators cheering for me, clapping and waving their flags, as I flung around. It only added to the ever-growing pressure.

'Don't let that get to you,' John French told me after practice. 'We have a really good car and an equally good chance of winning. Those signs, those people, they don't mean a thing unless we can do the job.'

Frenchy and I came up with a plan. We wanted to settle the car on the Saturday; we weren't out to set lap records or blitz the field. We wanted to run all our parts in and qualify well enough to be somewhere at the front.

We accomplished our plan, qualifying in second place, giving the car a solid but not overly demanding work-out. KB, in his Channel 9-backed Camaro, took the top spot; Brock, this time more menacing, just one place behind me on the grid.

With a new pre-run engine and gearbox strapped in, I took to the grid, a strange calm shielding me from the burning expectation. I had done everything I could for preparation: the car, the lead-up, the plan. Now it was all down to my ability, and in a way I took comfort in that. I knew I could do the job.

In an instant the light was green and another Bathurst was underway. I belted off the line, a perfect start, smoking both Brock and KB to the first corner. Again I was leading the greatest race in the land, and it felt every bit as good as it did the year before. I was determined to stay in front.

But soon the full force of my competition became apparent, with KB hanging to my tail and quickly making ground. I thought about a Lakeside-style play, with me ducking and weaving. I figured there was no point. This was a war of attrition, not a sprint, and I would only ruin my car. KB passed me coming into the final turn, wheels squealing, car rumbling.

Brock tried to pounce but I held him out momentarily, the Bathurst king swooping on me soon after. This was short-lived, however, with KB slamming into a little Gemini and sending the fellow Holden end over end like a skittle on lap 16. KB was forced to pit with a broken axle. He was done and dusted, laps down and out of contention.

My focus now shifted to KB, and as always he was all elbows out and full throttle. The race looked as if it would be a two-way war between me and him, although Bob Morris was looming and doing a good job.

I stuck on KB's tail, not letting him out of my sight, and in an instant the race changed again. His car bucked for a moment, a clip from a backmarker sending him arse over tail. I only had a second to react, yanking violently on my steering wheel to get out of the way. His car sped off the track and collided hard into a wall.

KB was injured but not out. He limped into pit-lane and, on national TV, said he was going to walk up to the bloke who had taken him out and punch him in the nose. KB was out for blood and in the mood for a blue, asking around as to who the culprit was.

'It's Ronnie Wanless,' someone said of the ex-pro boxer turned race car driver.

KB suddenly went quiet. Naturally, he didn't go looking for a fight after finding out that he had swapped paint with the best fighter in the paddock.

Right there and then, I thought I had won the race. With only Morris behind me in the horizon, I figured I could back right off and ride it out to the end. Frenchy and I decided that we would pull it up and conserve the car. There was no point going hell for leather and risking another catastrophe when we could just ease our way around and put the foot down if we were challenged.

So I pulled off the throttle, caressed the brakes, and slowly and cautiously pushed the car into gear. We set ourselves generous lap times and went to a plan. All was going well until I came in for a stop and shut the engine off, as was the rule.

'Bit of oil, Dick,' someone said.

We quickly worked out that it wasn't a concern. We had a dry sump, and one of the lines from the oil tank leading to the pump had sprung a leak. It drizzled oil when the car was stationary, but under suction the small hole meant nothing. We marched on, not a care in the world.

And on lap 121 all hell broke loose.

'They've gone in everywhere,' someone said. 'It's utter carnage and there's no way through! At least six cars. KB and Morris are in it.'

We went and looked at the vision. Chris Gibson's and Bob Morris's cars collided violently, smoke and metal spewing into the air. In their wake another four cars bashed and barged into each other, collecting rear ends, walls and steel. You could tell they were tugging on their brakes desperately to avoid the dangerous dance in front of them. It was complete chaos. Officials frantically waved flags and stopped the rest of the pack in the nick of time. The remaining drivers parked their cars behind the carnage, bottlenecking the track.

We got straight on the radio to John, who was driving at the time and thankfully was nowhere near the mess.

'Mate, take it easy,' I said. 'There's a big one at the top.'

We found out exactly where it was and told John.

'Get ready to pull over,' we said. 'There's no way through.'

John slowed over the Cutting and was directed to stop. That's where he stayed for an hour, until they cleared some of the mess and called him through. The terrible six-car pile-up had taken out Morris, who was coming second, and the early threat, KB. We were leading by 38 seconds at the time; only a mishap could have stopped us from winning.

After about an hour, a lane was cleared and John took off. Smoke poured from the car. With the engine off for so long and no pressure to push it through, the dodgy line had spilt oil onto the engine. It raised an eyebrow or two, with people suspecting we had a critical problem. We didn't.

John brought the car in and we stood around, helpless and unsure.

'What the fuck are they going to do?' I said.

'I have no idea. I reckon they'll have to start it again.'

We worked on the car, preparing for another race should it come up. It was a scene of total madness. People were running around with calculators and rule books. Engines were revved and spanners turned. Fans were screaming and shouting, demanding the drivers return. Battered cars came back to the pits – what was left of them, anyway.

The teams were all called to a conference. Bathurst promoter Ivan Stibbard stood in front of an anxious mob of drivers, who hung onto his every word.

'Under the international rules,' he said, 'after seventy-five per cent of the race has been run, we can declare a winner. And we can declare that Dick Johnson and John French have won.'

What? I thought. *Really?*

I had to check myself, making sure my ears had sent the right message to my brain.

It had.

'Yahoo,' I screamed, leaping out of my skin. 'We've won Bathurst!'

I was convinced they'd start the entire race again like John had said, re-gridded and had a shorter affair, so I was genuinely shocked when I heard the news. I began to cry tears of joy, the reality still not sinking in. To suddenly be announced the winner, even though I hadn't crossed the line and known for sure, was like being stung by 50,000 volts.

Jillie ran over and grabbed me, almost throttling the life from my shaking body. The crowd around the podium was enormous, heaving. I was in nirvana.

I took to the podium, a lifelong dream realised. And man, did it feel good. I sprayed champagne and cheered. I was king for the day.

Some negativity started not long after my jubilation. A lot of people were questioning the rule, claiming the result was a farce. Some people downplayed the win, calling it the Bathurst 121 or whatever, but I didn't care. I had won Bathurst 1981, and my name was going down in the record books. Sure, it would have been nice to have crossed the line and get the chequered flag, but that's not how it worked out and I was fine with that. Fuck the knockers – I was the champion of Bathurst!

We celebrated one of the biggest achievements in Australian sport with a few cans of XXXXs in a little shed out back, high-fiving and backslapping each other.

As the dust settled in, I thought about the win and the prize money.

'Sixty thousand dollars,' I said, letting it sink in. 'Wow. Let's put it back into doing it all over again.'

Motor racing was just so addictive and a thrill worth

chasing to the end. And after years of heartbreak, it was now well within my grasp. I was in a position to win in 1980, and now I had won. It seemed all a little bit too easy, and I wanted more.

I felt like a man at the peak of his powers, even though I was 36 at the time. Looking back, and considering the age at which most blokes call it quits, I should have been thinking about retirement, not about how many more Bathurst titles I could win. It's bizarre that my career was kicking off just four years shy of my fortieth birthday. I didn't think about it at the time, but I can certainly look back now and say that I did something very unique – winning and gaining so much hunger at an age when most sportspeople would've been thinking about the end. I guess I had struggled for so many years, and to finally get it right was just bright sun and rainbows. I really felt like a teenager, and the win, and my situation, made me feel like it was the start, not the end.

The guys today are wimps. They get to 35 and think they're dead. That's one of the things I admire about Russell Ingall. He lies about his age – he must be almost 50 – but he's still going.

I also respect John Bowe, who's still at it, and God, he must be 100.

I had so much motivation to continue, and it mostly came from Brock. My long-time dream was to beat him, and I wanted to prove that I was every bit as good as he was. We were only a couple of months apart in age, and as long as he kept on racing, I would too. It wasn't as if I didn't like the bloke or anything like that. I was just bloody competitive and he was the guy to beat. To win you had to beat Brock.

My mind was finally clear. I felt as though the pressure was off and I had paid back those people who had supported me. My body was also good; I was as fit as a fiddle. This was the beginning of the next chapter for Dick Johnson, and what a ride it would be.

Again my mailbox was full when I arrived home, the front porch also overflowing with hessian bags stuffed with mail. But this time there was no money, just letters of congratulation. Jillie and I sat on the bed and read every one. I welled up with pride as I thought about the joy my feats had brought to people, my fans. To think that a battler from Brisbane could bring a smile on someone's face, his achievements meaning something to their lives, was overwhelming. As I said, I love my fans and I will never forget them.

My life has changed forever with the win.

I can no longer walk down the street without being recognised. I wasn't particularly comfortable with it, and I went red at times when people made a fuss. But it was something that came with the turf and I just looked at it like I was making a new friend. Some people change when they are confronted by fame; I didn't. I suppose it helped being 36, because I was mature enough to think about it and deal with it. I was the same bloke I was when I was running around in 25th and besides, Jillie would have kicked my arse if I became a tosser.

Some people are really up themselves, especially today, and think dealing with fans is a chore. They don't want anything to do with Joe Blow, and I've seen disgusting things from Australian athletes – not in our sport, thank goodness – like when they pretend to talk on their mobile phones just so they can brush fans off. That is rude and pathetic. Back in my day it was never that bad, but still some drivers thought they were above spending time with the people who ultimately paid their bills and gave them the opportunity to drive. I was never even in a position to think of being like that, because I would have retired in 1980 if it hadn't been for those who now wanted a bit of my time.

18

UPS AND DOWNS

Rice Burners

Red, white and supposedly full of dynamite, Allan Moffat's Mazda RX-7 roared out onto the track for the first race of the 1982 Touring Car Championship. We gave it to him before he took to the track.

'What's that little thing, mate?' we asked. 'I'd like to see you put the family in the back of that, whack on the trailer and go for a holiday. It's a rice burner.'

Undeterred, he confidently dodged and weaved his way through the track, sending heat to his tyres and fuel to the car's little belly. He revved the rotary, not that we knew what that was, pulling a surprising roar from the tiny 1.2-litre engine. It was a far cry from the whopping 5.8 litres he had at his disposal in the GTHO – the beast that had helped make him famous.

Allan hit the gas and sprang into a corner like lightning.

He also got out at the speed he came.

Bang!

An almighty clunk rang out, stopping him and his new toy in its tracks. We roared on past the incapacitated midget of a car, and laughed.

Allan Moffat was one of eight drivers to roll up to the first race of 1982 in a Mazda RX-7. With factory support behind him, he was among several drivers who had smelt a revolution. Competing in the 3000 cc class, they also thought they could give it to the big bangers with 6000 cc at their disposal. George Fury and Fred Gibson rolled out in a thing called a Nissan Bluebird Turbo. Half the field had put their faith in a new brand of Japanese machinery – lightweight cars with small engines. They had things called 'computers' and 'turbochargers' that manufactured horsepower in spite of size. We thought it was a load of crap, especially when Allan's car shat itself in the warm-up.

We later found out that these rotary things really needed a lot of warming up. Not like our tried and true, you had to do everything and anything to get heat into the engine, and for Allan that meant strapping a bra, a big bit of material, over the hood before going out. Only problem was, the silly bugger left it on when he went out and the car fried!

We thought these new things were a joke and were determined to wipe them off the racing scene. A touring car was supposed to be a big car. It was the type of vehicle that the average family drove, fit for three kids, a dog and a holiday. These new Asian cars were sports cars, and should have been competing in the sports car category, but at the same time, we didn't think they were going to be a threat with their tiny engines and no straight-line speed. So we didn't kick up a stink or argue about their inclusion; these new cars were nothing but speed bumps.

We continued working on Tru-Blu following the Bathurst win, trying to extract every ounce of its might. We knew the other teams, especially Brock's, would be coming for us, and we couldn't afford to stand still. I was still a privateer, but I now had the success and the budget of a bigger team. I was never going to be able to compete with factory teams when it came to funds, but I had a top team all the same and we went about acting like one. We started looking closely at our set-up at the beginning of 1982, and tried to be as professional as we could. We figured there was more to racing than just being fast, and started treating our team like a business.

Full of confidence and ambition, we went out and won the first two races of the season at Sandown and Calder Park. Brock was of course shaping up as my biggest threat, and won the third race at Symmons Plains. He also claimed victory at Oran Park, and that's when the season officially became a farce.

Brock was running his own team since Holden had pulled out in 1979, and with the support of several dealers, he had paid $50,000 to buy HDT for himself. Brock was producing his signature model cars for the market, and he made and sold enough of these machines to homologate them to race. He was able to engineer all sorts of trick bits for the road car, which would then be applied on his race car.

But apparently he went a bit too far with his manifolds, illegally modifying the inlet on his race car, at least, according to CAMS. For whatever reason, he was in their sights in 1982 and it sent the entire championship to hell. I think Brock was actually leading the championship when the drama reared its ugly head. It wasn't by much, but he was in front and posing a very serious threat. They told him he had been excluded from Calder and would not earn a point from Oran Park to Surfers Paradise. He was out of the season. But Brock vowed to fight the charges and commenced legal action, so the championship was a disaster.

I won another race, the second-last in Adelaide, and went into the final round in the lead over everyone else, other than Brock, by a large margin. I came out of the last race the unofficial champion, but was not crowned for nearly two months later when Brock withdrew his legal action. It was a massive let-down and a total non-event. To win the championship but not be able to celebrate it for eight weeks was a joke. And to not win it by beating the best was also a hollow victory. I took the title, but there will always be a question mark over it, thanks to CAMS and their drawn-out processes. I have no doubt Brock was running illegal equipment, but why they couldn't have jumped on the problem and made him fix it as soon as it arose stumps me to this day.

The category was in a pretty bad way and lacked leadership and brains. Politics got involved and problems weren't thought about until they occurred. There was no future planning and it was really hurting.

1981 was no fluke, but to win my second championship in this way sucked. Big time. Now it was time to go back-to-back at Bathurst. At least that was the plan.

Goodbye, Baby

I handed my next-door neighbour the keys.

'She's a beauty, mate,' I said. 'The best I've ever had.'

I grabbed the cheque for $45,000, turned my back and walked away.

I sold my 1981 Bathurst car after winning the championship in 1982. It was an emotionless transaction and I had no regrets parting with what would become one of the most famous cars in the sport because it was time to upgrade to the XE. The car is now worth in excess of $1 million, and if I had known this, I would never have let her go. But back then race cars were treated like spanners, hammers and chisels. They did the job for a while, and were then tossed aside. Race cars weren't considered collectable items, and we needed whatever money we got from them to develop a more superior version.

So the famous 1980/81/82 Tru-Blu was gone (for now), and it was time for a more developed model. Or so we thought.

We went to Bathurst in 1982 full of fear and apprehension because the new car just wasn't right. The XE had a new back end on her and we had big trouble making her as good as the car we had just sold. We tried our best, sourcing shocks from the US and playing with rear arms. And while it had improved, it still wasn't great.

We rolled the car out for practice and it was using oil like a baby goes through nappies. The shit was everywhere. We poured litres upon litres into the thing, but had no idea what the problem was. We pulled apart the engine into a thousand pieces on the Saturday night before the race and put it back together, complete with rings, bearings and new rubber, none the wiser.

We qualified seventh, and while the car was good enough to make it home, it wasn't good enough to finish first place. We wrung the life out of her just to make it to third position. It was disappointing not to win following our domination in 1981, but a podium was a fair result given the drama we had. Little did we know there was more to come.

We were stripped of our result on the Monday after being pinged for using illegal cylinder heads. It was bullshit. Doug Jacobi, our parts man at Ford, had made the components, which were available on the road car. Any investigation would have proved that the parts we used were indeed legal. But we didn't have the money to fight the charge and copped it sweet. It would have been a different story if I had won the race instead of Brock, who had racked up a record sixth Bathurst win.

The Rising Sun

1983 was a shit year. Terrible. Let's start with the Touring Car Championship.

Coming off my win the year before, I expected to give the thing another shake. The car still wasn't where we wanted it, but we thought it would have been good enough to get the job done. It wasn't.

And none of us could have ever predicted why.

After their debut year in the 3000 cc class, the Mazdas and the Nissans moved up to the new Group C category.

Allan Moffat had turned his RX-7 into a ridiculous rocket that went on to win four rounds of the season and to take out the championship. Allan Grice won two in his Commodore; Brock, two in his Commodore. Grice would have won the series thanks to a beneficial scoring system for cars with smaller engines. However, he boycotted the final round after finding out the system would be scrapped the following year in a move that would put turbo engines on a level footing with the rest of us. I could only manage two third placings in my ill-handling XE and went on to finish sixth in the championship. It wasn't pretty.

We were quite stunned by the rise of Moffat and the RX-7. With plenty of money from Mazda, he had developed the car into a flyer: it was small, nimble and fast. The RX-7 struggled on the flat-out straights, but there weren't enough of them on the circuit to do any real harm. They were also better on brakes and tyres, which we continued to shred.

I had a lot of reliability issues with my machine, and was quite ashamed of my car and my performances. CAMS saw that we were struggling and attempted to give us some relief, finally succumbing to my plea for bigger wheels and brakes. The car ended up improving, but it was too late for the championship. It was all going on the line at Bathurst.

We weren't so concerned about the RX-7 and the Nissan leading into Bathurst. We knew that they would struggle for power and would not be a major threat. Moffat knew it too, controversially lobbying CAMS to go from a 12A engine to a 13B. Some even suggested he foxed during the season and went slow to convince them he needed more.

It was about this time we got a new truck, and like my

year so far, it was also a dog. In fact, we almost missed our own launch thanks to the ball-less beast. Heading to Oran Park to start our endurance season with a new-look car, we arrived six hours late. A trip that should only have taken us 12 hours took 18, because the new truck had no power. We were hoping to get a good omen of things to come in our brand-new car – Greens-Tuf.

Trees, Trees and More Fucking Trees

I was the second-last in the shootout, full of steam and ready to roll. I was determined to forget about the horrible year of 1982 by landing pole, and hopefully winning the only race that mattered.

I was flat-out across the line, pushing my green beast, Greens-Tuf, to its limit. Hard onto the brakes at the first, my car spewed out onto the dust, shaking violently until the grip returned. The crowd cheered, my heart raced. Brock had been quickest all week, and he was to come, so I knew I had to extract every inch from my 550 hp machine, hit every line, every kerb, and make this one count.

I was quickest through the first section, absolutely blitzing it. I was a second and a half up on the frenzied mob that had gone before me. The time was given to me over the radio.

'You're flying, Dick,' the message said. 'But don't back off; Brock's coming.'

I was giving it my all, wheels screeching, engine thumping. I knew Greens-Tuf was fast enough to be on pole, and probably even quick enough to win the race. It was understeering a bit in the lead-up, but I just had to throw it around and do the best I could.

I first noticed the understeer coming through the Dipper and going over Skyline, but I couldn't back off because I knew the lap was going to be good; I wasn't about to throw it away.

I came through Forrest's Elbow and the understeer forced a mistake. I was caught a bit wide and, coming out, the camber went from a positive to negative, and I was going a fraction too quick. The car drifted dangerously towards the wall.

Bang!

It wasn't much of a wall, so I thought I was going to be OK. I kept on the throttle.

Whack!

That's when I hit the tyres. The tyres that shouldn't have even been there! The bastard things were just put in for non-race days so punters wouldn't smash into the end of a wall when they were driving up the other way.

My front tyre hooked onto the bundle, blowing it out, and my steering broke too.

A 1500-kg out-of-control missile sent me rocketing into the grass at more than 100 k/h. Trees, big, thick and ancient, sprang from the earth. There was nowhere to go and I was going to crash. Hard.

Somehow my car speared sideways to avoid the first two trees, the biggest and most menacing of the lot, but soon I was slapping against wood. Pieces of metal flew from my car and it felt like my body was being smashed around like an egg.

Crunch! Bang! Slap!

I ducked down and braced, fearing that after this, I would never move again. There was nowhere to go but into something hard and the car smashed and bounced through the wooden hailstorm with violent force. All of a sudden the car stopped. I was alive, and I had no idea how. I shook my head.

You are one lucky son of a bitch, I thought, relieved that all my limbs were still attached.

I pushed at the driver's door. It was jammed, so I crawled over the console and the TV camera, which was mounted on the passenger seat. I got the door open and fell out. Apparently I tore my helmet off and threw it at the wreck in frustration, but I can honestly say I do not remember a thing. I'm at an absolute blank after getting that door open; I can't even recall the events of the following day. Maybe it was from shock that I've completely wiped that moment from the hard drive.

What I do remember is walking through the back of the pits with Jillie and John French's wife, stunned and shocked to my core.

I later found out that Brock, on his warm-up lap, saw me and stopped, genuinely concerned. I was OK but on the edge of the road in a rage. He bundled me into his car and gave me a lift back to the pits.

My car was completely gone. We pulled it back to the garage and figured there was no way it was going to race. *Ever.*

'We have to do something,' said Ross. 'We are not giving up on this.'

Ross, eager to promote his new product 'Greens-Tuf' (which the car was named after), went about pulling off a miracle. He refused to give up on his dream and came up with what seemed an impossible solution.

'Let's buy another one,' he said. 'Surely we can get something.'

Although Greens-Tuf was ruined, most of the parts inside were still good. He figured we could get a new car, whack all our stuff in, and buy a ticket into the Bathurst lottery.

So Ross approached a competitor.

'Can I buy your Falcon?' he said to Andrew Harris. 'Money isn't an issue.'

Andrew didn't say no straightaway. 'Mate, I have a commitment with Bendigo Nine,' he said. 'A contract. I have to run.'

'But does it have to be in that car?' Ross asked. 'In a Ford?' He knew he could easily buy a Commodore, ready to race, but that was no good for me with my Ford deal.

'I'll sell you the car but you have to find me something comparable that I can race,' Andrew replied.

Ross smiled. 'Done'.

He bought the Commodore for Andrew, I can't remember who it belonged to, and we took hold of the Falcon, minus the engine and bits. And then we went to work.

It was a mammoth task. With less than 16 hours until the green light, it was almost mission impossible. We stripped the car in record time, gave Andrew his stuff and went about bolting on all the things we salvaged from our wreck. It was an ex-Bob Morris car and we knew it was good. But we also knew we were pushing shit up a hill.

We whacked it together in the nick of time. Engine, gearbox, electrics done. But we couldn't do the paint job.

We had to get all our sponsors back on, make it look like the thing we wrecked, and the local TAFE came to our aid, lending us their facility and gear.

We rolled out onto the grid as the sun edged over the horizon, and were greeted with tremendous cheer, not so much from the crowd but from our rivals. They couldn't believe what we had done. It was a miracle. I was so proud. The crowd also went berserk, but it was the sight of the rival crews applauding that almost brought me to tears.

We started tenth, and despite being optimistic, we were never really hopeful. We couldn't have possibly won this great race with just 14 hours or so to prepare. The battery kept on going flat and we didn't know why. The thing had a bung fuse, and it eventually finished us.

As I said, 1983 was a shit year.

19

GREENS-TUF

Mean Machine

With fat wheels, aggressive guards, chunky arches and all the good stuff from our 1983 disaster, the new Greens-Tuf was a mean machine that would help restore big banger pride after the rice burners ripped us apart.

CAMS had helped. They let us get away with bits and pieces, fearing another year of domination from the Japanese invasion. They didn't want to see a one-horse race and, after our struggle the year before, gave us a bit more room to make the car a proper race machine.

And it was.

We came firing out of the blocks, the car surprising us with its stunning straight-line speed. The glowing green gas-guzzler was all power and punch. And although the car lacked some finesse, it was able to blow the competition away, except Brock in his Commodore at the opening round in Sandown.

It was evident from the first race on the new level playing field that George Fury didn't stand a chance in his turbo-charged Nissan, bombing out with a DNF (Did Not Finish). Moffat finished third, but his season was to be short-lived with a crash at Surfers Paradise resulting in a serious hand injury.

The 1984 championship came down to a fight between me and my old foe Brock exchanging blows for much of the season. He ended up winning two races against my one win, but that was good enough to get me my third championship. I never finished off the podium, consistency landing me a rare hat-trick.

Things could have been different if Brock hadn't missed two rounds to compete overseas, but that was his choice and I ended up beating him by 38 points. I couldn't have been happier. Following a poor season the year before, I had bounced back and proven that my previous feats had been no fluke. It would have been easier to throw my hands in the air and pack it in, but we stuck at it, backed ourselves and came up with a ripper car.

I would go as far as saying the 1984 Greens-Tuf was as good as Tru-Blu. It's hard to compare cars across different eras, even if they're just a couple of years apart, because the rate of development was just staggering. Tru-Blu did 2.21 at Bathurst, while Greens-Tuf went on to do 2.17. That's a huge difference in speed in a small amount of time. I would have to say both cars were equally good, my two favourites of all time.

The season was in full swing when CAMS dropped a bombshell that would send us into a frantic panic.

'Group C is over,' they said. 'We're moving to the international "Group A" formula.'

CAMS were desperate to be recognised internationally as a motorsport authority and told us to dump $150,000 worth of race cars and gear, and start again. It was the future, they said, and we were given no choice. None of us were happy about it, considering we had spent years building our cars according to a category that worked. Sure it needed some tweaks and changes, but this was like throwing the baby out with the bathwater.

The decision meant that the Falcon was dead and buried. There was no way we were going to be able to compete against the new Group A cars in a Falcon since it had gone to a six-cylinder engine only. We would have been flogged.

Brock was still going to be able to use the Commodore because he was building a V8-model signature edition and sold enough of them to satisfy the rule.

We had a hell of a decision to make. Given we were still aligned with Ford, we had two choices.

The first choice was to go and get a Ford Merkur XR4Ti, a turbo-charged machine that was paving the way for the Sierra. The Sierras were the cars of the future when it came to world-tour car racing, but they were bloody expensive and we had no money. We also didn't know a thing about computer chips or turbochargers, either.

The second choice was to jump into a Mustang, which is what we eventually did. Fearful of chips, timers and electronics, we decided to go with what we knew. The Mustang had five litres with a 302 Windsor V8. We weren't ready to experiment with new technology and thought that something that had a carburettor strapped to its belly was the best way to go.

We found the cars in Germany, bought them off a team that had raced them in Europe. Now, we knew that the Mustang was never going to be as good as the Falcon – it didn't have as much horsepower and we didn't have time to develop it. Regardless, we were convinced the machine was going to do well.

Two Mustangs arrived the week before Bathurst and we were able to throw one in for a few test laps. The car really surprised us. We thought it would struggle big-time on the horsepower-heavy track, but the Mustang clocked a respectable 1.18. Maybe things would be OK.

Meanwhile, things weren't so great for the Falcon in its last run in the soon-to-be-dead Group C. I pushed hard, floored the beast and sailed on past Larry Perkins for the lead. Things were looking good and then the car died. The Falcon was thrown onto the back of a tilt tray and after some CPR on a fuel pump we got her back out. We were in a hopeless position but decided to soldier on. I was back underway and cutting down the field. I jumped on the radio and did an interview with former senator John Brown, the bloke who is said to have shagged a sheila on his parliamentary desk.

'What's wrong, Dick?' he asked after I failed to respond to a question.

The car had shat itself again, on live TV with me looking the fool. That was the end of the Falcon, at least for now.

I had experienced the highs and lows of Mount Panorama during the five most eventful years of my life. I had gone from heartbreak to ecstasy, to heartbreak again. I was a bit down when I kissed the Falcon goodbye. It was a great car and I wasn't sure what I was getting myself into next with the

Mustang. And I couldn't help thinking that I hadn't made the most of what I had.

Between 1980 and 1984, I really could have walked away with five Bathurst titles; instead I left only with one. Most of it was down to bad luck, but I also made a couple of costly mistakes. I had missed a few golden opportunities and was kicking myself as a result.

I thought I would never win again.

Mustang Sally

The flies were relentless. Swarming, they darted across my face, clung to my arms and stuck to my back. I swatted at them, catching nothing but the sweat on my brow as the heat burnt my skin through the suit. The stinking hot breeze blew dust everywhere, although it didn't deter the black plague of pests. I began sneezing uncontrollably, my body shuddering with each sneeze, which was enough to shake the flies off for a moment.

Welcome to Winton in summer: flies, 40-degree days and filthy pollen-laden winds.

We arrived to the first race of the year packing our Mustang and it was a pretty cool-looking thing. Going from the old Falcon – sheepskin seat covers, AM/FM radio, heater and handbrake – the Mustang was certainly an upgrade in style. For one, it actually looked like a race car, with everything stripped and only the essentials left behind. It was a sure sign that we'd moved away from the road-going model, where everything in the road car had to be in the race car. I now had lights that flashed at me when I needed to change and other instruments specifically designed for helping the car move faster. But that didn't necessarily mean we were actually going to go any quicker.

We pulled the Mustang apart not long after its encouraging show at Bathurst.

'Oh no,' I said, looking inside the rocker cover. 'This isn't good.'

It had been built by Jack Roush. I continued to dig around in the engine.

'Fuck,' I yelped. 'Chevrolet rocker arms.'

The deeper we went, the worse it got. The car was a mishmash of parts and full of illegalities that would have seen the scrutineers throw us out in a heartbeat. This car was 100 per cent illegitimate and it was pretty evident the Europeans didn't give two shits about the rules. We were sent into a mad scramble, first sourcing and buying the approved parts and then making an engine out of them.

The official paperwork that came with the car said the engine had 328 hp at 6500 rpm. Before we pulled all the illegal modifications off, we whacked the engine on the dyno. It appeared the Europeans were telling fibs because we could only pull 283 hp, and even less when we put the standard parts back on.

It was clear that we were going to be up against it. The top guns in Europe were the BMWs, the Jaguars, and the Volvos, and that's what most of our domestic rivals went for. We were obviously contracted to Ford and had to stick with them. With big budgets, Colin Bond and Allan Jones went for the Alfa Romeo. Garry Willmington went for the Jaguar. But we suspected Jim Richards would be the best of the bunch, opting for a BMW 635. The German car was well established in the European touring car scene and Jim had great contacts with the manufacturer. He was also one hell of a driver, so we thought he would be the bloke to chase.

Still, we entered the season full of optimism. The Mustang had been good at Bathurst, and while not overly successful in Europe and being outgunned by much more advanced machines, we thought the Mustang might actually suit our smaller, more technical tracks. And we were going OK at Winton . . . until the engine overheated.

The flies were fucking annoying, but it was the heat that killed us. We first became concerned in practice, even ushering in a fire truck to blast our radiator with water from its ample hose. None of that helped; the Mustang ceasing and recording a DNF on its first outing. We were right about Jim, however. He proved to be the pick of the new cars, scoring an emphatic win.

We fared much better away from the crippling heat, where the Mustang actually proved to be a reliable car, moving us smoothly in and out of the corners and keeping us in the mix. But there was no catching Jim and we didn't manage to win a race. We were content landing podiums, and thanks to our consistency we ended up coming second to Richards in the championship. It wasn't the result we wanted, but it was still pretty good considering what we had and how we'd got it.

Rocking up to Bathurst without a Falcon just didn't seem right. For so many years it had been Ford versus Holden, but now I was looking around at Jaguars, BMWs, Toyotas and Volvos.

The international invasion CAMS had hoped for finally happened. Five drivers from the UK turned up to Mount Panorama, as well as one from Germany, another from Belgium and even a bloke from Venezuela. They came with big reputations, well-developed cars and astronomical budgets.

The V12 Jags, shipped from Britain, came with 40 tonnes of spares. They had a $550,000 budget for the one race.

This is our race, I thought, desperate to show them how it was done.

The problem was, we were playing in their cars and by their rules. All the machines were homologated in Paris, the regulations were set there too, and bloody hell, we even had European officials! Despite our determination to send them scrambling back to Europe, we didn't.

A bloke called Armin Hahne won the race with John Goss in a XJ-S Jaguar – they just had too much power. I'm still not sure how legal the car was, but their names are in the record book and that's all that counts. A burly Scot called Tom Walkinshaw, who had quite a reputation, came third.

CAMS had got what they had wanted, but I couldn't help thinking they'd taken a backwards step. The Group A cars were actually slower than what we had the year before. Greens-Tuf would have smoked the lot. I ended up finishing at a disappointing seventh. We were OK at the top but had nothing on the straights. The only consolation was that we beat all the Commodores.

Thunderbox

The police officer walked up my driveway and glared at me.

'Mr Johnson,' he said. 'Can I have a word?'

People were often stopping by my house, my race workshop was in the garage, after all, so I thought nothing of it at first.

'G'day, mate,' I said. 'What can I do for you?'

He grinned. 'It's more what I can do for *you*,' he replied, matter-of-factly. 'I'm not on duty at the moment, but I will be tomorrow when I come back with my partner to ask you some questions about a matter that's come our way.'

My heart sank to my stomach.

'It appears you might have been involved in an incident in Tasmania.'

I shat a brick, thinking about the drama that all started a year ago . . .

'This is it,' I said to the promoter. 'The last time. If you don't get those stinking toilets fixed, we're never coming back. *Never*. You got it?'

The toilets at Symmons Plains were an utter disgrace. Old pieces of corrugated iron slapped onto a rotting wooden frame, the building was ready to fall over. But it was the inside that had me and the rest of the paddock fuming. Well, more spewing.

You could not walk into the toilets without dry-retching. The stink was out of this world – think dead, rotting, and hot. The urinal was nothing more than some tar on a slope. The piss went in and pooled at the bottom since there was no drainage. You would have to hold your nose with one hand while you aimed with the other. The splashback forced you to pee from a distance, also leaving the rest of the floor covered in piss.

But the crapper was the real disgrace. A prehistoric thunderbox, the toilet was nothing more than a wooden frame, a toilet seat and a 10-metre hole. Someone had simply dug a gigantic pit and shoved a seat over the top. Seriously, you'd find better toilets in Ethiopia. The hole was teeming with decades of hell, mountains of shit and piss that emitted the worst possible stench.

And then there were the animals.

The hellhole was rat infested. There were also cockroaches, spiders and sometimes snakes. It was one thing making us use it, but the women's toilet, adjoined to the other side, was exactly the same, maybe even worse. Some of the driver's wives were wetting themselves in the pit-lane because they refused to enter the rickety house of delights. Enough was enough.

'It will be fixed, Dick,' the promoter said. 'We promise.'

We came back the next year and nothing had changed. We were pissed off.

So we all agreed to take matters into our own hands.

A couple of blokes from the teams and I waited until after sunset, the dark giving us cover and the punters all gone, before grabbing a couple of trucks and going to work.

Whack!

The old filth pile came crashing down as they blasted through the rotting wood and rusted iron. The next truck flattened the shit-heap entirely. Job done. We laughed and left content, but the smile was wiped off my face the next day when the police officer stood in my driveway.

'Seems like I'm in shit,' I said. 'Excuse the pun.'

'Oh no, mate,' he replied. 'That's why I'm here. I am off-duty now, but I won't be tomorrow. I'm going to ask a bunch of questions and here's what you should say . . .'

'Absolutely not,' I said to the very same police officer the next morning, partner in tow.

'I did not drive a truck on that night. I heard of the commotion, but I absolutely did not drive a truck. Not near the toilet, not anywhere.'

It was the truth. Someone else was driving the truck. I was outside directing him, egging him on.

'That's all we need to know,' the officer said. 'Thanks for your time.'

I didn't hear anything about it after that. I owe that fine young officer a beer or two.

I wasn't so lucky in 1986. We did our best to improve the Mustang, flying to America to try to homologate a fuel injection system, but our efforts were denied by CAMS.

A new Mustang model was out, but all we really got were some new headlights and a grille. We worked hard to get more horsepower and we managed to take the thing from 282 hp to 348 hp thanks to a loophole in the laws. It was legal to remove metal, not to add metal, but we worked out that we could pretty much do what we liked if we glued the pieces back on instead of welding them. But it wasn't enough.

We ended up finishing the Australian Touring Car Championship in sixth place, our worst result in almost a decade. And to make matters worse, it was won by a Volvo with a Kiwi behind the wheel. Robbie Francevic became the first non-Australian to win the title when he wiped away the field in his Volvo. He was also the first to win the championship in a turbo.

Robbie was only packing two litres, but with the help of a turbocharger managed to beat my rumbling five-litre V8. It was an eye-opener to say the least. Robbie was just impossible to catch in 1986. With water-cooled brakes, computer chips and fuel injection, his car went fast and had great suspension. I didn't have a chance. I'm not sure how legal the car actually was, but I was having a shit year anyway. Our reliability was a real flaw.

Robbie was a character too, a real salesman who could have matched it with Muhammad Ali. He was a decent driver, but I reckon anyone could have won in the Volvo he had that year. Still, he got the job done and deserves to be recognised for his feats.

Bathurst 1986 was not much better than the championship. I qualified sixth and snuck home to finish fourth, but I was never going to win with my Mustang's horsepower. Allan Grice won in a Commodore that year. Strangely, it was nice to see a Holden win. After watching foreign machines reign the year before, the win seemed to restore some sort of normality among all the craziness. But something else happened that changed the history of Mount Panorama Circuit forever.

Death at the Mountain

My car shuddered as I hit the brakes and began washing off the 270 k/h I had picked up storming down Mountain Straight. For some reason I looked into my rearview mirror, and saw the beginning of an incident that would lead to a drastic change in the circuit layout, shaking all the drivers to their very core.

I first spotted Mike Burgmann's Commodore as it was attacked by Garry Willmington's Falcon. They were coming down the straight at jaw-dropping speed; Willmington was doing close to 280 k/h as he pulled alongside Burgmann, attempting a high-risk overtake. I'd seen such moves before, and knew that the pass was fraught with danger. I kept on watching, aware that they were now both in an awkward position, and sensed that something was about to unfold.

You had to be really cautious coming down the Mountain when you hit the bumps – we didn't have shock absorbers like you do today – otherwise your car would shimmy and shake all over the place. You were also likely to fly into the air as your 1500-kg machine smacked into the small bumps and sail towards the sky before returning to earth with a thud. There were no aerodynamics on our cars to speak of, nothing to pin them to the ground. If two cars were close enough to each other, a vacuum would be created that would suck the two vehicles together like gigantic magnets.

Both Burgmann and Willmington's cars left the ground at the same time.

My heart was in my mouth.

In a split second the situation became deadly. As both cars hurtled through the air, the vacuum sucked them together and they touched – the impact sending Burgmann flying off the road in a violent spin towards Dunlop Bridge.

When I came around to the Bridge, my fears were confirmed. Emergency workers picked him up out of the back left-hand corner of the car. They didn't stop the race and they didn't tell us officially until after, but we already knew Burgmann was dead.

These sorts of things can happen and I tried to shrug it off, even though I was a bit angry because it could have been avoided. Burgmann was a personal friend of the track promoter Ivan Stibbard, who was, understandably, in a bad way.

'You guys don't believe me when I say these cars are going dreadfully fast now,' I said. 'Without our aerodynamics they become aeroplanes.'

Bathurst organisers eventually changed the racetrack, putting in the Chase on Conrod Straight, but it was too late for Burgmann, dead at 41.

I think this could've been the first racing death I had encountered while in the car. It was a horrible feeling, and I was so upset for Burgmann and his family. But it didn't leave me scared, it made me more angry than anything. I guess that's what we drivers do – turn our fear into something else. We can't afford to think about the incessant dangers.

20

SIERRA

Shelling Out Some Clams

Time had come to move up to the Sierras – problem was, I didn't have any money. I'd already spent all I had on the Mustangs, and the new Sierras were going to cost me a heap. I spoke to Ross, my long-time sponsor and friend, but he wasn't in a position to give me what I needed. He suggested I approach Shell. Knowing nothing about business, I got help from Ross to put a proposal together. We then went down to the head offices at Shell and presented our case.

I was bloody lucky because a bloke who loved motorsport had just been appointed as the company's retail marketing manager. John Rowe had just moved from Ireland, where he had huge success using motorsport to market the brand. I went in and told him of my plan, about the Sierras and how we were going to conquer the world. He bought it and agreed to give us $1.1 million a year. It was a huge deal and I was absolutely floored by the amount – with that budget, I could run two cars instead of one. I wasn't a factory team, but with a deal like that I was going to be close. I now had the means to become a real force and an outfit to be reckoned with.

Now I just had to find some cars.

I had impressed Rowe earlier, in fact, which probably helped me seal the deal. It's a story worth retelling . . .

On the front row of the grid, I looked across at Formula One superstar Gerhard Berger. I wondered what the fuck I was going to do because I couldn't see a thing. I was in my Mustang, a left-hand drive, and because of where I was, I couldn't see where the start lights were.

We were at an exhibition race in Adelaide before the F1, and while it wasn't a championship race, it was still a very big deal. For the first time, the eyes of the world were on us, and 100,000 people sat in the stands. Berger had jumped in a touring car and the megastar was expected to win. I wanted to show him who was boss, but I was panicking because I thought I was going to miss the start. How embarrassing would that be with all the Formula One stars looking on?

'What do I do?' I said over the radio. 'I'm going to get swamped.'

I was met with cold silence.

I unbuckled my seatbelt and leaned across the dash. With my arse out of the seat and my body stretched across the cabin, I could see the start lights. But I couldn't reach the clutch and could barely touch the wheel. I thought about giving it a go, but I wasn't too keen to blast down the straight without a seatbelt on.

The panic grew.

I stayed there, full of indecision, until the first start light came on. Almost a natural reaction, I jumped back into my seat and clipped the belt back in. Again I could see nothing. I decided I would guess. I counted to three and dropped the clutch.

In a minor miracle it was the best damn start I had ever had.

I had timed it to perfection. It must have been a fraction from being considered illegal because I took Berger by a mile. And I was never headed. I won the race and my name was up in blazing lights. At this point of time I was already with Shell in a minor way (they provided me with free fuel) and Rowe was over the moon. Shell was sponsoring McLaren at the time and all the company bigwigs were there. It looked good for him and I'm sure it helped me score the massive deal.

As I said, Ross didn't have the budget to give me a million dollars in 1987, but he soon made his fortune. His story is quite remarkable. His father, Les Palmer, made stairs that were uniquely designed and featured a single steel tube situated in the middle with platforms on top. He bought tubing, an evil necessity of the design, from Broken Hill Proprietary but could never get enough. They charged him a fortune for the metal and mostly told him they had run out of supply.

So one day he told them to fuck off.

'I'll do them myself,' he steamed.

BHP laughed and wished him the best of luck. They had no idea a fierce competitor was about to be born.

Les went about making a machine to construct his own tube. Through trial and error, grit and determination, he was able to build one that made tubing and which ran from underneath his house. The machine ended up working: rolling cold steel into a square before welding it along the crack.

Les was a funny old bloke – passionate, he had a dry sense of humour and was a bloody genius when it came to working things out. His machine was a success, but he had a moment or two early on.

The machine had an automatic cutting mechanism that severed the steel at a certain length. One day it failed, and the machine kept on feeding the steel through, inch after inch, metre after metre. The big heavy tube poked its head from under the house and edged its way into the place next door; cutter prone, asleep. Like a hungry snake prowling in the sun, the steel marched ahead. Continuing to grow, the hard, uncompromising tube ended up smashing into a neighbour's house. Les heard the wood and glass breaking, and went for the emergency shut off.

It was then he decided he needed a factory.

Les had no idea what he was on to, but his son Ross did. Ross was an extremely bright, quirky fellow, and he knew the money wasn't in the stairs but in the tube. He was a straight-A student, and recognised an opportunity when he saw one. Ross threw away his promising career as a banker, a big deal back then, to sell his father's offcut tubing.

He sold the excess off in an instant and went looking for more. With money to make, he secretly took the main bits of tube, which were destined for his father's stairs, and sold them too.

Les, who had built the machine because he couldn't get enough tube off BHP, didn't have enough of it again. He was *MAD*.

'Dad, stop with the stairs,' Ross said. 'The money's in the tube.'

Les fumed before going at his son with raised fists. I was there watching on as they traded blows, a fair dinkum fight.

'Don't bother with your stupid steps,' Ross shouted mid-punch.

Father and son eventually tired.

'You give me $30,000 and you can have the machine, you little bastard,' Les said. 'But you can't leave me with no supply. Under no circumstances.'

That was the birth of Palmer Tube Mills. Dad was never left without supply, and son went on to make millions and millions. They made more machines, got in bed with Japanese giants and took it right to BHP. Ross was a genius and innovator. At his height he would have been worth 100 million dollars.

I'm sure I helped him make his mark somehow with the success I had in the early 1980s, his products splashed across my all-conquering cars. But Ross was the one who sponsored me and leveraged the deals for maximum profit. Ross was a brilliant mind and a good friend.

He was also a mad rooter in his youth. Ross was the first person in the country to modify the gear lever in his Volkswagen so he could collapse it and make room for shagging women across his front seat!

Without a Paddle

I put on a brave face. Publicly, I said everything was fine.

'Let's get a couple of the Sierras and go racing,' I announced, beaming. 'Can't be any harder than what we've done before.'

Privately, I was a wreck.

First, there was the matter of the $1.1 million I had in the bank. Now that shouldn't have been a problem, but in the blink of an eye I had gone from the battler punching above his weight to the well-funded race car driver and team owner with a large backer expecting results. I was also about to go into a two-car team and had to hire staff, find somewhere other than the garage in my home to work from, and think about becoming a legitimate business owner, responsible for not just himself but for his employees.

Second, I had to build a car I knew nothing about. I was genuinely afraid of moving away from carburettors and distributor caps – things I'd spent my whole life working – to computer chips and turbochargers. I had delayed the decision by taking on the Mustangs, but now I was left with no choice. I also had to find all the parts to build them. I couldn't just walk down to the corner shop and get what I needed; there were only a couple of blokes who knew everything about racing Sierras and they were all overseas.

So I gritted my teeth, grabbed my passport and headed to London. The season finished after Bathurst, when I went straight to the UK. Andy Rouse was the main man when it came to Sierras and he was the first bloke I went to see. On a dreary English day, he told me what I was up for when it came to the engine and parts, racing a Sierra.

'It will cost you about 200K for all your engine management systems and parts,' he said. 'I'll ship the entire thing to you and provide you the support you need.'

I agreed.

I then went and saw Alan Barnes, who was the contact for Nordic Supplies. They were the guys that supplied Ford Motorsport parts for race teams and I bought the rest of the gear from him: panels, seats, wheels, the dash, etc.

While I was in Europe, I also bought myself an RS Cosworth Sierra road car for my daily drive. Not only would it be a brilliant car to rip around in, it would also provide a good guide for helping me build my race car. I seriously didn't know what went in where for these machines and there was no race car building manual.

And although I could have bought a complete race car from Andy Rouse, I didn't have enough money even with my new budget. Andy charged through the roof! Besides, I'd been building cars for years, so it couldn't be that hard.

All the bits and pieces finally arrived in our new race shop at the back of Ross's factory, Palmer Tube Mills, in Acacia Ridge, where he had generously built us a two-car garage as I clearly didn't have enough room at home. And the team went about building a race car that we'd hoped would be good enough to win me another Bathurst.

I hate to admit it, but it was me who came up with the idea to build a car that could be driven in both left- and right-hand sides.

'It's all about weight distribution,' I explained to the team. 'We can use the left-hand drive for the predominantly right-turning tracks and a right-hand for the left.'

We had a big budget and I was determined to use it.

In the end, and although it seemed like a good idea at the time, it turned out to be a dumb, expensive and pointless exercise. Needless to say, we eventually converted the left-hand drive back to a right.

We built the roll cage with Greens-Tuf tubing and it was outstanding. Ross even advertised the tubing's success in his marketing campaign. The rest came together fairly easy. There was a bit of trial and error, but the pieces gradually fitted and we had something that looked like a race car after a couple of days. The engine was probably the easiest bit until we got to the computers – we just didn't have a clue. Luckily, we'd hired an ex-Gibson employee, who had experience with the Nissan turbo, and he became our go-to guy, setting up the computer program for us. Still, the idea of it was a nightmare.

For my entire life, I'd gone on steadfastly believing that the power of a car could be controlled by the carburettor, which in turn controlled the amount of fuel, and the distributor, which provided the spark. Now all that was done with a computer? We were totally reliant on what Rouse gave us in the way of computer chips and I didn't like it one bit.

I was also ignorant. It's to my detriment – and probably the worst mistake I have ever made – that I refused to learn the new system. I understood the principle of the new technology, but to me it was just weird electronic shit, and I decided then and there to leave it in the hands of others. It would come back to bite me in the arse, of course, because that was the moment I relinquished a lot of my engineering control.

Not wanting to fully learn the new technology, I stepped back and hired Neal Lowe to be our team manager for 1987.

I felt that I was out of my depth and also thought it was about time I concentrated on my driving and leave the day-to-day operations to someone else. But it was a mistake. A big one.

The year didn't begin well. We couldn't get our head around the electronics in the car and went into the first race with an underpowered vehicle. Glenn Seton flexed his muscle in the impressive Nissan, winning at Calder Park, and we limped home to finish ninth. We didn't improve in the second race at Symmons Plains, again coming ninth. (While the car wasn't much chop, the toilets were a lot better!) We fared even worse at Lakeside, bombing out with a DNF as Jim Richards showed the might of the BMW.

It was pretty evident early on that we were outclassed by the BMWs and the Nissans. I think the BMWs had a bit of an advantage because they weren't using turbos, and the rest of us were struggling to unleash their full potential – with Nissan being the exception, as Seton and his team took it to Richards and his BMW.

We needed more horsepower but had no clue how to get it. We weren't able to program our computer (even the ex-Gibson employee wasn't up to speed with the equipment we had) and, like I said, we became dependent on Andy Rouse and his company in England.

So I called him up in desperation.

'Mate, we need more power,' I said. 'We're getting flogged.'

'No worries,' he said. 'I'll send you the new customer chip. It'll do the job.'

We sent Rouse $1000 for the new chip, waiting anxiously for the parcel to arrive from England and thinking it was the solution to all our problems. We thought we could whack the little card into the engine and the car would be going two seconds quicker each lap. But we were wrong.

The chip did little. We didn't have the machinery to program the thing ourselves and could do nothing to adjust the engine. I called Rouse once more and forked out another $1000, but again the new chip was no silver bullet.

The situation was a complete joke and we were being held to ransom because we operated under the Zytek engine management system, and the chips he sent us weren't specialised for this particular program, but simply upgrades he sent to everyone when he felt like making a buck. We tried to go around the problem by tricking the computer into making changes to other parts of the engine. It worked in theory, but in practice it was a disaster. We ended up blowing 37 turbos in the first year!

I was at my wits' end and grabbed Jillie and my passport and jumped on the plane to the UK looking to start a fight.

'This is bullshit,' I said, striding into Rouse's offices, trying hard to keep my cool. 'I need to be able to have the machine in order to program the chips myself. I'm getting belted over there and this is the only way forward. I'm willing to pay you whatever you like so I can control things myself rather than rely on the customer chips you send out.'

He shook his head.

'What do you mean no?! I've spent a fortune on this!'

Rouse stayed silent and shook his head again.

I could feel my blood boiling.

'You are the biggest c*%t I have ever met in my life!' I screamed. 'You can jam the whole deal right up your arse.'

Jillie was there too and reckons that was the angriest she had ever seen me. I don't think I'd ever used the c-word in my life, and right there and then I blurted it out in front of my wife. I walked out of the office, feeling totally dejected, and with an icy breeze chilling me to my core, I looked to Jillie.

'We're stuffed,' I said. 'This could be the end because I really don't know where to go now.'

Desperate, I called Doug Jacobi from Ford and told him of my seemingly hopeless situation.

'It's a long shot,' Doug said. 'But since you're there, why don't you pay John Griffiths a visit? He's involved with the Sierra program for Ford.'

So I followed Doug's advice and Griffiths ended up putting us in touch with the man who would become our saviour: Graham Dale-Jones.

Graham was contracted to Ford to do the rally engines and he had a few tricks up his sleeve. I told him of our problem, and he said he could sell us a 1.2 Bosch system that would do the job, and even offered to set it up for us free of charge. He said it wasn't as fancy as the other system but effective all the same. Graham went over to America for a rally, and as promised, dropped by Australia on the way home to set it up and teach us how to use it. What a legend!

We were now in a position where we could make adjustments to the engine. We weren't experts straightaway, but through trial and error, we worked the thing out and began making some real gains. We recorded our first race win for three years at Adelaide. It was a big improvement and provided some much needed hope.

We had a real shocker at Bathurst 1987. It began with qualifying when we failed a fuel check. We'd filled out churns in Brisbane, and although it was of a lower grade than the mandatory fuel and gave us less power, we were robbed of our time. It was a dumb decision to disqualify us but we copped it. Even without the penalty we would have qualified seventh, while the European Sierras took out the top five spots.

Greg Hansford, who was driving my second car full-time in the championship, and I recorded a DNF in the race. It was a shit way to end a shit year, one of the most trying in my career.

21

THE CHAMP IS HERE

Bullets and Christmas Cards

I grabbed a glass from the cupboard, threw in some ice and filled it to the brim before tipping my head back and downed the high-proof bourbon. I poured another and passed it to Greg. I waited until he had a sip and then I gave him the bullet.

'What I have to say isn't real nice, mate,' I blurted, the warm bourbon in my belly giving me courage.

'But I have to say it. I've been talking to the boys at the top, and we've come to the decision that we have to go in another direction. You won't be driving for us next year.

'I'm sorry.'

Greg went white. 'What do you mean?' he said. 'Are you serious?'

'Afraid so. It isn't totally my decision, but this is the way it has to go.'

The poor bugger took it hard. He looked as though he was going to cry. I felt terrible.

I had never sacked anyone in my life and to fire a bloke like Greg was just heartbreaking. He was a good driver, and we had only given him a year to prove himself in what was ultimately a shit car.

I felt for him but had no choice.

Greg was in complete shock. He said nothing for a while, sipped on his drink, and then pleaded for another chance. But it was too late. The decision had been made. Shell was tipping in huge money and was very disappointed with the year we'd had. Greg was an easy target and they told me he had to go. My hands were tied.

Giving Greg the bullet was one of the hardest things I have ever done. He was a terrific bloke, but unfortunately he was the sacrificial lamb for our poor season. Shell demanded both cars had to be competitive and they thought Greg wasn't up to the job. It was harsh because the cars weren't great and I would have liked to have given him another year.

I sacked Greg at the Jack Newton Celebrity Pro-Am, a charity golf tournament on the North Coast. It was an extremely awkward day. I hit woods and irons, fired balls into the sand, crippled by anxiety. He was with me the whole time, not a care in the world, and was really enjoying himself. I was a wreck because I knew what was coming. I meant to tell him on the course, but I couldn't work up the courage so I waited until I had a stiff drink in my hand.

Greg really was a great driver and I wished him the best. I didn't like what had happened, but the deed was done.

It was time to move on.

Not long later an envelope was lobbed over my way. Inside was a Christmas card, which was strange because I'd never received one addressed to the workshop before.

'Merry Christmas, Dick,' it said. 'Heard you have a drive going? Would love to be involved. Best wishes, John Bowe.'

I had a bit of a chuckle when I put the card down because John was pretty good when it came to playing the game. He was one of those blokes who was always hanging around the bigwigs, loitering with the journalists, and doing anything he could to further his name. He even had his own personal public relations agent, a bloke called David Segal, known as the 'seagull'. I would go as far as saying John Bowe was the best politician in motorsport.

He probably didn't need to send me the card because he was already in my sights. John had been hanging around the Shell brass, never one to miss an opportunity. He told them how good he was and what he could do for the team. Even before we told Greg he was no longer required, Shell had earmarked Bowe as their man.

I had known John for a while. He was a good driver. We had an epic battle back when I was in the Mustang and he was in the Volvo at Bathurst – we swapped paint, banged panels and warred. I knew John could drive and I also thought his outgoing personality would be helpful for the team. Soon after the card-lobbing, he was hired.

I can remember sitting with him on the way to the first race of the year.

'No, you drive, mate,' he said. 'I have work to do.'

He pulled out this gigantic machine, all black box and twisted cords.

'What's that?' I asked.

'A phone,' he said, surprised I didn't know what his Motorola MicroTAC mobile phone was.

He spoke on the damn thing the whole way to the track, selling and buying cars. When he wasn't making calls, he had his head buried in the classified ads. He was every bit the used-car salesman. Needless to say, a good one at that.

Red-Faced and Ready for Revenge

I was utterly embarrassed after 1987. We had been towelled up in the Touring Car Championship. Bathurst was rock bottom. I was supposed to be the big gun of the Australian racing scene; the international drivers came fearing me and my reputation. Instead, they left thinking I was a joke and that the Australians were just a bunch of colonial backwater plebs.

It burned.

Both my cars failed to fire a shot, out within a couple of laps. I was a laughing stock, and the European drivers thought the world revolved around them. I felt as though I had let my nation down, and for the first time in my life I was embarrassed to call myself an Australian.

We were better than that. *I* was better than that.

I entered the 1988 season with vengence on my mind. Rather than fold, be weak and go for the easy option, I took the bit between my teeth and challenged my team to rise from the ashes and prove we were the best.

The first job was to sort out the car.

We really had problems with the Sierra. The computer

was the first issue, but after a hasty trip to the UK, and with some good friends and luck, we got that sorted. We now had the Bosch system and were growing more confident with our ability to control it with every passing day. But computer aside, there were still problems with the car. With the help of Dale-Jones, we had more power, but we were still blowing things left, right and centre. Components were breaking and we needed to improve them if we were to redeem ourselves. The biggest issue was the diff: we were using an extremely expensive Rudi Eggenberger model and it was rubbish. Apparently the best Ford bit in the world, it had a limited range of ratios and there was always something wrong with it. The piece of metal just couldn't handle the power.

So we decided to build our own. I spoke to master engineer Ron Harrop and he came up with an idea.

'I reckon a nine-inch ring and pinion will do the job,' he said. 'It will be strong, and it'll give us flexibility with the ratios.'

He built it and the diff was ironclad. Indestructible. But we still had to homologate it. We rang Ford and they agreed to help.

'Send it over and we'll get the job done,' they said.

Ford did and the new diff was bulletproof. A godsend.

With Ford's help we also homologated a Hollinger six-speed gearbox. The Getrag model we were using was hopeless, the sort of thing you would find in a BMW road car. The Hollinger was another giant leap forward and gave us reliability and added performance. We had also upgraded from the RS Cosworth Sierra to the RS 500 Cosworth.

It came out with a larger intercooler, a bigger turbocharger and a better inlet manifold. It also had stronger con rods and a state-of-the-art oiling system.

Ford had finally developed the car they had wanted. It looked as though it was going to be a real weapon, and we had the best of the best thanks to some Aussie ingenuity.

The RS 500 also boasted a whopping 580 hp in race trim. It was a huge leap considering we had 200 hp when we ran the first Sierra, and really quite amazing to pull so much power from a four-cylinder engine. I struggled to believe that such a small block produced so much grunt.

One day we pulled the turbo off and ran the engine flat stick on the dyno. Revving the absolute shit out of it, we managed to pull 90 hp. We whacked the turbo back on, cranked up 2.4 bars of boost, and the car produced an incredible 680 hp.

It floored us all!

It will come as no surprise that we went into the season full of hope, brimming with optimism. We had the cars, the drivers, the money and, most importantly, a point to prove.

The Shell Ultra-Hi Racing Team dominated the 1988 Australian Touring Car Championship. Beginning with a crushing display at Calder Park in the opening round, I went on to win six of the nine rounds. John Bowe won two of the other three, with Tony Longhurst, the only man to stop us from winning them all, who was also in a Sierra!

I can still remember the look on Allan Moffat's face when I lapped him at Adelaide International Raceway. I was running first and Bowe second, the next challenger ten seconds behind. I came into the straight and saw Moffat in front, almost a lap behind. He was driving a Sierra, an Eggenberger car he had paid more than $1 million for. Moffat was halfway down the straight when I turned the corner. With my foot flat to the floor, I passed him.

Whoosh!

My Sierra looked like an F1-11, his like a Corolla. I could see the steam pouring from his ears, the anger consuming his face. Moffat had the shits and I was over the moon.

The only blight on the season was a DNF at Winton Motor Raceway. It wasn't my favourite place in the world, still isn't – it's like running a marathon around a clothes line. My dislike for the dust bowl grew on this day when my old mate Larry Perkins took me out. I was powering along just fine until he decided to T-bone me coming into the hairpin. I was pissed and let him have it afterwards, but it wasn't all bad because John went on to win.

I was crowned the champion at the end of 1988, and boy, did it feel good. I was totally humiliated the season before and to come back in such devastating fashion made me feel confident about who I was and where I was going. I had been through so many ups and downs during my career, but I can honestly say 1987 was one of my most trying years. I didn't know where I was heading, or what would happen, but we really proved what a team we were a year later. From that moment on, we knew we could get through anything.

I didn't think too much about the prospect of equalling the record for the most Touring Car Championship wins – I was now on four, one behind my idol Ian Geoghegan. I was just so stoked that we were able to pull off a one-two in the championship with John Bowe finishing second. It was only our second year as a two-car team and we did something utterly rare and outstanding. It seemed so long ago that I'd thought my career was finished – *again* – after meeting with Rouse in the UK, even though it was less than 12 months before. We had a little bit of luck, but mostly our fourth championship came from complete determination and our Australian fighting spirit.

Britain and Barry

I had never seen so many rabbits. Maybe they were hares. What the hell did I know? I was used to kangaroos and wombats. Whatever they were, they bounced across the lush green grass, over the rolling hills and endless plains of the English Midlands, which led to one of the most famous motor racing tracks in the world.

The Silverstone Circuit was legendary. Stirling Moss, Jack Brabham, Juan Manuel Fangio, Jackie Stewart – they were all part of the magic.

I had conned my way there, intent on restoring Australian pride, and flogging these arrogant know-it-alls. It began when I phoned Ross Palmer.

Ross Palmer was launching his company in the US and the UK, and was about to hit the two whopping markets with a product called Redkote.

'What better way to launch yourself in the UK than have me go over with a car and give it to them?' I said.

'You reckon you can match it with the Europeans?' he replied.

'My oath. You know I can.'

He agreed. Shell also offered to pay.

The race was for the Tourist Trophy at Silverstone, and took place on 4 September 1988.

With a decent budget, a dream and a truckload of Aussie fighting spirit, I loaded all my gear into two air-freight containers, grabbed my passport and headed straight into enemy territory.

I had never been to Silverstone and was astounded by the magnificent track when I arrived. Surrounded by rich verdant countryside, rabbits (or hares) roaming the plains and rain lashing the ground, I edged through the gates and was met by one of the most prestigious circuits in the world. Built on an old World War II airstrip, the track was long, fast, sweeping and technical. Being a naive Aussie, I asked a local a dumb but important question.

'Clockwise, of course,' he answered, when I queried what direction we would race. 'How could you not know that?'

I smiled.

I began testing on the Tuesday. After unloading my gear and piecing it all together, I took to the track – and made sure I went clockwise. I was cautious at first, learning the long straights and the hard braking points, and figuring out just how fast I could go into the sweepers. I soon had the tyres squealing and the brakes burning. After a few laps I felt I was doing OK, when I noticed a high-profile spy.

Sitting in an F1-like compound, full of computers and technology, Rudi Eggenberger's team engineer was hunched over endless screens monitoring my every move. I had no idea why he was doing this until someone told me I was nudging the lap record on my very first fling.

I beamed.

Full of fire, and revenge firmly on my mind, I went out and ragged my Sierra. These guys I was up against knew Silverstone like I knew Lakeside, so they must've been embarrassed when they found out I was more than a second up on them. The entire European field shook their heads in disbelief and went back to their elaborate computers.

It only got better for this proud Aussie in qualifying – I hosed them by 1.5 seconds. I kicked their arses and it was one of the sweetest moments of my career.

I was on top of the world. To watch people like Rouse, the bloke who had dudded me, look panicked and scared, was just priceless. I had them in a spin; I had shown them what a convict Australian could do. It got even better when the race roared to life.

With plenty of confidence and nothing to lose, I screamed off the line and left them in my dust. I was more than 200 metres ahead of my nearest rival before the first turn. I had the fastest Sierra in the world, no doubt about it, and man, did it feel good.

Unfortunately, a failed water pump ended up costing me the win, but make no mistake about it, despite the setback, I had put Dick Johnson Racing and Australian Touring Car Racing on the map. The Europeans were in absolute awe.

Shell were impressed. They decided they would start using me in ads to promote their products and brought in a bloke called Barry Sheene, the two-time 500 cc world motorcycle champion.

Barry was a legend. He moved from the UK to Australia in the late 1980s because the cold weather in England was hell for his long list of injuries. (He had broken just about every bone in his body and was crippled with severe arthritis.) Barry joined Darrell Eastlake on the Channel 9 commentary team and developed quite a following. For some reason Shell thought that he and I would make a good team. They were right.

Barry and I hit it off from the get-go. A media agency called George Patterson was hired to produce the ads, and they took the two of us out on a fishing trip to see how we got on. Their original plan was to cast me as the joker and Barry as the serious guy. Please!

I reeled in fish after fish and Barry caught a cold, complaining about everything from the sun to the brand of beer in the fridge. The casting agent quickly changed his mind about the roles we were to play, and Barry of course became the joker for the 20 or so ads we would film over several years.

Barry was a serial pest – and I say that in a nice way. He was forever complaining. We would go to a restaurant and he would have the waitress rattle off every ingredient in every dish because he claimed to be allergic to garlic. After all that, he would then order veal and ask for a side of garlic bread! He appeared to be rude and obnoxious but funny at the same time. Barry could call someone a prick and tell them he didn't like them, and this person would laugh thinking Barry was their best friend. If I did that, I'd be punched in the face.

Barry was also a chain-smoker, fag always in hand. Of course, that made filming the ads difficult because he would want to be in and out quickly so he could go and have a smoke.

'Come on,' he said in his thick cockney accent. 'I want to go first. Let me do my little bit and then you get on with yours. Right, yeah?'

I agreed.

He was done in two seconds flat. I did my spot in about five minutes and then went out front to get in the limo that had been hired to take us both to the airport. It was nowhere to be seen. I called the driver.

'Where the hell are you?' I asked.

'Oh, Barry told me he had some type of emergency and he had to get to the airport asap. I'm stuck in a bit of traffic but will be there to collect you shortly.'

Barry and I were booked on the same flight to the Gold Coast. By the time I arrived at the airport, the plane was long gone. The next flight was three hours later. I called Barry, fuming.

'You right, gov?' he answered. 'I'm just about to tuck into a baked dinner at home.'

I asked him what the emergency was that made him take the limo early.

'I was hungry,' he said.

That was Barry. He could be a pain in the arse sometimes, but there was never a dull moment when he was around. I was absolutely gutted when he passed away. Dead at 52, claimed by cancer. He will always be missed.

22

TIMES FIVE

Going Out with a Bang

The windows exploded.

Whoosh!

I grabbed at my face, trying to wipe the searing heat from my brow. I looked around and half the garage was destroyed. Wheels rolled, toolboxes were tipped over, makeshift walls had fallen to the ground.

'What the hell was that?' I screamed, my hair singed, my skin feeling like it would melt.

I looked at my car, panels scratched from the flying glass.

And then I ran.

With fuel splashed all over the garage floor, I was frightened the whole thing would blow. One of my crew was refuelling the car at the time.

'Get out,' I yelled to the others.

Everyone scrambled and rushed outside into the cool

dark of night. We waited a moment, expecting all hell to break loose. Silence. Nothing. Coast clear, we grabbed a fire-extinguisher each and bolted back, dousing the entire garage in a sea of white foam.

I thought my Bathurst campaign was over.

Bathurst in 1989 was still prehistoric. Forget concrete towers, state-of-the-art plumbing and electronic roller doors. The complex was a maze of hastily erected tents and dirt. We tried to work out what had happened.

The swearing chef gave it away.

'Fuck,' he screamed, running out of the catering tent, swiping at invisible flames. Think Ricky Bobby from *Talladega Nights*.

'Man, was that you?' we asked, not bothering to ask if he was OK.

He nodded, red-faced and reticent.

The catering tent was located right beside our garage. Turns out the hire gas oven was faulty and was leaking gas. He hit the pilot light.

Bang!

The oven could have killed us all. We were OK but thought the car wasn't looking so good.

The mad scramble began.

We worked throughout the night and by the time the sun edged over the Mountain, burning away the early morning fog, our car was back together and ready to roll. The team was utterly exhausted and so was I, but for their efforts won the best-presented car.

But there are no room for excuses at Bathurst.

Complete with windows, a fresh polish job and an engine that had finally reached its peak, our car conquered all as we floored around the Mountain. It drove sensationally. Full of grunt and roar up the hill, balanced and precise across the top, and lethal coming down, we recorded a stunning time of 2.14.58. We were the car to beat with the quickest time. Brock was also ominous, less than a second behind in his Sierra – that's right, a Ford – but more on that shortly.

We moved into the Tooheys Top 10 and pulled out an almost perfect lap. Under immense pressure, we clocked a 2.12.898, which was good but not good enough. Thanks to some devious trickery, we were relegated to second place. Bordering on illegal, Brock discharged his halon-gas fire-extinguisher, which was angled across his intercooler, giving him added horsepower going up the straight. He copped a $5000 fine but kept his pole. We weren't concerned because we knew we could outlast and outrace him the following day.

What came next was one of the best races of my life. It was complete domination. We led from start to finish and were never challenged. I recorded the fastest time, lapped countless cars and won my second Bathurst 1000, finishing the epic race in 6.30.53. It was the most satisfying victory of my life, a day when everything went right. The car was a weapon and Bowe was fantastic. After powering away to a commanding lead, all we had to do was cruise home.

I was now a two-time Bathurst champion and this win was free from controversy.

It was really surreal. After my shocking seven-year run, I was absolutely elated. I really thought I could never win at the Mountain again. I suspected I was cursed, resigning myself to the fact that I might leave the sport as a one-time winner. But I was OK with that, because it was already a dream fulfilled. There was something, though, maybe it was the magic of the place, that kept me going, kept me coming back for more. I didn't think too much about the win at the time. Sure I celebrated, but I pretty much just took it all in my stride.

I wasn't the type to look too far into the future. I was more a simple guy who took it one race at a time. I was nearing 50 by then, but I felt like a teenager. I never got the shits when I lost. As long as I gave it my all, I was OK. But boy, I never tired of winning.

I also won my fifth touring car title in 1989. I must say it wasn't as easy as the year before, because the rest of the field had come along. Bowe won the first race of the year, laying down the gauntlet, and I responded by winning the next two races. Bowe won another, but I managed to win four of the eight races and seal a record fifth championship. The worst I fared was a seventh position, and aside from that I was never off the podium. Bowe was good enough to finish second in the championship giving us back-to-back one-twos.

The 1989 championship was very special. It was a real buzz to equal my idol Ian Geoghegan's record of five Touring Car Championship wins, not that I gave it too much thought. Funnily enough, Ian and I also shared the same birthday and called each other without fail on that day.

Looking back, I probably achieved a little more than him, no disrespect intended to a brilliant driver and a better bloke. Back in his day, the championship consisted of a single race, not a season, and he won four of his five in a single event, whereas all of my championships were fought over an entire season.

I was 49 when I won my fifth championship, but I seriously thought I could win a few more. Today I would be considered old, maybe I was, but I was at the peak of my powers. I was fit, hungry and had mastered my craft. A few of the reporters had thought I was finished and told me I should retire. I think they were sick of the same old faces and wanted to give some of the young blokes a go.

Needless to say, I ignored them. I also might have told a few of them to get nicked.

As I mentioned, Brock was in a Ford in 1989. It caused a huge outrage and is something that not too many people think of today. It might be time to tell you a yarn or two about my old mate Peter Geoffrey Brock, King of the Mountain. Peter Perfect. Legend.

Brocky

I sat on the Sandown start line, fiercely focused. I pressed my left foot onto the clutch, revving and roaring with my right.

Vroom! Vroom!

The rest of the field followed suit, a chorus of churning metal filling the air. And then, from the corner of my eye, I saw a flashing hand. I looked over to the other car on the front row. Inside the roaring cabin was Brock, waving frantically in an attempt to catch my attention.

'What?' I yelled uselessly through the thundering noise.

Brock smiled before pointing to the crowd. I glanced towards the heaving throng: flags were waving, people were cheering. I looked back to him again and shrugged.

But he kept pointing, this time with more intent and

what seemed like frustration. I looked once more, my eyes immediately focusing on the huge pair of tits that were swaying in the wind.

Bounce. Bounce.

I wondered how I had missed this perfection of boobs and nipples on first glance. They were spectacular. I began laughing and looked over to Brock, who was also pissing himself.

Whoosh!

While in our own little world of breasts and boyish behaviour, the race had started and cars were rushing by. Smile wiped from my face, I shoved the car into first gear, dumped the clutch and burnt rubber as I roared from the line. It was too late. The entire half had passed us by. Brock and I, the two greats, were far behind. I shrugged my shoulders and laughed. After all, they were good tits!

This was Peter Brock the larrikin. The drinking, smoking knockabout. The man who loved his racing, his women and good times. But Peter was a complicated man, with as many personalities as he had cars.

I first met Brocky back in the Zupps days. He was already established and I was a nobody. I can't say we hit it off like a house on fire, but he was polite, friendly and came across as a very good bloke. We had more to do with each other as the years rolled on. We began a rivalry on the track and formed a mutual respect for one another, even though our banter was restricted to racing.

I suppose I was envious of Brocky in the early days. Envious but not jealous. Not ever. I had to fight for everything I had, scrape together money and build cars with the spare change I had. Meanwhile, Brock had everything.

Aligned with Harry Firth, Brock had access to the best cars and a budget I couldn't even comprehend. Firth gave him his real start in a factory-backed Monaro at Bathurst in 1969. Firth called him at his Diamond Valley Speed Shop and asked him if he wanted a drive. At first Brock thought it was a joke and told Harry to get nicked. He thought it was a mate trying to wind him up, but of course it wasn't. Brock had been smacked in the arse with a rainbow.

The kid, who had first gone to Bathurst as a spectator six years before, scorched his way to third place with Des West. Some say he would have won except for a brake pad stop that wasn't needed. Either way he had arrived.

The legend was born.

At the same time I was battling my way around Queensland in the old EH Holden I had built myself. I didn't have the cash to compete at interstate tracks and while Brock was getting the best and most expensive gear, I forked out $1800 to buy my next car, the Torana LC.

As I said, I may have been a little bit envious but I wasn't jealous. At that stage I really didn't look ahead. I took it a race at a time and was happy to do my own thing. I didn't ever think I would get the opportunity to compete with Brock. And I wasn't worried; I just wanted to race.

Of course, things would change.

I first went against Brock in 1973. He had been racing at Bathurst for four years, but he didn't make his Touring Car Championship debut until that year. The scruffy, long-haired lout had been blasting around in his beloved Austin A30, racing the car that would go on to make him one of the best drivers we have ever seen, whenever and wherever he could.

We both lined up at Adelaide in LJ Torana GTR XU-1s. I really didn't consider him for a moment. I knew he was good, but I was more focused on myself than anything. He came first and I finished sixth.

By the time I made my Mount Panorama debut in 1973, he was already a Bathurst champion and a fan favourite. He was with HDT and I didn't expect to get close. He came second and I finished fifth.

After years of hardship and struggle, I thought I was about to join Brock at HDT in 1974. With Brock in his new SLR 5000, Firth gave me a trial in one of the old HDT XU-1 GTRs. I had Brock smoked until a mechanical mishap, the bad luck relegating me to third. I thought I'd done well enough to earn a full-time drive with the all-powerful team for 1975, and was expecting my fortune to finally change.

But I was wrong. And that's when I switched to Ford.

I suppose our rivalry, now famous and revered, wasn't born until 1980. On the tenth of August to be exact, at the CRC 300, Amaroo Park. Brock was the dominant force in the sport, peerless. He had won three Touring Car Championships and four Bathurst titles. I had won only a couple of races back then, but on that day, in front of a huge crowd, me and my 351 Cleveland engine blasted to the lead and showed Brock that he finally had a competitor. My tyres faded late in the race and he won. But he knew I had arrived. He told me as much after the race, strangely happy knowing I had him beat.

He dared me to continue.

Tim Pemberton fuelled the duel, the PR man whipping the

press into a frenzy with the whole Ford versus Holden thing. The fans were sick of Brock winning everything and creating his rival would help renew interest in his man. I didn't care about any of that – I just wanted to win the race, and to do that I had to beat Brock. It's fair to say he became my focus; Brock was the best and he stood in my way. I did everything I could to run him down, my day in the sun finally arriving in 1981, when I held him at bay at Lakeside in a heart-stopping battle to win the Touring Car Championship. It was a gripping fight, both of us giving it absolutely everything we had. And it was on that day Brock forever earned my respect. He could have punted me from the track or made excuses for not winning, but he didn't. He simply came up, shook my hand and told me I had deserved to win my championship.

Our rivalry went on until he retired in 1997. He came back later, but I was gone by then. The height of the hysteria was the early 1980s, when Brock and I were both at our strongest, and often it was utter madness with the fans and the press. We had many a great battle on the track, although we were in vastly different machinery at times, which made for less of a fight. Brock was a mere shadow of his former self when I had my best years in the Sierra, having had a nasty split with Holden, ending up in a BMW and then a more expensive but inferior Ford. He can thank his crystals for that, and probably his ego too. Brock believed in his own bullshit and wouldn't listen to a word anyone said, not even from his closest mates. It ended up costing him his relationship with Holden and a win or two.

He was a wild man in the early days. Brock and the HDT boys had crazy parties after every race and all sorts of shit went on. Once he invited me to a hotel in western Sydney after a meet at Oran Park, and they were ripping in, empty cans and cigarette butts everywhere. John Harvey, Brock's right-hand man, went to the toilet and left his drink sitting on the bench. One of the HDT boys pulled out his cock and pissed in it. Fly still undone, Harvey, known as Slug, had a couple of sips before throwing the beer against the wall.

Back then, Brock was a drinker, a rooter and a wild man. I dare say, every story you have ever heard about him is true. I think he went off the rails for a while after the breakdown of his first marriage, which didn't last too long. Then Brock was engaged to a girl named Karen McPherson, so it must have been a surprise to her when he came out in the papers saying he was about to marry the newly crowned Miss Australia, Michelle Downes! The union was a disaster and ended up driving Brock mad. Apparently the Channel 7 weather girl liked to party and left Peter at home. Peter got jealous and mad. Things didn't work out well.

He was never to marry again but he did meet Beverly McIntosh, a woman he ended spending almost three decades with. He still got up to all kinds of shit, but I think he was genuinely happy and he was in a stable relationship. Bev turned a blind eye to his secretaries and affairs.

It was Bev who put him onto a bloke that would change him forever – and help ruin his relationship with Holden. Peter – probably thanks to 30 Marlboro Red cigarettes a day, binge drinking and a relentless schedule – didn't feel well in 1984 and was driving like a busted. He looked so bad that some people said he had cancer. Bev put him onto a bloke called Dr Eric Dowker, a chiropractor, who had been treating her, in an attempt to sort him out. Dowker got him off the smokes and the grog, and turned him into a vegan. He also introduced Peter to crystals and a bunch of hippy crap.

Jillie and I went to Peter's unit in Port Douglas one day for a rare visit. They were waving crystals around, conducting an off-the-cuff magic show. Both went on about the power of the things and made me hold my arms out before pushing them down. They then put the crystal in my hand and did it again, this time failing to lower my hand an inch. Needless to say, I thought it was a load of bullshit and told them as much.

All fruit and veg, Peter embraced his new life and took Dowker everywhere. We thought he was a weirdo, but Peter was adamant he was the man.

No one knows exactly who built it or when, but Brocky began talking about a thing called an Energy Polariser in 1985. It was a box with a couple of crystals and a magnet in it, held together by resin. He began putting this polariser in his cars, claiming that it somehow rearranged the molecules of the vehicle and made the car go faster. Everyone had a laugh at his expense. I had a go at him one day telling him it was a bunch of shit. It didn't go down well, but I thought it needed to be said, not that he listened. Another bloke who had the balls to say something was then Brock employee Larry Perkins, who told Peter he was acting like a loony and it cost him his job. Larry drove with me at Bathurst the next year!

Most people were too scared to voice their opinion and Brock ended up taking the device to General Motors in America to have it tested. They found that the Energy Polariser had no effect on the car, but that didn't stop Brock from pushing it. To cut a long story short, he went against the wishes of Holden and built a production car called the 'Director', with the device at its core. It didn't see the light of day and Brock lost the support of the company that previously thought he was God. Looking back, it was stupid. Brock had Holden at his beck and call – all he had to do was smile to get what he wanted from them – and he threw it away for a stupid box and a bunch of baloney.

The turbulence didn't stop Brock and me from being on-track rivals, or from being off-track friends. We were always hanging out at races and I enjoyed his company.

We were sitting at a bar in Adelaide after a race, having a quiet drink with the publican. Brock looked towards the door, which was in full view.

'Have a go at that bloke,' he said, pointing to the man dressed in full leather, a couple of hefty gold chains dangling from his neck. 'He isn't coming in here.'

The publican gave the bouncer a nod, and the husky man sent the leathers-and-chains guy packing. Brock and I erupted in laughter; we were in hysterics. I almost fell from my stool.

'What?' the publican said. 'What are you two on about?'

'Do you know who you just kicked out?' Brock asked.

He shrugged.

'It was bloody Billy Joel,' I screamed, laughing even harder.

The publican darted out the door and ran down the street. He tried to convince the American rock icon, an absolute superstar at the time, that it was all a mistake. Billy told him to get fucked.

All in all Brock was a good guy, genuine, honest and humble. He had his flaws, his weaknesses. He was a man who was many different things to many different people. But to me he was a guy I considered a friend, even though we never once called each other on the phone. He was also a fierce driver who helped inspire me and drove me to become my best. Brock was a champion of our sport, and I enjoyed every moment that I shared with him.

23

DAYS OF THUNDER

Racing Revolution

Bob Jane sat us all down and told us of his $54 million plan
to bring the National Association for Stock Car Auto Racing
to Australia. He told us it was going to be a revolution and he
wanted us in.

We all nodded and agreed.

The four-time Australian Touring Car Champion and
tyre tycoon brought NASCAR-style racing to Australia in
1988. With speedway-inspired racing booming in the US,
he thought ovals were the future and went about building
the Thunderdome at Calder Park. It was a high-speed oval
surrounded by towering stands, and had a purpose-built
1.8-kilometre track with 24-degree banking on turns one,
two, three and four. The Thunderdome was completed in
1987, and that's when Jane sat down with the country's best
drivers to reveal his dream.

He knew he had to have all the big names of Australian motor car racing involved, as well as some American stars. Jane didn't offer us money, he merely sold us the dream. I really had no choice but to go and race. My backer, Palmer Tube Mills, was about to hit the US and they thought this series might eventually be their ticket into the lucrative and large American market. Jane also told us that we had to mix it up in the demonstration races to get the fans in. He didn't want one bloke winning every time because the new category would turn into a bore. Jane wanted to create some excitement with loosely scripted races and we were happy to oblige.

My car was a Ford Thunderbird, which was bought and imported from the US by Ross Palmer – there was no way I was putting in my cash. The Thunderbird had about 750 hp and was specifically built for NASCAR, a very different brand of racing, all high speed and rolling left turns. It wasn't great by NASCAR standards, but I was pleasantly surprised when I jumped behind the wheel. I thought it would be heavy, stiff and horrible to drive, but it wasn't bad. I quickly found out it wasn't the car that mattered but how you set the machine up, as well as the way you drove.

A road course involves rushing into corners, breaking hard, turning violently and getting out as fast as you can. Meanwhile, the ovals are a completely different beast. Instead of flogging into a corner, you roll in, slow and steady, gently touching the brake. You wait for the car to bite, the rubber to grip, and then get back on the gas and roll out again.

It sounds easy but it's not. On road tracks there is one to one and a half racing lines. The quickest way around the track is on the one line, and you can get away with going half a line out, a whole at most, if you need to make a move. In NASCAR, there are up to four lines. You sit side by side, four cars wide, lap after lap, all while doing 300 k/h. I really struggled to get my head around it.

I first raced the Thunderbird during a practice session at Calder Park, where I discovered that setting up a NASCAR car was a completely foreign thing to me. The oval stock cars are 100 per cent set up for going around left-hand corners; the steering is so biased towards the left, that if you let the steering wheel go while driving in a straight line, you move to the left. It is so fixed in this direction that you don't need to fight while going around the bends; rather, you hold it neutral while cornering. It's on the straights where you really need to focus, tugging the wheel back to the right.

I did quite a lot of races. We had all types of meets, but the more serious ones were the Lightning Strikes events. Five were held in 1988 and my best overall result was second position, but like I said I never took the series to heart. I also knew it would never work in Australia, where speedways were dirt tracks, and it was always going to remain that way.

Poor Bob Jane lost millions – Calder Park as a place of NASCAR racing now a run-down, derelict and broken dream – but his idea did pave the way for a two-year adventure I will never forget.

You Prick

All Levi's 501s, Marlboro Man and John Wayne, Richard Petty is an American legend, the greatest driver NASCAR has ever seen. But as I peered over the wheel of my Redkote Ford Thunderbird, powering towards the snakeskin boot-wearing stars-and-stripes cowboy at Sears Point Raceway, I didn't give two hoots. I was flying and about to put a lap on him.

Smashing my foot into the pedal, I braked hard and late. I yanked at the wheel and sent my groaning No. 38 sailing past the icon who, to this day, has won more NASCAR races than anyone. It was a perfect move. I was about to plant my foot back down and floor my way onto the straight.

Whack!

My head shot into the side of my seat, the impact knocking my hand from the wheel. I grabbed, twisted and turned at the wheel, but there was nothing I could do. I was off the track as the other cars whizzed on by.

'Hey,' I called out to my crew chief Ray Evernham. 'You see what that prick Petty just did? He ran into me.'

Whoops.

It was then that I realised I was still miked up and had just called an American icon a prick on live TV, the heat-of-the-moment comment beamed directly into the homes of millions of American NASCAR fans.

And so began my NASCAR adventure in the US.

At the urging of Ross Palmer, I signed on to go to America in 1989 to compete in five top-flight NASCAR races in the Winston Cup. Truth be told, I didn't want to go, but I was left with little choice. I knew it would be a distraction and feared it would hurt my chances of winning another championship back home. I also thought the cars were bloody dangerous and wasn't really interested in learning a whole new craft at my age, but Palmer was paying the bills and had just launched in America.

So off I went.

With Jillie, Kel and Steven in tow, a family holiday in the offing, I arrived in the US after a 16-hour flight. Our first race was at Sears Point, near San Francisco, and the connecting flight was delayed. We were piled into a limo after landing and the first practice session was already underway. I arrived at the track, frantically changed into my race suit and jumped in the car.

'Man, what the hell is this?' I said, looking down at the gigantic steering wheel.

Ray shrugged.

'This looks like it should be on a London bus,' I said. 'Not on a race car. What the fuck?'

It was at least 65 centimetres wide.

I went out despite the shit wheel and found that the car was pretty good. Ray was a bit of a pioneer when it came to shocks, having worked for American racing giant Penske. After some intercontinental discussion, he helped set me up with a very good suspension package that no one else had, and upon my request, had also gone outside the NASCAR circles to find and install brakes that were far superior than anything out there. NASCAR guys had little regard for brakes, and on some ovals, they only used them to pit.

I immediately turned heads when I cut my first lap. I smashed into the kerbs, driving right over the top of them, finding the quickest way around the track, while the others drove around them, having never seen a car on two wheels.

'What's that all about?' someone said. 'You're like a hopping kangaroo.'

I kept quiet, knowing that if they tried the move themselves they would end up breaking their cars. Unlike them and their stiff and staunch machines, I had the shocks that allowed me to attack the kerbs. Although I was going OK, there was still that damn cumbersome wheel.

I asked around and found out that they used these gigantic beasts because steering was hard and heavy on the ovals. Without power steering, drivers needed to sit right on top of the wheel, as close as they could, to turn the thing around. The huge wheel allowed them to use their shoulders, backs and any other muscle that was willing and able to get the weighty machines through the fast, slight bends. The thing was, we weren't on an oval and the wheel was still shit, so I turned to Ray.

'I don't care what you get or where you get it from,' I said, 'but go find me something smaller. I can't turn left and right with this. It's like a tug of war.'

Ray went to an auto shop that night, found what he could and bolted it on. The new wheel made a world of difference, and along with the good suspension and brakes, as well as 20-odd years of experience on road courses, I was able to bluff my way through the foreign machinery, competition and unknown track to qualify eleventh in my Thunderbird. It was a staggering result, considering there were more than 60 cars all up with only 43 making it into the race.

I surprised the Yanks and, in turn, myself.

An Australian company I knew was in the US at the time was setting up NASCAR with in-car cameras. The Americans didn't talk in the car, and many refused to have the equipment installed. After my decent effort in qualifying, they approached and asked me if I was happy to have a camera put in my car. I agreed; I'd been doing that sort of thing for years and was quite comfortable having a chat while driving. So they wired me up, installed the camera and off I went.

I didn't stop to think what I was getting myself into. I was about to be beamed, *live*, into homes across America. NASCAR, as you probably know, is kind of a big deal. Massive, even.

I found the race quite easy in the first stint. Everything was working well and I pushed forward, claiming four spots with very clean, standard passing moves. I was in seventh when I got my first taste of a caution, which they call a yellow flag. I don't know what caused it, but all of a sudden the entire field was charging towards the pits.

It was crazy. Forty-three cars bolted into a lane barely wide enough for two cars, with only 20 bays to stop at. You do the maths.

Luckily I made it in, locked on some new wheels, copped a load of fuel and motored on out.

All good. Or so I thought.

'Ray,' I said. 'What's going on? I was seventh before, and now I think I'm twenty-second.'

'That's NASCAR,' he replied bluntly.

I shrugged and got on with the job. Again I charged through the field, working my way up to twelfth. The yellow flag came out again, prompting madness. This time I only lost five places, but I was still pissed. Red mist hovering, steam coming from my helmet, I went for it.

And that's about when I found Petty. We both went flying off and I called him a prick on national TV.

I finished the race in thirty-second place, and although I was disappointed about that, I was just happy to get through my first race. It wasn't until I pulled into pit-lane that I learned my comments about the American legend had been broadcast. Live, uncut, and to millions.

Man, was I embarrassed.

I thought I was going to be chased out of the country with pitchforks and iron bars. When I got out of the car I walked through the paddock with my head down, eyes on the ground. Somebody slapped me on the back and I braced myself for a punch in the face.

'Yo,' the driver – I'm not sure who – said. 'That was awesome. We were all laughing our heads off. Can't wait till your next race.'

The drivers thought it was just the funniest thing ever. And so did the fans. They had never seen or heard anything like it. I was previously anonymous, a novelty waiting to be crushed, and now I had guys like Darrell Waltrip and Dale Earnhardt Sr coming up to greet me.

As for Petty, well . . . it took me six races to convince him 'prick' was a term of endearment in Australia.

I should have learned my lesson. But I didn't.

'Ah, fuck,' I said in another incident, careering off the road at 200 k/h as I headed straight towards a wall.

The impact threatened to launch me into the air. Again I'd been doing well, again I had crashed, and again I had a microphone strapped to my helmet. The ESPN commentators ignored the f-bomb and started a conversation with me.

'I fired up in there a little quickly and just slipped off the road,' I said. 'It's as slippery as a butcher's block. There's more gunk on there than a kitchen table.'

'Dick, you had a great run until that point,' the ESPN commentator said. 'How did your day go?'

'Well, I'm just waiting for these turkeys to lift me out of here,' I replied, my car still buried in the wall. 'I just want to get back into the race and have a go. I didn't come all the way here to be sitting around.'

'Dick,' the commentator continued, 'we like your accent. Welcome to the Winston Cup.'

NASCAR weren't so pleased with me afterwards. I was dragged into a room and told I was the first person ever to drop the f-bomb live on national TV. The NASCAR people were all very religious, from the Deep South, on the Bible Belt. You were excluded from racing if you didn't go to a NASCAR-sanctioned church service on the morning of the race. In the end, though, I got away with it because both the drivers and the public found my remarks hugely amusing. I was the crazy Aussie bogan giving the sport a big shake.

I had caused a stir, and also shown some potential.

'Man,' said Dale Earnhardt Sr to me one day, 'you teach me how to drive on those road courses and I'll teach you how to drive them ovals. We could be quite the team.'

Snap It Back In

I left the track and in an instant I was buried in a concrete wall, the impact reverberating through my body and my brain, momentarily knocking me out. I would have stayed unconscious had it not been for the pain in my knee.

'Arrrgh!' I screamed in agony; it was like nothing I'd ever felt before.

My knee was burning, hotter than the fires of hell. It felt like a shotgun had been fired point-blank into my knee, the shrapnel bouncing and hitting the rest of my body. My foot was jammed into the brake and the 800-kg cement block had sent all its fury straight into my leg.

I summoned the courage to reach down and grab at the source of pain, but the gun went off again.

Boom!

I screamed and decided to stay still. Strapped in the car, the minutes felt like hours, and I was able to figure out what was wrong. I had a dislocated knee, a bit of bone floating on top of jelly. I think I passed out, such was the pain, until I was eventually dragged out of the car through the window, my leg dangling.

Bang!

The shotgun fired again and I yelped.

Next thing I knew I was in a medical centre, a frightened Jillie waiting outside. The doctor grabbed at my knee. Now the pain felt more like a grenade than a high-powered gun.

Arrrgh!

I could sense Jillie cringing, my agony almost too much to take. The doctor looked down at my face, which was red and wrangled with hurt.

'This is bad,' he said. 'You'll have to go to the hospital.'

'Fuck that,' I said bravely. 'No way. You grab that thing and you push it, rip it, pull it. Do whatever it takes, but I am *not* going to hospital.'

He nodded.

I gritted my teeth as hard as I could as he went in for the kill. I clenched every muscle in my body, closing my eyelids so tightly that my ears felt like they were going to pop right off.

He went in and snapped the bone back into place. And again I screamed, this time a terrifying shriek that knocked Jillie to the ground. The pain left my body in an instant. I gathered my thoughts, said thanks and walked out.

I wasn't trying to be tough, but I was shit-scared of American hospitals. First, I didn't know if I was insured, and second, I'd heard about the horrors that occurred there. I just had it in my head that I wasn't going near one, so I told the doctor to do whatever it took.

I have never been afraid when it comes to driving. Not even after the crash in Greens-Tuf, a violent dance through the trees that could have easily left me dead. Jillie was shaken to her core after that one, and for a moment thought I was done.

I must admit I was a bit concerned driving for NASCAR, because it was bloody dangerous. Aside from the chaos on track, all four-wide, cowboys dashing to the pits on a yellow, the cars were completely unsafe. They were so rigidly built with steel bars and metal that they didn't crumple, and the poor bastard behind the wheel would end up absorbing the brunt of the crash.

The seat was also a massive problem; it looked like it had been pulled out of a church hall.

'We have to do something about this,' I said. 'I don't want to end up in a wheelchair.'

I'd often wondered why the Americans were always

breaking their legs and hips, but after seeing all this I wondered no more. The seat offered absolutely no protection, and I tried to bring over a carbon-fibre seat like we had back home.

But NASCAR wouldn't allow it, stating that the seat had to be metal, so I built my own. With the help of an American mob, we constructed a seat that had side protection all the way to the floor. It supported my legs, stopping them from flying about the cabin in a crash. I should have patented it, because they all use it now.

Just Cruise-ing Along

I sat back having a chat with the CEO of NASCAR, John Cooper, Jillie by my side. We talked about how I was going, what I thought about the series, and whether I would come back for more.

'By the way,' the boss said, out of the blue, 'Tom Cruise is going to be here tomorrow.'

Jillie almost fainted. 'What?' she cried. 'TOM?!'

'Yes,' the boss said. 'He's doing some research for a NASCAR movie he's starring in. I can introduce you if you like.'

Sure enough, he took both Jillie and me to meet Tom the next day. All Ray-Bans and perfect hair, he was every inch the Hollywood star. He extended his hand, Jillie instead plunging in for a kiss. She was like a giddy schoolgirl. They spoke for about two minutes, the box office drawcard asking all about Australia and telling Jillie it's a place he really wanted to go.

After shaking Tom's hand, I just stood back and let Jillie have her moment. I didn't give two shits about meeting him;

I'm not into dudes. I can remember having a quiet chuckle because Jillie was taller than him. That was pretty funny.

Tom's NASCAR movie eventually came out. It was called *Days of Thunder*. I thought it was shit . . . until the cheque arrived.

'Have a look at this, Jillie,' I said, rushing from the letterbox, envelope in my hand. 'The movie mob have just sent me 1100 US dollars.'

Turns out they used vision from real races for the film and little Dick Johnson and his No. 38 Redkote Thunderbird made the final cut. I was in the movie for exactly six seconds and that earned me over 2000 Australian bucks at the time. I decided it was a great movie after that. Thanks, Tom, you're short but a star.

While I certainly had some fun during my NASCAR days, I do have some regrets. I can say without a doubt that the NASCAR experience cost me at least a championship that would have seen me become the only driver in the history of the sport to win six titles. I did five races in 1990 and six in 1991. My best result was a twenty-second position, and I crashed out in five and failed to qualify for two. I travelled between Australia and the US for each race, sometimes racing in America on one weekend before going back home the next. I was absolutely exhausted and was left with nothing on the track. My racing went to shit, and as a result cost me the 1990 championship.

I later offered Marcos Ambrose advice before he left V8 Supercars to try his hand at NASCAR. He was a two-time V8 champion and was leaving at the peak of his powers.

I told him that he had to befriend all the people he was

about to meet because they are a law unto themselves, that it wouldn't be easy to meet the right people, let alone get in with them. Without a good team he was going to be nothing, and he wouldn't get that without making friends.

Marcos must have listened, because he has gone on to do remarkable things. He went about it the right way, starting in trucks and progressing from there. I reckon he has done a sterling job and deserves much praise. He really is a great driver, and who knows what he would have done if he stayed here? He may have ruined his V8 legacy by leaving, but it's fair to say he's pretty happy with where he is now. Marcos wanted to spread his wings and go on to do bigger and better things; America was his choice.

He certainly did better than me.

24

REVOLT AND REVOLUTION

Touring Car Entrants Group of Australia

A storm was brewing back in Australia. Dark clouds hovered, thunder cracked, and a red, white and blue Nissan was set to reign.

Jim Richards beat me in the 1990 Touring Car Championship in a GTR E32, a monster Nissan that would soon be known as 'Godzilla'. Richards, and his mate Mark Skaife, would end up changing the face of the sport. I would have defeated him had it not been for my constant draining trips to the US. I hardly stood a chance from there, the Nissan going on to conquer all.

But let's back up a bit. Before we get to the stories of Richards and Skaife, beer cans flying, 'pack of arseholes', and some Bathurst bullshit that still leaves a foul stench, let's talk about the thunder, the lightning and the storm that threatened to bring the motor racing sport to its knees.

Australian motorsport was in a bad way in 1988. Fans weren't turning up to races, the media wasn't interested, and nobody watched us on TV. The racing was one-sided – only rich teams won races – and costs were spiralling out of control. As drivers, we knew the sport was going downhill, and over beers at a bar or a garage at a race, we discreetly talked.

The general sentiment we had was that fans just didn't understand the cars we were driving. You couldn't buy a Sierra in Australia or many of the exotic delights that were roaring around then. We felt as though the fans no longer connected with the cars, or with us.

CAMS were in bed with the Federation of International Automobiles (FIA) – the international governing body – and they thought they could put us on the world map by following what was decided in Paris, ignoring where we had come from and what had made us. Our sport was huge in the 1970s and early 1980s, and it was thanks to Holden and Ford. They were the cars people drove, and the brands they wanted to support.

Personally, and somewhat selfishly, we were also furious about all the cash we were being forced to put in. Whenever CAMS came out with a new rule or direction, we were forced to throw everything in the bin and start again. Adopting the international model was bloody expensive, buying Sierras, GTRs, BMWs and Volvos – it was sending us broke. This would not have been a problem if this formula had worked and we'd made our money back through sponsorship, but that wasn't the case. The drastic drop in attendances and TV audiences was smashing our bottom line.

As investors, we felt as though we had no say in our sport or in which way it was going. We were the blokes who put on the show, the muppets who were paid to build and drive the cars. But we had no input in the sport, which was now rapidly in decline. We also didn't make any money, and made the best that we could from the sponsors and track promoters, while CAMS took the rest. We didn't get sanction fees or receive a cut from the tickets sold or cash from TV deals.

But these weren't the reasons why I called a meeting in Wellington in 1988, put the word out to the likes of Brock, Richards, Perkins, Tony Longhurst and Fred Gibson, to come meet me in a lunchroom on the top floor of a rickety wharf in New Zealand, Shed No. 4. It was because our sport was about to die, and I wanted to do something about it.

I *had* to do something about it.

Here, on a chilly day, the Touring Car Entrants Group of Australia, or TEGA, was unofficially born, the biggest guns of our sport sitting around a table, finally deciding enough was enough.

'Guys, we have to put our heads together and fix this thing before it falls over,' I said.

There were nods all around the room.

'We are the ones spending the money, yet we have no voice. We can't keep on lobbying CAMS and have our opinions and concerns fall on deaf ears. We need to come together, look at things and work out where it should go.'

Everyone agreed. We shook hands and vowed to take action. Once we returned to Australia, we set up TEGA and CAMS got wind of it and shat a brick. The confederation was fearful that we were establishing a vigilante group intent on bringing them down. But that was never the case. We just wanted to have some direction, some control, and to be able to work with all the warring parties to ensure our sport survived.

We hired some lawyers, the wigs hastily filling out the paperwork. We also rented an office in Melbourne, where we met once a month, with no great plan at first but the need to analyse what had gone wrong.

'Let's look back,' said an old hand, 'to why the sport was so popular in the late seventies. Why did they love us then?'

'Because we had bloody cars they could understand,' someone else answered. 'Things that they drove and loved.'

Another butted in. 'It was Ford versus Holden, and that's what it should be now.'

He was right. Everyone in Australia drove either a Ford or a Holden, both brands providing the most popular cars in the country. If you weren't putting your kids, your dog or your missus into the back of a Commodore, you were putting them into a Falcon, greasing up the tow bar and whacking on a trailer to go on an end-of-year trip.

The future of Australian motorsport was clear: we all needed to get into a Ford or a Holden. We had to bring back the great old rivalry, the two-way fight that had made and defined our sport.

But that was easier said than done. We were a powerless mob with no money. I put in 100K, which was matched only by Fred Gibson. We hired Ken Potter and Paul Berringer to run TEGA, but still we had little teeth.

As I said, we never set this body up to be vigilantes and

we knew the only way the hastily formed organisation would work was to get CAMS involved. They thought we were a threat and were determined to beat us back into the ground. We eventually invited them to sit in on meetings, all cloth-hats and patches, snotty-nosed, which we thought would help ease some concerns.

Aside from CAMS, there was another important set of players on the scene – the promoters, who owned the tracks and marketed and promoted the events. They also took the gate receipts, and were shocked when they were asked for a sanction fee. Sensing a power play, they set up their own organisation, leading to a three-way war between us, CAMS and the newly formed Promoters' Association. What a shit fight.

We never meant it to be that way and that's what no one understood. Even though we were drivers, who some probably thought were dumb, we knew that all three parties were important. There was no future if we couldn't find common ground. That wouldn't come for another nine years, when a bloke called Tony Cochrane came in and kicked some heads. But we did reach a historically important agreement for the 1993 season, due to the disintegration of the international touring car deal that left CAMS with no choice. A new formula was needed, and with our sport left in a lurch, it was a no-brainer.

CAMS finally agreed that it was time to return to the Holden versus Ford war. It wasn't that simple, and concessions were made. But before we get to the events of 1993, let's talk about 1992, the year that I was ripped off, when a decision took place that has left me fuming to this day.

Pack of Arseholes

The rain began belting down. A trickle at first, it became a deluge, water bucketing from the sky. The track threatened to become a river.

John Bowe and I had run the perfect Bathurst race. Packing a Sierra now past its use-by date, and vastly inferior to the Nissan 4WD GTR that had been supposedly impossible to beat, we'd made up for its weaknesses with pinpoint driving and precise strategy.

We'd made the right calls at the right time.

'I'm coming in,' I yelled over the two-way, on lap 143, 18 laps shy of the end.

'This is going to turn to shit. Get out the wets, and let's win this thing.'

I slipped, slid and aquaplaned into the pits, a ferocious storm unloading and unleashing all of God's might. The heavens didn't just open, they collapsed, sending a tsunami of water onto Australia's most famous and brutal track.

I wasn't taking a chance. John Bowe was due to drive the final stint, but the chaos meant we had to be in and out. After a lightning stop pushed out by my crew, I powered up the Mountain and passed many cars, which were useless and utterly dangerous on slicks. We were in second place, chasing Jim Richards and Mark Skaife, who'd overtaken us on lap two, but we refused to give up the fight.

Cautious but still powerful on the rain-friendly tyres, I floored my way towards Forrest's Elbow, only backing off when I saw the yellow flags. I came through the bend and saw a mess of cars – Corollas, a Commodore and the number-one

Winfield Nissan that I'd been chasing – all smashed and slammed against a concrete wall. I kept on, now in the lead.

Bathurst 1992 was going to be mine.

With my competition ruined, wrecked and going nowhere, I backed off and completed lap 145. And that's when the red flag came out. I'm no genius, but I knew the rules. I thought the officials would go back a lap, before the chaos and carnage, but that was fine because I'd taken Richards on lap 144.

I fist-pumped and fired through, sticking my hand out the window to salute the crowd. I rolled my war-torn car, a smoking heap, into pit-lane, where I was met by my crew and their high fives and thumbs ups. I had won my fourth Bathurst 1000.

Or so I thought.

I leapt from the car and embraced my crew. It was a wonderful moment, maybe the greatest considering what we were up against. Neil, my team manager, slapped me on the back, a frown from ear to ear.

'Dick,' he said. 'Calm down. I don't think we won.'

'What?' I shouted. 'You're kidding, right?'

Neil proceeded to tell me officials had counted back two laps, not one, and the race had been won by Richards and Skaife.

'How could we be beaten by a car that's in a wall?' I demanded. 'That's bullshit!'

I was absolutely furious at first, but my heart sank towards my stomach and I felt utter despair. Neil went to plead our case, leaving a glimmer of hope. The rain continued to belt down and I retreated to my truck. I sat there, head in hands, struggling to comprehend what had just happened. I was in complete shock.

I can't believe they can do this, I thought. *How can they?*

I was dragged from the truck and told to make my way over to the podium. Fans were cheering and patting me on the back.

'Go, Ford!' one screamed.

'Well done, Dick,' said another.

I didn't say a word, walking with my head held high, my shoulders back and straight. I stood on the podium, and my fate was sealed when I was announced as the runner-up. I took my consolation prize and looked towards the crowd.

All hell broke loose.

Fans were screaming blue murder, shouting, yelling and booing. And then beer cans flew, forcing Richards and Skaife to duck for cover. I had never seen Jim lose his cool, though I did expect that from Mark, a young hothead with a short fuse.

I was later told that Skaife strapped beer cans into his race suit, telling Richards he was going to throw them back at the mongrels if one hit him. Richards, the calm statesman, ordered Mark to put them away and warned him to keep his cool. In the end it was Richards who lost his shit, and the first time I had ever seen him blow a fuse.

'I'm just really stunned for words,' he said. 'I can't believe the reception. I thought Australian race fans had a lot more to go than this. This is bloody disgraceful. I'll keep racing, but I tell you what, this is gonna remain with me for a long time. You're a pack of bloody arseholes.'

Slamming the non-Nissan-loving crowd sparked pandemonium, the fans going even wilder, chanting 'bullshit'.

I kind of thought it was pretty funny and agreed with their sentiment, but not their behaviour.

The outcome of Bathurst 1992 burns me to this very day. We did everything right and were beaten by a car that didn't make it home. I will never get over the decision, not in this life.

While I was filthy with the officials, I wasn't dirty on Jim or Mark. The farce wasn't their fault; they just went out, did their job and received the race win, albeit angrily. I still believe I'd won, and it was a huge achievement against a 4WD supercar that shouldn't have even been on the road.

The Nissan was never sold in Australia, admittedly neither was the Sierra, but it was a Japanese monster that had us all hopelessly outgunned. When CAMS finally accepted TEGA's proposal to return to the classic Holden and Ford rivalry, Class A Australian-produced V8 cars, the Nissan was gone. I think it got the send-off it deserved.

Jim is an absolute gentleman of our sport, a legend and a top bloke. Mark would go on to equal my record and become a great driver himself, even though he was someone we loved to hate, a bloke we liked to stir up, all attitude, ego and fire.

Bad Boys

Paul Cruickshank was drunk. Known as 'Pinocchio', my Dick Johnson Racing (DJR) staffer had downed more than his share. He looked across the bar and saw Mark Skaife.

'I reckon I should go over there and give him a barracuda,' he slurred.

The rest of us laughed before egging him on.

Skaife was standing at the bar in the Hunts Motel in Western Sydney. He was being loud and typically obnoxious. We all watched on like schoolboys as Pinocchio snuck towards him. We didn't think he had the balls.

'Arrrrrgh!' Skaife shouted as Paul sank his teeth right into his arse. 'What the fuck?'

Paul had picked Mark up and bitten him on the bum, hard enough to draw blood, and Skaife exploded, his short fuse on fire.

He cocked his hands and went in for a swing.

Bang!

Before he had a chance to unload, Mark was fired into the reception wall. Another DJR employee, a tough, beefy man, had grabbed the young gun and flung him across the room. He held Skaife up and looked him in the eye.

'Mark,' he said, calm and collected. 'I have a bad feeling that someone here is going to get hurt. And I'm pretty sure that person is going to be you. I think it's best you walk away.'

Skaife took the advice, reluctantly retreating.

I can still remember Skaife's first drive in a Laser at Amaroo Park in 1984. I was there watching on, witnessing the birth of one of the sport's greatest careers. Skaife would go on to win more races than anyone in the history of the sport and equal my record, but he was always a controversial figure, not widely liked.

Skaife came into the sport as a young gun in 1988, and the blokes that worked for me disliked him from day one. It wasn't that he was a bad guy, it was just that he came across as arrogant and cocky. He was also quick to fire up. Skaife was the sort of bloke who couldn't take a joke, especially when it was on him. He would always blow up and that made him a target. He also niggled and got up the nose. So I think a lot of people went after him, knowing he was an easy stir.

A little like Brock, he was also lucky enough to be gifted with the good gear. He was picked up by Fred Gibson in 1987 and was never left wanting for a decent car. I suppose other drivers were envious that he'd walked into a superior team and always received the best toys. But I reckon you make your own luck, so good on him. There's no doubting he was a talent and he worked hard to earn his wins, ending up with powerhouse HRT in 1998.

Mark's a lot like his dad, Russell, in many ways: a man I came close to having an altercation with. I was never a fighter and did my best to make friends, not enemies, but Russell really got up my nose and we almost came to blows after a few beers back in the day. I don't recall exactly what was said, or how it started, but Russell and I ended up pushing, shoving and threatening to swing at each other. Russell used to race Capris around Sydney and he was a bloke I never liked. He used to get juiced up and have a go at anyone and everyone. I think I told him he was a wanker at one stage and that's when the shoving began. It was broken up by racing identity Tony Warrener, but I did walk away from that and called him an arrogant prick.

Now, I don't judge a son by his dad, but it's probably fair to say Mark got his mouth from his old man. He doesn't shy away from a thing and doesn't mind a blue, and maybe they are some of the traits that helped make him a great.

Looking back, I can't remember too many stand-out blues. It was pretty common for drivers to confront each other and shout and scream, but it was all left out on the track.

Larry Perkins was one bloke who didn't mind having a go. He was pretty placid in the early days, back when he was my teammate, but he became cranky more and more as the years went on.

I am no angel and have had my fair share of blues. I have gone months without speaking to people, the writer of this book included. I gave News Limited reporter James Phelps an almighty serve at Sandown, calling him every name under the sun after a story that almost killed my race team. But a couple of years later, I agreed to let him write this book, honouring one of my favourite sayings: 'You only get a sore neck by looking back'.

Life is too short to have enemies, and nothing good comes from holding a grudge. Better to forgive and forget.

25

BACK TO THE FUTURE

Game-Changer

The V8s were back – big, bold and loud.

Bloody brilliant.

Sitting behind the wheel of a sparkling new EB Falcon, I planted my foot to the floor and ended seven years of foreign machinery and fading crowds.

The first race of the 1993 season, on February 28 at Amaroo Park, marked our 'return to power' and the official birth of what would soon become known as V8 Supercars.

The Sierras and Skylines were gone, replaced with thundering five-litre V8s; Falcons and Commodores. Officially, there were three classes: Class A for Australian-produced Holdens and Fords, Class B for two-litre cars and Class C for normally aspirated 2WDs.

We couldn't force everyone to throw their expensive equipment in the bin, so we made concessions to allow the likes of Tony Longhurst to continue. Tony was backed by BMW, and there was no way he was going to be able to put together a racing budget if we made it all Holdens and Fords. We decided to have a 'phasing-out period', and gave the non-4WDs and non-turbo-powered cars two years to adapt or die.

For Ford, it wasn't a fair fight. There were only four Falcons compared to 27 Commodores. The Commodores had competed in the former category, making it an easy transition for them. My old mate Perkins had the market cornered when it came to building Holdens; he made a motza.

We had to build a completely new car, but our first effort was knocked back by CAMS.

'Not a chance,' they said, after we blasted the outrageously speedy machine around Bathurst during a test.

'It's too bloody fast.'

In the end, it became a showroom car, too good to be considered, our hard and expensive work tossed in the trash. We were sent to the floor. Neil Lowe was the man responsible for building the first weapon; Ross and Jimmy Stone taking over the day-to-day duties and giving me a Sierra speedy enough to take it to the Godzilla Nissan the year before.

The second car was a compromise and not the machine we wanted, but we still thought we'd be in with a fight.

And we were right.

I won the first race of 1993, my teammate Bowe taking out the round after I failed to finish the second.

But from there, it went all downhill for DJR.

We struggled to develop the car and we were left behind. Glenn Seton and former F1 world champion Alan Jones went on to score a remarkable one-two in the championship. They did a tremendous job, Seton a worthy winner driving his Ford.

A DNF at Bathurst ended an unremarkable year. And although it was a tough, trying and challenging period, it was great to be back in a Falcon. The hastily built EB was heavy and difficult, a work in progress, but it won the attention of fans, whose interest in the sport had been revived; the dark clouds from the past years of the Australian motor racing industry blown away by the thunderous crack of 31 V8s.

That's what this sport is all about. Strip away the rhetoric, the bullshit and it becomes simple. The stunning sound of a big block engine is what the punters want – music to the ear, with its glorious roar and raw power. This is one of the major principles CAMS forgot about when they went about changing the rules – not necessarily for the better – and what almost killed the sport.

We started the revolution in 1988, but our Gettysburg moment would not have happened without Wayne Cattach, a great and remarkable man. Shell recruited Wayne for me a couple of years before because they were concerned, and rightfully so, about the state of my business and decided I needed help. I was a race car driver, not a businessman, and the size of my outfit had outgrown my ability to do paperwork.

After 19 years with Shell, working both here and aboard, Wayne lobbed in my workshop, shocked with what he found.

'Mate, you have a brilliant race team,' he said. 'Full of bright, enthusiastic and hardworking people, but your business is shit. You might win races, but you won't make money.'

Wayne was a godsend. He came in and fixed the figures, balanced the sheets and increased the bottom line, restructuring DJR and turning it into a formidable financial force. Soon after, he turned his attention to the organisation born in a wharf, which at that time was powerless and without bite.

'TEGA won't go anywhere the way it is,' he said. 'The structure's all wrong. The concept is right, but we need to dismantle the whole thing and rebuild it. That's the only way it'll work.'

So Wayne ripped it apart and restructured the hastily formed organisation into a powerful motorsport authority, becoming the first chairman, responsible for changing the sport forever. In fact, he was so good that we eventually lost him, the former sales and marketing man going on to become the CEO of the sport. Our loss was V8's gain and, later, our pain.

Craig Who?

I grabbed the radio and let loose.

'John,' I screamed, 'there's no way you're going to let some snotty-nosed kid beat you. '

I was furious. With only 14 laps to go, some 20-year-old Bathurst rookie had just ballsed his way past Bowe towards Mountain Straight. I couldn't believe it.

'Who the hell is this kid?' I said, panic rising in my voice.

Turns out this kid was called Craig Lowndes.

'Pull your bloody finger out,' I continued to roar at John. 'We're not losing to a nobody!'

We went into Bathurst 1994 full of confidence. The Touring Car Championship had been going up and down, but we had scored an emphatic victory at Sandown and arrived at Mount Panorama ready to roll. All was good.

Until we hit the track.

'This car is shit,' I realised after the first practice session.

The EB Falcon, backed by Shell, was unbalanced, down on power and a shadow of the car it should have been. It was never a world-beater, but we had developed the machine to the point where it was meant to be a serious contender. Ross and Jimmy Stone worked their rings out, trying to sort the car out.

Nothing changed.

For two days the EB was an absolute heap of junk. The best we could do in the shootout was tenth, which was more my fault. I was going OK until I clobbered a concrete wall.

Heads were down, egos flattened. We were a long way off the pace and despite tireless work, and 101 theories, we didn't have a clue how to improve the car. I almost gave up there and then. I went back to my motel and slammed my head into the pillow. But I couldn't sleep, tossing and turning all night. Tortured by what was to come.

I arrived at Bathurst on Sunday morning a defeated man. I jumped into the car for the pre-race practice session and steeled myself for despair. Hitting the accelerator, I floored towards the first corner and then tugged at the wheel. The car did exactly as I asked. I powered up the straight, all punch and push. The EB Falcon danced across the Mountain, a high-octane ballerina with balls. I flew down the straight and pitted.

Ross and Jimmy smiled.

I don't know how they did it, but the two clued-up Kiwis had fixed my car. The darkness at the end of the tunnel was gone, replaced by a brilliant white light. I wanted to kiss them both but I didn't, of course. That would have been poofy. Instead, I slapped them on the arses and looked to Bowe.

'It's go-time,' I said. 'We're back in this thing.'

And we were. I was about to put a lap on this upstart Lowndes, who just three years before had begun his career in a Formula Ford. I was 50 metres away from passing the HRT recruit when a safety car was called.

Craig Lowndes, born on 21 June 1974, had won the Formula Ford Championship in 1993. His success in the open-wheeled class scored him a test drive with the Holden Racing Team. He was a surprise Bathurst entrant, and that's all I knew about him. I never considered him a threat.

Not until 14 laps to go.

With a move we had never seen before at Bathurst, he'd charged past Bowe. 'You get him back,' I demanded.

The commentators were in shock.

'This kid is dynamite,' they said. 'Never have we seen a rookie do this.'

With my verbal spray fresh in his ears, Bowe took the bit between his teeth. He hunted and hounded, never leaving the back of the widest Commodore ever seen, for a brutally stressful lap. Bowe was right on his arse, coming into the straight. A back-marker, the No. 42 Commodore, caused Lowndes to baulk, if only for moment. But it was all JB needed. Seconds later, he gobbled up the unknown at Hell's Corner, taking the lead and restoring order.

I was a wreck.

There were 11 laps to go now, and the difference between victory and defeat was up to a bloke who often walked around my house practically naked. In an attempt to relax, I shrugged my shoulders and took a deep breath.

After the next lap, it was clear that the fight was over; Bowe pulling away as the kid dropped off. I think HRT might have been struggling for fuel or something was up with their tyres, but that was their problem, not mine.

Bowe crossed the finish line and I had won my third Bathurst title. I jumped in the air, hugged and kissed everyone on my team. *Again*. I had won two here before, but the thrill was as good as the first. *Nirvana.*

I was now an old man, still determined and fierce, but there were days when I thought I was spent. To stand on the podium, to reclaim the sport's ultimate prize, was justification for all the battles we had fought, and all the shit we had dragged ourselves through.

Needless to say, we partied hard. But still I gave it to Bowe for being passed by Lowndes. 'Man, I can't believe a kid almost had you beat,' I said.

Lowndes later admitted that the spectacular pass was a complete mistake. He went to slam down the brake but grabbed the throttle instead. Regardless, he showed true talent and determination, and through this heart-stopping race, I had witnessed the birth of another legend of our sport, even though I hardly knew him back then.

I knew much more about another rookie who made his Bathurst debut in 1994.

He was Steven Johnson. SJ. Junior. My son.

Steve

'Thanks very fucking much, Dad,' Steve said, moments after I told him I had hired Cameron McConville to drive my second car at Bathurst in 1993. 'That's just great!'

Steve thought he had scored a seat in my second EB Falcon after a good showing at Lakeside, when I tested a few young guns. He hadn't.

While he showed plenty of pace and potential, young McConville was quicker, and he got the gig over my son. Clearly, Steve wasn't terribly pleased and he begrudgingly came to Bathurst to join the pit crew, changing tyres, washing windscreens and pouring fuel. Watching on as McConville charged around Mount Panorama fired Steve up, and made him desperate to work on his driving to land a seat for the following year.

I'd always thought Steve would follow in my footsteps and become a race car driver. As a kid, he would hang out in the garage, watching me work on my cars. Steve, the toddler, grabbed at hammers, wrenches and whatever else he could reach, doing his best to lend a hand.

Steve had a little blue pedal car, which he rode every day, blasting down the steep driveway at frightening speed. He would turn and slide at the bottom, getting the thing up on two wheels, which given this daily ritual was quickly worn down from hard plastic to steel core.

I never pressured him to race. Not once. I told both him and my daughter Kel that I would support them no matter what. All I asked was that they choose something they were good at and to give it their best shot. Steve cut his teeth in karts. I thought his motorsport career was over when he asked me for a car.

'I'll have a Suzuki Vitara,' he asked after passing his HSC.

'You'll have a what?' I shouted.

'Yeah, a little soft-top mini 4WD,' he said. 'You know, a Vitara.'

I looked him up and down. 'You are yuppie wanker,' I said. 'But whatever. A Vitara, it is.'

As an incentive for Steve and Kel to do well at school, I offered to buy them each a car if they passed their leaving exams. Kel passed easily and we got her a Ford Laser, a neat little girlie car.

Steve, on the other hand, wasn't much of an academic achiever, but he worked hard – and I ended up buying him a neat little girlie car too! I gave up on him becoming a race car driver the day he brought it home. But three days after buying the poof mobile . . .

Bang!

He was crunched. A car came from nowhere and T-boned the Vitara, turning it into a wreck of twisted metal. Thankfully he wasn't hurt.

'You have three options,' I said. 'The insurance company has said they will replace it with a brand-new car. We could do that, or we could have them pay out the policy, then we buy the wreck and rebuild it ourselves. That way you can keep the change. Or we could buy an old shitter for you to drive around in, and spend the rest on a race car. I'll give you a couple of days to decide.'

'I don't need a couple of days,' he said. 'Let's get the shitter. I want to race.'

We bought Steve a Datsun 1600 and his career was born. We put a 12-A rotary in the little four-door boxy-looking car, and off he went. He showed talent and skill from the get-go, blasting his way to twelfth position in the 1993 Australian Sports Sedan Championship, where he raced against more experienced drivers with better gear.

This was the same year I invited him to test for an endurance drive, but he just wasn't good enough. However, his despair was to be short-lived.

'You're going to be driving the endurance rounds,' I said to him, sometime in 1994. 'Oran Park, Sandown and Bathurst.'

Steve was over the moon.

And so, my son made his V8 debut in 1994, at Oran Park, where he qualified twelfth, impressive for a rookie who had driven the car in testing just twice. Meanwhile, I had been going like a busted with a couple of DNFs in the previous rounds and I ragged my way to fifth in the pre-race session.

'What's that all about?' Steve asked. 'You were driving bad, down in the dumps, and all off a sudden I come along and you find your form!'

He may have given me a bit of motivation because there was no way I could let him beat me. It was a strange feeling to be racing against my son. I was proud, but still very focused on my job. We didn't cross paths on the track, although I did keep an eye out for him, occasionally catching a flash. He ended up in eleventh and I thought it was an outstanding debut. I finished third, the young buck refuelling my rusty tank.

I didn't give Steve a pep talk before the race, or a big emotional speech. That's not my style. I just looked him in the eye.

'Boy, I don't mind if you have a scrap,' I said. 'But make sure you don't bang with me or Bowe. The golden rule in racing is you don't hit anything sporting the same paint.'

I may have been his dad, but I think JB was his mentor. Steve thought I drove like an old man, all right arm on the windowsill, sitting back on a couch. John Bowe used to get right up on the wheel, ripping and tearing at close quarters, always looking busy. Steve wanted to be like him, not me.

Bowe basically lived at our family house for 11 years. Hailing from Tasmania, he stayed in our spare room for weeks at a time. He was renowned for waking up at 3 am and grabbing a drink from the fridge, wearing nothing but his lucky red undies. Seriously, he only owned and wore one pair. Steve survived this nightmarish scene and JB became another father-figure for my son.

I suppose it's never easy taking advice from your dad; as a kid you always think you know better. It's also hard giving advice as a dad, because you worry about placing too much pressure and too many expectations on your greatest love. Steve really listened to JB and they became extremely close. I really have to thank JB for what he did for my kid.

Of course, I was accused of nepotism from the start. A lot of people thought the only reason Steve got this opportunity was because he was my son, and it's this 'jobs for the boys' criticism we've been copping ever since.

It is complete bullshit, and they can all go and get stuffed.

Steve got a drive because he was good, plain and simple. I overlooked him in 1993 because he wasn't ready, but in 1994 he was. His racing times should have immediately shut everyone up. He finished seventh at Bathurst in his Mount Panorama debut, and I think that silenced some.

I am a family man above everything. I love my wife, love my kids and love my friends. I also love all those people who have worked for me and have been loyal over the years. In the end, life is nothing without the people around you, and I am blessed to have had an incredible bunch. I make no excuses for being loyal to the important people in my life. I will always fight for them, and my fans.

By 1995, Steve was offered a full-time position from Garry Rogers Motorsport to join their emerging team, but SJ knocked it back. So GRM went and hired their second choice, future champion and now HRT driver Garth Tander, who has gone on to become quite the gun.

I honestly think Steve should have taken their offer. I reckon it was his biggest mistake and this would have given him the chance to free himself from my shadow. But he was loyal and desperate to drive with me at Bathurst, and I didn't want to say anything to him or try to influence his decision. It was his dream – mine too – and SJ knew that if he left he would never get the opportunity.

I was a year-to-year prospect by 1995. I had started thinking about retirement and only three things were keeping me going: Peter Brock, my sponsors, and the chance of driving at Bathurst with my son.

Brock and I were the same age and had such a big and famous rivalry that I thought I could have the last victory by outlasting him. I was also being pressured by my sponsors to keep going; a lot of the team's income depended on me being in the car. I had to put DJR in front of me.

When SJ turned down GRM, he knew he'd have to wait in the wings at DJR. Bowe was well established and not going anywhere, and so Steve knew he wouldn't get a full-time drive until I retired. If he wanted to wait, that was his choice. I don't think he suspected I would go for another four years!

26

TOO OLD TO DRIVE

Finished

I suited up, grabbed my helmet and opened the truck door. I looked down and the ground was a river, the rain belting down so hard it looked like the water was actually shooting from the puddles and firing into the sky.

I went to take step, just 20 metres between me and the garage where my car waited, primed and pumped.

Stunned and silent, I couldn't move.

I checked myself, shook my head and stepped into the pouring rain. Forcing myself to put one foot in front of the other, I dragged my body, which seemed as though it was anchored to the truck, to the garage.

I was numb and utterly drenched when I arrived in the pits, which were a hive of activity, all busy bees and roaring metal. I looked at my car and froze again.

And that's when it hit. I was having a panic attack.

A whisper crept into my ear. 'You don't want to drive.'

I shook my head again in an attempt to shake the voice off.

'YOU DON'T WANT TO DRIVE,' it screamed, furious I had tried to ignore it.

This time I listened, and left with no choice.

I was totally spent and exhausted.

And for the first time in my life I was afraid to get behind the wheel.

It was 1997, on a dark and extremely wet day on Phillip Island, when I knew my time was up. I didn't want to get in the car. I was seriously afraid I would lose control on the drenched racetrack, firing off at high speed into who knows what.

I wanted to retire then and there, but I couldn't. I jumped in the car and fought on, battling my fear, even though I felt like a shadow of the driver I once was.

Every sportsperson has to confront the end. Retirement is as certain as taxes and death. Age eventually weakens the body, reflexes fade and muscles deteriorate. You can't compete when your body burns and your joints ache. The young are full of energy, enthusiasm and what could be. The old are tired and weak.

But for me, aged 52 in 1997, it wasn't so much my body letting me down, but my mind.

I was still fit. Fast-forward to 1999 and I was one of the few drivers who were left standing at the end of a gruelling V8 Supercars debut in Adelaide in 40-degree heat, the rest of the field retiring to ice baths and drips. I jumped out of the car and signed autographs for an hour.

But mentally I was fried. My motivation had gone, and in my head, I was struggling. I couldn't pinpoint one driving skill I had lost.

These signs of mental fatigue were already showing as early as 1994. Rushing into a corner at 250 k/h, I no longer had the nerve to go that extra ten metres before hitting the brake. I would slam my foot down early, not brave enough to risk not making the turn. I had lost trust in my ability, and in this sport that can prove the difference between coming first or last.

It came to a point where I began questioning myself. I really thought I would screw up if I pushed myself too hard. The only thing that gave me a jolt was my 1994 Bathurst win, momentarily giving me the confidence to go on. Still, the sense of an ending loomed large, even though it would take me a long time to reveal my feelings. I suppose people close to me could see it at the time, though they wouldn't dare to bring it up.

I didn't believe in myself, although plenty believed in me.

1995 was a trying year, the Kobe earthquake in Japan destroying the Dunlop factory contracted to supply us with our specialised tyres. Dunlop went to the ends of the earth to supply us with rubber, eventually finding us some wheels in the UK, but the tyres we got were no good, either too hard or too soft for the Australian tracks.

Despite these difficulties, Bowe delivered DJR with another championship, and I was very happy for him. We gave him a great car and he was an accomplished driver on the rise, truly tremendous.

But I was already done. I would have given him a run five years before, but in 1995, I was a spent force, and was really only good at two tracks – Lakeside and Bathurst – which I knew like the back of my hand. There, I was more than happy to jump behind the wheel, and could match it with Bowe, Skaife and Lowndes. Even now, pushing 70, I could give Jamie Whincup and Mark Winterbottom a run at those two tracks.

The writing was on the wall: the young guns were appearing and I was fading.

Looking back, I should have retired in 1994 after my Bathurst win, when I'd defied my wearying mind and body to pull off the sport's biggest coup against all odds. Not many sportspeople get to go out with a fairytale finish and that could have been my chance.

It would have been a fitting finale. It also would have given Steve the opportunity he deserved. He had matured, was ready for the drive and, unlike me, was confident in his abilities. Instead I went on and did little: the Eastern Creek 12-hour event win in a Mazda RX-7 alongside Bowe. The next four years hurt me, and they also hurt Steve. I honestly think he would have become a champion had he been given a full-time drive in 1995. It is one of my greatest regrets to this day.

But my hands were tied back then. I was only a team boss, and my sponsors called the shots. They wanted star power, with Bowe and me to lead. And that's what we did. Well, until JB did a deal elsewhere on the quiet and ended an 11-year association. But more on that in a minute.

First, let's relive the best things that happened to me post-1994, including the moment I finally got to drive with my son Steve at Bathurst.

Maybe the proudest moment of my life.

Cat's in the Cradle

Steve, who had been waiting patiently in the wings for years after rejecting offers to go elsewhere, had two dreams: to drive with me at Bathurst, and to take over from me when I retired so he could continue the Johnson legacy in the famous No. 17 car.

One of the greatest days in my life was telling him that one of those dreams was about to come true.

'Steve,' I said. 'It's time for you to step up. We're going to race the endurance season together.'

I was beaming as Steve kept his emotions in check. He knew he was ready and had accomplished everything required to team up with his dad, having done a great job in his three years as a Bathurst co-driver, and had earned his spot along-side me. I'd had a partnership with JB for ten years up to this point; now it was time for me and my son to have ours.

Practically it made sense. In terms of physical appearance, Steve and I were pretty close, sharing about the same height and build, which made swapping seats easy. I'd also paired JB up with young gun McConville, who were also similarly built. I thought I was doing JB a favour by teaming him up with someone other than me – I was on the decline, whereas both he and Cam were on the rise.

Shell, our major sponsor, agreed with the move. There was obviously mileage in the whole father-and-son thing, but it wasn't about publicity for me. I wouldn't have done it if I didn't think Steve was ready, and I truly believed I was giving our team's two partnerships an equally good chance of taking out the greatest race in Australia.

Bowe was kept in the loop the entire time, and told me he supported the move. Privately, he might have thought otherwise.

This was a golden opportunity for Steve – if he did a good job of it, he'd have the chance to eventually take over from me and earn a full-time seat in the car. I made that clear to him.

'You have to step up,' I said. 'You have to do everything right. This is your chance to prove yourself and the time for you to make your mark. If you do badly, it could all be over, and I don't want that. People already think you got the drive because you're my son, but I want them to see that you have the ability that I know you possess, that you've shown to me.'

The rising pressure we predicted was piled on before the race. The media made a big deal of the father–son duo, and rightly so. It's not often a father takes the sporting field with his son, very rarely at the biggest event the sport has to offer. It would be like Wayne Pearce playing a grand final in the same team as his NSW State of Origin son Mitchell.

Steve and I did all the press, posing for pictures and dealing with the hype for our first partnership in the 1998 Bathurst 1000. I was very concerned about the faceless people whispering 'nepotism', and in a sport like ours, people were always going to take a shot. I knew Steve had earned his drive, and so did all the serious motorsport people that bothered to look at his previous times and results.

Still I was worried for my son.

'Mate, this is a big deal,' I told him. 'This could make or break your career.'

So Steve went out and proved the knockers wrong. In the lead-up to Bathurst 1998, his times were as good as mine, sometimes even better. He had stepped up to the plate, showing everybody he had a big future in motor racing, competing with and even beating me at a place where I still felt I was at my best.

The day of the race finally came, and we were going along fine, everything running to plan, when we were struck down.

Bang!

From nowhere Steve was clobbered.

The flags were out at Forrest's Elbow, and Steve hung out wide trying to avoid the mess, when he was T-boned by Tony Longhurst, who came through fast and without control.

I was shitty. Not with Steve but with the result. Bathurst is my Mecca. *My* race. And I was totally filthy with the crash and the subsequent DNF. JB and Cameron also didn't finish, ending off a horror year.

It was the last day of the event, and I felt that I was over racing and needed some space. I slammed the door on the truck and stormed out of there. I'd already decided that the following year, 1999, would be my final year, when I'd give myself one more chance.

Bye-bye, Bowe

I finally worked up the courage to confront my Bathurst disaster and walked into my truck two weeks after the heartbreaking failure. I trudged up the stairs, unlocked the transporter and started thinking about the year ahead.

My first job was to pull out the now stinking race gear and

give it to Jillie to clean. I opened my locker and threw my mouldy suit, undergarments, gloves to the floor.

I then pulled open JB's door.

It was empty.

'What the hell,' I fumed. 'Where's his gear?'

For 11 years I'd been taking all the smelly race garments and giving them to my wonderful wife Jillie, who'd wash, press and returned them good as new. I'd normally do this the day we returned to Brisbane, but this time I waited weeks, such was my despair with what had happened.

Never had JB's gear not been in the truck. He was a lazy bugger, didn't do anything that could be done for him. I got straight on the phone.

'What the fuck is going on?' I demanded. 'I just went to the truck and your gear's gone.'

'Nothing,' he said. 'I just took it out.'

I pressed him, knowing he was talking shit. 'Nup, I'm not buying it,' I said. 'You're leaving, aren't you?'

JB beat around the bush for a while, telling me he had an offer he was considering, but I knew immediately he was gone. He wouldn't have cleared his gear unless he had a done deal.

Turns out he did sign on with someone else months ago. He'd been secretly going to Perth to test with a bloke who had offered him the world. I don't know how much he had offered JB to drive the Caterpillar Ford, but it must have been more than the 100K or so a year I was paying him, huge money back then.

I cracked it.

'That is low,' I said. 'You were part of this team, part of this family. How could you do this?'

344

I considered JB to be one of my best mates. He was my son's mentor and a bloke I would have done anything for. I wasn't angry at what he did, but at how he did it. If he came up to me and told me he wanted a new challenge or had a bigger offer, I would have understood. I would have tried to talk him out of it, but ultimately I would have sent him away with my best wishes and understanding.

But I could not cop him being secretive and underhanded. I told him to get fucked.

It hurt like hell. I thought he was the future of the DJR team and rated him highly as both a person and a driver. My retirement also depended on him being part of DJR and Shell hit the roof when they found out, trying to make me reconsider my plan to quit in 1999. That wasn't going to happen. JB had always been a team player and I couldn't understand what he had done. I wiped him there and then, and we didn't speak for years, at least not as friends.

I was now left to find a replacement – Steve, the obvious choice. But the oil giant disagreed and demanded a name, so they chose Paul Radisich, a bloke I was never keen on.

Paul was a handy steerer, but he was always hard on equipment and I didn't think he was a star. He had driven for me before and I didn't feel he was up to the job. I was left with no choice, and Shell got their way. 'The Rat', as Paul was known, was my teammate for my final full year, not that my swan song was certain until the bitter end.

I had planned to go out with a bang, and had organised a busy schedule of dinners and farewells. But JB was a big part of my exit strategy and all of that was tossed in the bin when he left unexpectedly.

I eventually forgave JB and we are now mates. He's a great bloke and still a terrific driver but he made a horrible choice. He will openly tell you that if you ask.

27

BUSTED, BROKE AND BITTER

The Storm Begins

Now comes the part of the story where I lose nearly everything I own: my boat, my house, my factory, my famous cars and my health. My dignity. The sad tale of an ex-race car driver who was conned out of $9.1 million and left in a long battle to save his beloved race team. It hurt then and it still hurts now. I can't wait for the pain to go away, but I suspect it won't. I'm sure it will eventually kill me.

It might floor you to know that I haven't drawn a wage from my business since 2008. Some people think I'm a rich racing legend, worth a fortune. But my wife and I have been living on a paltry sum – just enough to cover for food, petrol and bills. Sometimes I have something left over to fly Jillie to watch our son Steve race. My only income comes from the factory space I rent to the team. I have nothing else. I lost it all in a dodgy deal.

I was happily retired and things were going well. I had two cars racing and my son Steve was finally behind the wheel. As a driver, I was totally done. A lot of sportspeople regret the day they retire, struggling to deal with losing the adrenaline rush and reluctantly fading away from the burning bright light. Some spiral into a world of hurt and regret. My mate John Bowe was one of those. He was diagnosed with depression once he called it quits, and continues to deal with the illness to this very day. I had no such concerns.

After four decades behind the wheel, I was well and truly finished and never wanted to return, even though I was forced into a one-off cameo in 2000. I suppose having Steve replace me helped me deal with the end. Through him and my team, I was still able to be closely involved in a sport I truly loved, putting my energy into preparing race cars and giving Steve every possible chance. I was in a unique position because I was able to relive all my highs and lows through my son. Steve ensured the Johnson legacy didn't end with me. I was able to stand in pit-lane, smell the rubber, feel the rumble and cheer on my boy. It was quite special.

Still, I think I robbed Steve of his most important years. He sat on the sidelines waiting for me to retire for six seasons, and I think he was quite overwhelmed when his opportunity finally came. Steve didn't know what it would take to compete for an entire season and struggled to find the consistency and commitment required to be the best in this sport. He was much better during his second year, working on his fitness and skill, and went on to win his first race.

The first blow, a mere jab compared to the uppercuts that would follow, came in 2000 when I lost my good friend and general manager Wayne Cattach to V8 Supercars. Wayne was the best operator I had ever met. Appointed by Shell, he walked into my garage at Acacia Ridge one day, and I threw him the keys to the factory and my chequebook.

'It's all yours, mate,' I said on my way out. 'I'm off to the UK to buy some bits to make us go fast. You take care of the rest. Oh, and by the way, you need to hire a driver to race with us at Bathurst. See ya.'

Wayne was shocked. He didn't even know who drove for us, let alone who was on the market. But he was an extremely talented man, responsible for transforming my business into a V8 powerhouse. I was never one to live beyond my means and only spent what I had to; I never lived large. Wayne was the first person to think of my financial state, coming in and restructuring my business and life so that I could one day walk away and be able to survive.

With limited notice, Ross Palmer booted us from Acacia Ridge. I had been fortunate for so long to have had his backing, never having to worry about rent, since he'd allowed me to set up my race team workshop at his Brisbane-based plant. One day he decided he was no longer able to do this, and his executives asked me to leave. It was quite a shock and we could never work out what his reasons were. We later found out he was quite ill.

Wayne went about building me a factory that would not only be for my business, but gradually become my nest egg. He wanted to ensure I had some sort of financial security, constructing a state-of-the-art facility for my race team that the business would pay off and would also act as my superannuation fund should anything go wrong. With my blessing he built a $1.3 million V8 super factory at Stapylton, Brisbane. It wasn't only a workshop but a museum that was open to the public and housed all of my famous cars, the attraction of which brought in revenue.

Wayne also restructured and re-engineered the business to a point where we could not only go fast, but also make some money. I had always put whatever spare change we made back into the cars to make them go even faster, and Wayne's motorsport background meant he understood my desire. He gave me what I needed to build competitive cars but was also able to financially manage things so some money went into the factory to create an asset for my future. I only took a moderate wage from the business, just enough for me and my family to live each day.

He was the best operator in the business so it was no surprise when V8 Supercars came knocking and asked him to be the sport's CEO. It was a blow for me, but Wayne wasn't about to leave me high and dry. He went out and recruited his successor, Steve Horton.

Horton was with me for the next two years and was an extremely good business operator just as Wayne had promised. He was an accountant, a brilliant one at that, but had no background in motorsport. Horton was all about the bottom line and was more interested in making money than having the team win races. We suffered on track as a result, but our bank balance boomed. I had $4 million in the bank by 2002 and the factory was completely paid off, totally mine.

I wasn't fussed about bank balances or bricks and mortar, and had always thought we should have been spending money on better cars for our drivers SJ and Radisich, who really didn't stand a chance because we weren't investing enough in the machinery. So in that very same year, I began talking to Steve Chalker, a Carlton & United Breweries (CUB) executive, who I had met through events like the VB challenge. All of a sudden he became very interested in my business, telling me what I should and shouldn't do. He shitcanned Steve Horton, claiming he was doing a terrible job. Despite the money in the bank, I agreed. I eventually hired Steve Chalker to be my general manager in 2002.

It was the worst mistake of my life.

Everything began to unravel in 2004, an uppercut rocking me and leaving me dazed and desperate. The sneaky right came from nowhere.

'We're out,' said Chris, a Kiwi, who was in charge of Shell's motorsport operations at the time. 'We're pulling the plug.'

It was in my office where he'd matter-of-factly broken to me that I'd lost $2.5 million a year. Shell had changed the way they did business and were now running on an international model. Chris told me they were scaling things back in Australia and my multimillion dollar deal was done.

I had four months to find someone to rescue my team.

Westpoint

DJR announced Westpoint, a finance company from Western Australia, as our saviour on 8 February 2005. It was a last-minute $12 million four-year deal that was to ensure our survival until 2008.

Or that's what I thought.

Chalker had sourced the deal through his next-door

neighbour Steve Wooldridge, a Queensland-based entrepreneur who operated a call centre. Westpoint was a property development business that raised finance to fund all their projects, using Wooldridges's call centre to source the money, mostly from mums and dads investing in their scheme. I knew little of the business and was simply relieved to find a company, worth an estimated $1.7 billion, to back me for the next four years. I didn't care where Chalker had found the money, or how he had gotten it, although it was Wooldridge who was responsible for putting Westpoint and DJR in touch.

I had no concerns about Westpoint and no reason whatsoever to think of them as anything other than a legitimate backer that was going to help our race team. We whacked their liveries on our cars and sent SJ and Glenn Seton out in the Westpoint-backed machines for the 2005 season.

DJR had enjoyed limited success over the past four seasons and after parting ways with Radisich, we punted on Brazilian Max Wilson in 2003 and then Warren Luff in 2004. We thought we were headed in the right direction and stable with a new eleventh-hour giant replacing Shell. Seton was also a big-name driver on the rise, and although we hadn't got the results we wanted in past seasons, we were ready for a big year in 2006.

Boom!

Without warning the blast that would forever change my life went off on 5 December 2005. I was told that Westpoint was about to go bust and my four-year deal was gone, just ten months after entering it. Turns out Westpoint were raising mezzanine funds that constituted a Ponzi scheme; they were using investors' money to pay off their interest. In short, they were a fraudulent company ripping the shirts of people's backs. I had no idea. Westpoint went into receivership on 2 February 2006, with 3542 people losing their money in an absolute disaster of a company. I was ashamed to be involved with them when the full extent of their operations were revealed.

But for me, at the end of 2004, I was left with just a month to save my team.

That's when my GM Chalker and his mate Wooldridge approached me with a solution they claimed would never leave me in the lurch again.

'You've now had two sponsors pull out and leave you in the shit,' they said. 'It's obvious you can't rely on something you yourself can't control to run your business. We need to set up a system that will help you service your race team without you having to worry about finding sponsors. We can use the cars to *promote* your business, not to support it.'

I asked them to explain. They told me that there was untold money to be made in the emerging mortgage-broking business, that I could be successful and big, even bigger than John Symond of Aussie Home Loans fame. Wooldridge said he had it all figured out and that his telemarketing company was the key. He had the tool to reach the consumers and he insisted that with my name, we could make a fortune. Wooldridge and Chalker also went on to tell me about the telecommunications business, saying they could use the call centre to broker deals between the consumer and the phone companies and make huge profits.

I was immediately suspicious. I listened to them before calling Wayne Cattach.

'Dick, I've done some research into the mortgage-broking industry,' Wayne said, 'and the people I've spoken to reckon it takes between three to five years just to break even. How you think you can fund your race team through a start-up first-year business in the industry seems impossible. My strongest advice for you would be to find another alternative.'

I told Chalker of my concerns. The very next day both him and Wooldridge were in my office with spreadsheets and PowerPoint proposals. They projected I could earn in excess of $45 million in my first year alone.

I am not a complete fool, but I was utterly desperate. The duo had me convinced. I knew we couldn't find a sponsor for the next year in such a short time and thought this was the only way forward. And although I didn't have to give them any cash, I did end up relinquishing 40 per cent of DJR for a promise and a dream.

Within ten days of losing Westpoint, I was signing papers that formed a new shelf company called Nanterre Pty, which would own FirstRock Mortgage Centre, V8 Telecom, DJR and ICCS (Inter Communications Connections Services). I was a 60 per cent shareholder in the new business, with Chalker holding 10 per cent and Wooldridge 30 per cent. I had given away almost half my race team for a majority stake in two start-up ventures and a call centre that I knew nothing about.

How they could pull the deal together in just ten days astounded me. It would later result in me losing $9.1 million. Before grabbing that pen and signing that contract, I'd owned a $2.1 million property, a $1.3 million factory, and I had $4 million in the DJR bank. I also had an expensive boat and two of the most famous and expensive race cars in the history of Australian motorsport: Tru-Blu, which I'd bought back in 1984, and Greens-Tuf.

I am now fighting to save my team and my house. The rest is lost.

On the Brink

With rookie hot shot Will Davison signed up to join SJ as driver, the promise of $45 million and a future free from reliance on sponsors assured, I entered the 2006 season full of hope and wonder. DJR had endured a few shit years, and while cautious, I had completely put my trust in Chalker and Wooldridge, the same way I had with Cattach a decade before. Steve ran with FirstRock on his car; Will with V8 Telecom. I promoted both businesses, doing whatever I was asked to do. In a scripted media release, I was reported as saying:

When I looked into it, I couldn't believe how much we were being ripped off. It didn't take us long to figure out we could give everyone a fair deal, and V8 Telecom was born . . . V8 Telecom is about reducing the cost of communications and making things easier . . . By entering into strategic part-nerships, V8 Telecom has negotiated wholesale rates with a number of networks so that we can pass the savings to our customers.

I had this to say about FirstRock Home Loans, which was named after my incident with the rock in Bathurst 1980:

Every Australian dreams of owning their own home, and that is something FirstRock can help everyone achieve. With the banks no longer dictating how the home loan market works, organisations like FirstRock now have the opportunity to offer everyone much more competitive rates on home financing . . . I have never forgotten the generosity of ordinary Australians that day [referring to the 1980 Bathurst incident] and have always tried to repay that support. I see FirstRock as another of those opportunities.

I said what I was told, in the belief that it would help me continue with racing and save my business. I was honestly hopeful that being part of these two new companies would give the public some value and also help my team survive. That's what I was told; I was never led to believe anything else.

Not until my money started going missing.

DJR charged through the year, business as usual, and at some point I was informed that the $4 million we had in our account was almost exhausted. I pulled my accountant aside.

'What the fuck,' I screamed at him. 'Where has all of this gone?'

With no satisfactory answer, I charged to Chalker.

I had a bunch of meetings with Chalker and Wooldridge, who together showed me the projections and said all was fine. They had a number of mortgages and future trails, but we had limited funds coming back, not enough to support the race team. They had dipped into the cash we'd held on to in order to keep operating for the year.

I wasn't happy, but I was a racer and the money was there to be spent on the team. I was assured we would soon see a profit and that everything would turn out OK, that the enterprise would become lucrative enough to float the DJR team and I would make whatever I had lost back. I never considered the $4 million in the bank as mine; it was only ever to go towards the team.

Alarm bells started ringing when I found out about a potential deal with Jim Beam. Through his former connections as an alcohol representative for CUB, Chalker had gone about enticing the bourbon brand to become our major sponsor for 2007. That was the first indication I had that our enterprise was on the ropes.

Why do we need to stop promoting our own brands and bring in a sponsor if all is OK? I thought. *Wasn't the whole idea of this that we didn't have to rely on any at all?*

The sirens really blazed when I heard that Chalker had offered the full sponsorship of both the DJR cars for $700,000, which were actually worth upwards of $3 million. It soon became pretty clear that neither FirstRock nor V8 Telecom was making a return and our V8 team would not survive without help. A series of meetings were held, and I was told what I'd been told before: that the business would eventually succeed, and we would achieve our desired goals. But this time, we needed some help in the short term.

Enter Jim Beam.

The US bourbon company was operating from a Sydney office with a staff of about 15 people. Phil Baldock, the Australian CEO, was leading the charge and wanted to become involved in V8s to leverage his brand. Tobacco giants, like Winfield and Marlboro, had once staged a ferocious marketing war using our sport (but had been consequently banned), and the alcohol brands thought they could do the same. Jack Daniels had linked with Larry Perkins the previous year, and now Baldock and Beam wanted in.

We had some discussions, and for them, it was more than sponsorship; lucrative pourage rights at events were on the line. Jack Daniels was reaping benefits both on and off the track.

Seven had just signed a $70 million six-year deal to join Australia motor car racing, and the future for the industry was looking bright. But Chalker had signed a paltry agreement with Jim Beam worth $700,000 a year, which wasn't even enough to support one car for six months. Too late. The deal had been done.

The Jim Beam staff, especially Baldock and Ray Noble, were very professional. We opened our books to them, and they came in and examined the business to make sure everything worked all right with their new major investment.

At our launch for 2007 at Melbas on the Gold Coast, young Jim Beam staffer Kel Constantine walked up and gave me a nod and a wink.

'Your future is assured until 2012,' she said. 'We'll make sure of that.'

It became apparent that the $700,000 a year contract meant little. Jim Beam knew it was grossly undervalued and were prepared to tip in as much as it took to get a return on their investment. That was a relief, momentarily, because they didn't know the future of my business was tied up in a shelf company that was set to collapse. Jim Beam didn't have enough money to save me, but I did – even if it was going to cost me everything I had as well as putting me into a debt I am still paying off.

Shit Hitting Fans

Chalker and Wooldridge approached me during the 2007 season and finally revealed how bad things had become. I won't quote them, but to paraphrase they told me they were up shit creek and the business was about to go bust.

They also admitted that they had taken out a $1.1 million mortgage on my workshop, the V8 super factory Cattach had set up to be my super fund. Apparently I had signed the documents, but I honestly had no idea. The money had been put back into the business and was keeping us afloat – for now. Chalker and Wooldridge had also enlisted a long line of creditors to prop up the enterprise, but they still couldn't pay their loans and could no longer get money. They told me my race team was gone, unless I could find some funds.

So in total, I'd already lost $4 million in savings, another $1.1 million on my workshop and nest egg, and now all I had to offer was my house and my cars. I took out a $2.1 million mortgage on my house. That was a lifeline for the moment.

But what I had to do next almost killed me.

I had to sell the cars that had made my name. The sweat-stained and battle-worn beasts that had made me the man I am.

My life's work and my trophies.

28

WHETEVER IT TAKES

Hey, Tru-Blu . . . I'm Going to Miss You

I walked through my garage, the front foyer that was now a museum: glass cabinets, trophies, news clippings and cars. The fluorescents slowly lit up the room, the fading sun retreating behind the cane fields and scrub.

I ran my hand over Tru-Blu, the car that had delivered me my first Bathurst title. A rock had ruined her the year before the life-changing win, but thanks to the public and their donations, she was sitting there, reflecting the dying rays of sunlight, looking as though the boulder that had almost destroyed her and my career had never been, while the 30-kg rock sat in a cabinet three metres away.

I turned to Greens-Tuf: the car that had almost seen me killed. I slapped at the hard cold steel that had saved my life.

I then looked at the Sierras, those tricky and troublesome cars that eventually helped me secure two championship wins and a Bathurst title. The smell of grit and determination still clung to the seat's fabric, a strangely pleasant stench. They were covered in the growing gloom, the sun gone, the fluorescents not enough to cut through the dark.

The Mustangs and the 1994 Falcon that took me to my third Bathurst win were slowly disappearing into the creeping darkness. Bowe's championship charge and an assortment of other memories – some failures, some triumphs – were slowly consumed by the black.

I paced around them, nervous steps, my stomach tied in knots.

They had to go. I was broke and busted and left without a choice. I picked up the phone and agreed to sell them all for $1.1 million.

Today Tru-Blu and Greens-Tuf are priceless; the rest of the cars are worth at least $10 million, although no one can actually settle on their true value, 'shitloads' being the accepted amount.

I had mortgaged my house, my factory, my boat and had spent my entire savings – all I had left now were my cars.

I had to sell them. In order to keep my race team alive.

I can still remember the day the sparkling transporter came to pick them up. It was tough, but I didn't cry or kick stones, because the bloke I sold them to, David Bowden, agreed that I would always have access to my cars and be able to keep at least four in my museum. David is a tremendous bloke, who understands what these machines mean to me, sheepskin covers, cracked dashes and all.

I was an absolutely shattered and desperate man when I signed the paperwork. I couldn't believe it had come to this.

It kills me more now, not realising how much they meant to me until they were gone. And although I still get to look at my precious cars, the fact that I no longer own them is just heartbreaking; it feels as if pieces of me are gone.

Looking back, I don't regret the decision because I had no choice. Those two bastards, Chalker and Wooldridge, had put me in a position where I had to compromise either my race cars – relics of my past – or my future. I had about 30 employees: my son one of them. If I hadn't sold the cars, all the people I loved would have been out on the street.

Nanterre Pty was in receivership and the creditors were demanding cash. I had to offer them everything I could, or my business would be done.

Chalker and Wooldridge had declared themselves bankrupt, and I was on my own. The other two failed businesses, FirstRock and V8 Telecom, were dissolved and I thought I had wiped my hands clean of them. Turns out I hadn't. The shelf company owned all four businesses, including ICCS and DJR.

I fronted the duo when everything had gone to shit, and told them the only thing I wanted to keep was my race team, that they could have the rest. I did the paperwork to clear myself of the mess, signing away my rights as a director for all businesses – except for DJR. But low and behold, Chalker and Wooldridge never filed the paperwork, leaving me with their $125,000 tax bill, and to face the angry creditors who had been tipped in the dump.

A receivership company was appointed and they organised a meeting with me and the 50 or so people who had backed the failed enterprise. I was financially exhausted, having sold my cars and assets to give them everything I had. If the creditors weren't to accept my offer, DJR would be gone, and I bankrupt and unable to start again. Meanwhile, Chalker and Wooldridge were out of the picture.

I've had many lows in my life, none more so than walking into a hotel to plead to a bunch of poor sods to take everything I had to give, my famous race team about to die.

Fitzy's Hotel

I drove to Fitzy's Hotel, near Logan, Brisbane on my own, steeling myself for the angry mob I was about to confront. I was utterly embarrassed with the amount I was going to offer them, but that was all I had.

On 8 March 2008, I met my creditors, who had the power to accept my offer, or reject it and kill off a race team that had been around for almost three decades. I walked into a makeshift boardroom, completely shitting myself. Only eight of the 50 or so creditors had turned up, but it was still enough to turn me white.

I sat at the table and the receiver introduced me and my plan, offering a minimal amount of return on the dollar. I was then asked to explain to the creditors what had happened with the failed enterprise and what I could do. Needless to say, they were pissed, asking 'How much?' and 'When will we get it?'. I told them what I had to give.

Thankfully they accepted.

It was damn right embarrassing. And completely terrifying. I felt like an absolute prick having to attend such a meeting, addressing these genuine, down-to-earth people who had trusted something I'd believed in myself.

And it made me sick.

I never for the life of me expected I would be in a situation like this. My parents had always taught me to work for everything I had. Dad was an Irish hardman, who never lived beyond his means, and he instilled the very same values in me. My parents would have been as disgusted as I'd been at what I'd gone through. It just isn't what the Johnsons are about. I had lived by the principle of hard work until Chalker and Wooldridge convinced me to invest in my future and not be reliant on others. I should have known that I could only ever rely on myself.

I walked away from the ball-busting meeting with a debt of $4 million. I had lost everything and was at the mercy of the bank. I could have retired from the sport a rich man in 1999, but all I had now was a multimillion dollar debt.

With DJR in voluntary administration, I had two choices: fold or start again. The administrator told me the business was finished and if I wanted to continue, I'd have to start up a new entity and go from scratch. I suppose the easy thing would have been to give it all away. To cut my losses and run. But I had my employees to think about, good men and women who relied on me. They had families and mortgages and I couldn't kick them out on the street. That is what ultimately made me decide to go on. So I picked myself up from the floor, dusted off my jacket and went about putting a shattered race team back together.

I am 68 now and I look old beyond my years. I am not a

healthy man, the reasons for which mostly stem back to that traumatic period of my life.

From the moment I hooked up with those guys I couldn't sleep, let alone eat. I constantly felt sick in the guts. I never believed in stress; I thought it was a myth. But from that day I have battled through pulsating problems that have made me older than I seem. It's hard to truly understand stress until you've experienced it. Stomach tied in knots, it's completely draining and all consuming. I've been dealing with this feeling for years now and it never seems to go away. I was never a big drinker, but around that time I turned to the bottle to help me sleep and forget my troubles at night.

I suppose I haven't been well since 1990, all those years of driving also taking its toll. I have had nine operations for sinus-related problems, which in the last ten years of my career got so bad that a piece of cloth rag was sewn into my race gloves so I could wipe away the muck pouring from my eyes. At times I couldn't see. I'd burst an eardrum almost every time I'm in the air flying to races, muck flowing everywhere at its worst. The sinus also gave me crippling headaches to the point where sometimes I had to lie down in the truck, buried in complete darkness before I jumped behind the wheel. I was in utter agony, but it never once stopped me from racing.

I am now paying heavily for those accidents and countless laps in my motor racing career. I have a titanium knee and a titanium hip. I have been in and out of hospital for years, dealing with infections and surgeons having to go back in to clean them up. I have been told not to travel, and I shuffle instead of walk. But still, I haven't missed a race.

To this day, I walk with my fists up, readying myself for blows. Every day is a challenge, but I am up for the fight. I know I have aged, I know I'm not well, but I'm determined to continue despite all that's affecting me. My family has kept me strong throughout my trials and tribulations, especially during that traumatic time of my life when everything seemed to have been taken away from me . . .

But amidst this hellish period a little bundle of bliss arrived, making me realise what life was all about.

My grandson Jett was born in March 2005. He is arguably the best thing that has ever happened to me. I was in the deepest shit, feeling completely desperate, and when he came along he made that all go away. I'd sit with him in my arms, and Jett would make me forget about everything else, and I was alive again.

Family is the one thing that has been constant in my life, and young Jett gave me the will to fight on. He is my inspiration, as are Jillie, Steve, Kel, Lacy and my brothers and my sisters. As was Jillie's mum and her dad; my parents too. And, of course, all my mates and lifelong friends.

I also made a quiet promise to myself, one I hope I'll be able to keep. As I walked out of Fitzy's Hotel, I vowed to pay back all those poor people who had lost their money in the failed company. We're not talking millions, and under law I'm not obligated to do anything. But that's not my style. I can't sleep knowing that I caused problems for these people, and if I get back on my feet I will give them every cent back. I dream of the day I will be able to call them into a room and put the money down on the table and apologise. I would love to show them just how much their support meant to me and that I am indeed genuinely sorry.

There's still a long way to go. But where there is life, there is hope.

Things certainly didn't get any easier when I received a phone call from respected News Limited motoring journalist Paul Gover.

'So, what do you think about Ford giving you the flick?' he asked.

'What are you talking about?' I said.

'Sorry, haven't you heard?' he replied. 'Ford have cut your funding. They're only supporting FPR and SBR next year.'

Sure enough, it was true. A Ford official called me soon after and said they were tossing me in the bin after more than 30 years of loyal service. In a cruel and unexpected blow, they wiped another $750,000 from my bottom line.

'You do what you have to do,' he said.

It was bloody rough and I couldn't believe it. I knew times were tough, but surely I had sold them more cars than anyone else in the sport and had done everything I could as a proud Ford warrior.

The reaction from the public was huge. They were outraged. Ford eventually buckled and gave me some minor support, but nothing in the way of cash.

I'm a loyal man, but it seems that that can only get you so far. I would seriously consider switching manufacturers if someone came to me with money and offered me their support. That may seem harsh, but my loyalty did not end up saving me when it came to Ford. I love the brand and the fans, but that was a bloody big blow and I still haven't recovered.

Where There's a Will There's a Way

I first met Charlie Schwerkolt on a plane. It was the mid 1980s and a mutual friend offered me a ride from Melbourne to Winton in his private aircraft after a scrappy and torrid affair. Absolutely beat, I gladly accepted. I was in no mood for a two-and-a-bit-hour drive. I boarded the small plane and sat in my seat.

'G'day,' he said, eyes wide and alert. 'I'm Charlie. Charlie Schwerkolt.'

It was obvious Charlie was a massive motor racing fan. He knew a lot about my career, which wasn't unusual, and as I chatted to him he struck me as a good down-to-earth bloke. We soon became mates, often meeting at races and also talking on the phone. Over the years we formed a solid friendship, and it was clear that his passion for motorsport meant he wanted to become more involved.

By 2008, Charlie was a rich man. He had his current business, Waverley Forklifts, and was living the grand life on the Gold Coast, having relocated from Melbourne. He was quite the businessman and had always done well for himself.

I knew I wasn't going to be able to survive on my own after being forced to start up again. DJR's sponsorship with Jim Beam was worth about $2.2 million a year, and we were receiving about $1.6 million annually in dividends from the Cattach- and Cochrane-led V8 Supercars, both of which were now going gangbusters. With the input of another minor sponsor, that added up to almost $5 million; so we were about $2 million short of what we needed to run a competitive two-car outfit.

All I had left was the factory I owned. It was mortgaged to the hilt, but it was still a booming property that commanded big rent. I was leasing it to the team for $24,000 a month and it was my only source of income. I wasn't drawing a wage from DJR and used that money to service my debt. I was left with only $1500 a month after I paid everything off.

The only way forward was to sell half of my business, and Charlie was willing to play ball; some say he was desperate to get involved. So after some brief discussions, Charlie sent his army in. They came from everywhere, looking my books up and down, studying all my statements and incomes. I thought his 'due diligence' was overkill but I was happy to oblige. I had no skeletons in the closest and everything was above board. I had cleared myself of any liability from the failed enterprise, and aside from my personal debt, the business was what it was.

He eventually agreed to buy half of DJR for a lowball $2 million. It was a small amount considering the Racing Entitlements Contract (REC) he was receiving as part of the deal was returning $800,000 a year in dividends from V8 Supercars alone. For his $2 million he was also buying a half share in the most famous business in the sport and all the equipment and intellectual property I owned, including the machinery, engine-building facilities, tools, cars and a panel shop – I can't even imagine counting up their entire worth. I thought it was a grossly unfair amount, but again I was backed into a corner with my hands up and left with no choice.

The only thing Charlie didn't get was the factory building itself. I owned it – well, the bank did – and it was set up as my superannuation scheme. By law I couldn't offer it for sale and no one could take it.

Having sold Charlie a half-stake in DJR for $2 million momentarily saved my race team. Apart from appreciating the money the deal had brought in, I was hopeful that as a result my mate could also bring in his business expertise and do 'a Cattach' – turn the business into the mighty enterprise it was before the dramatic fall. I wanted Charlie to help resurrect my Roman Empire.

It was March 2008 when a thundering white V8 Supercar at Eastern Creek blew the sense of doom and gloom away. It had been a week or so after I had met with the creditors and saved the business, and I'd still been feeling low and desperate. But the Jim Beam machine we prepared and delivered to the track in the most dramatic of circumstances powered away to one of our famous wins.

A kid called Will Davison delivered DJR our first win in seven years. It was race two of the three-race event and he clobbered the big-name field to record the win, going on to take out the round. I tried to fight back the tears.

'This is motor racing,' I said. 'From the outhouse to the penthouse in one hit.'

Davison cried, letting it all out after his debut win. 'Words can't describe how I feel,' he said. 'Not just for me personally but the whole team. It's amazing and I'm very emotional.'

I was riddled with debt and had only just saved my team, but this kid had come from nowhere and scored a remarkable victory. After years of pain, I finally cried tears of joy.

It seemed like DJR were back on track. We backslapped, hugged and vowed to get on with the job. We had Jim Beam, Charlie, Will and a bloke called Adrian Burgess, who I will speak a lot about in a moment. He was really the man who delivered us the success on track.

First to Will Davison, the kid who broke a seven-year drought with his efforts behind the wheel. Will is a third-generation driver whose grandfather Lex was an open wheeler legend who won the Australian Grand Prix four times. He came to us full-time in 2007 to replace fading force Seton, having run the endurance races for us the year before. Many would have considered it risky giving this young bloke a job, but I didn't.

I first noticed Will in 2004 at the Melbourne Grand Prix. He had scored a drive with Team Dynamic, and after trying to emulate his grandfather in an open wheeler, he strapped down in what would have seemed a difficult and heavy V8 for the first time in an exhibition race.

I thought he was brilliant. His team looked as if it was about to collapse, but in the very next round, Will went out and ragged the wheels off the thing. He managed to push into the top five against the big names of our sport and showed tremendous potential beyond his years. Will shone and made a mark for himself.

I found out Will was looking for a gig after his team folded at Clipsal, Adelaide, through his old man, Richard, who was also a racer. I was more than happy to give him one. Will was young, talented and hungry, and was our man. We signed him on for a three-year deal.

DJR's first victory in almost a decade in 2008 more than validated the decision to sign an unknown. Jim Beam were over the moon and it was such a relief to get the win for them. They had stuck by us and it was so good to see them happy, smiling, and realising we could offer them a return. It was also great for Will. He had only been in the sport for a short time but had done the job in a challenging period, up against the biggest and the best in the sport. He arrived that day and it was clear his future was bright.

Will became part of the DJR family and it was with great regret that we had to let him go at the end of 2008. He was bright and an enthusiastic team player. A star on the rise. But he got an offer from the Holden Racing Team and we just couldn't match it, or dare to stand in his way. Although things were on the up in our team, Will thought that for him and his career, he was better off going to the powerhouse HRT, where he had an opportunity to replace Skaife. Will had aspirations to make it to the top and I totally understood. I really thought it was the best move for him and didn't think we could do anything more to help him with his dream and hoped HRT could.

Of course, I was sad to see him go. But Will and his father Richard were upfront and honest about the move and informed us of every step along the way. As I said of my experience with Bowe, I am OK with anyone's decision as long as they are truthful about it. I am an understanding bloke but can't cop deception and lies.

Will has remained a mate of our team ever since and is still considered to be part of the DJR family and forever will be, no matter where he goes. I think we also earned Will's and his father's respect by not kicking up a fuss and being supportive of the move.

Will's departure was smooth. But the coming of our next driver ended up starting a war, an ugly four-year battle that again has left me fighting for it all. It ended a friendship and almost cost me my team (again). Get ready for the most dramatic, stressful and ugly chapter in my history.

Dick vs. Charlie. Mate vs. mate. Quite possibly what could prove to be the fatal blow.

29

THE FORKLIFT DRIVER, THE DANCING BOY AND THE MINING MAGNATE

Charlie

Charlie walked up to me and surprised me with some news.

'Mate, I've just signed up James Courtney,' he said, of the one-time *Dancing With The Stars* contestant. 'He's going to replace Will.'

'You what?' I said. 'You signed who?'

But I wasn't angry about that.

'We haven't even discussed this and you're telling me you've gone out and signed a driver without me knowing?' I said. 'This is supposed to be a partnership!'

Charlie went quiet.

'Well, what did we get him for?'

'$800,000 a year,' he muttered.

I swore, steam rising from my collar, before turning and walking away.

The amount Charlie had offered was just ridiculous. We

had never paid anything like that for a driver before; I never would've entertained the thought. For a start, we didn't have the money. We were still in a bad way and his outrageous wage would cripple the team. Second, James wasn't worth anything near that. He'd only had a couple of years in the sport and was yet to be a proven product; we could've signed up anyone for that amount.

What shitted me more than anything was the fact that Charlie had kept me out of the loop and had done the deal on his own. We were supposed to be in the business together, and he had gone behind my back and struck some agreement with James's manager Alan Gow – a bloke I'd disliked ever since he was involved with Peter Brock – which made it worse.

I was furious, and that's when the problems between Charlie and me began, leading to the row that would eventually split the DJR team. It was the tip of the iceberg that sank the *Titanic*. It seems to me that Charlie was more obsessed with being around famous people than anything else, and this is probably why he was in the sport. I thought it was a terrible decision and I let him know that.

It's not that I had a problem with James, who's always been someone I've liked. Although he's one of those self-promoting blokes, a little like JB in a way, he's also friendly and funny. James is an accomplished international driver, having started out as a junior karting champion who went on to test F1 cars. He had an opportunity to drive F1 full-time but knocked it back following a horrendous test crash that left him in hospital for a week.

James was with Stone Brothers Racing before he came to me, and I'd often talked to both Ross and Jimmy Stone about him. It was evident James had potential, but he could also be hard work and needed everything to be right. I didn't think we had the right environment for him, and I especially didn't think he was worth $800,000 a year. I mean, that's the type of money Craig Lowndes and Jamie Whincup are paid now.

But the deal was done and I had to live with it.

I tolerated Charlie and his know-all attitude and got on with the job. James turned out to be quite the talent, mainly thanks to his chemistry with our head engineer and race team manager, Adrian Burgess. Adrian had worked with James in Europe and the pair got on like a house on fire. They were great mates and Adrian was able to give him the car he needed. We'd recruited Adrian from the F1 paddock in Europe and he was a brilliant mind who had helped deliver Will's win the year before.

The peace between Charlie and me didn't last long. Again we were standing toe to toe, shouting the house down. Again he had gone behind my back, this time costing me $500,000 a year.

Charlie thought he was a smooth operator and took it upon himself to go to Jim Beam to negotiate new terms. Our deal with the bourbon company was officially up at the end of 2009, but I had their word they would continue until the end of 2012. I was happy with the agreement we'd had and it would have continued for the next three years. That is, until Charlie went in and demanded more cash – an extra $100,000 a year.

Jim Beam didn't like it one bit and ended up playing hardball, reducing the deal by $500,000 a year. He could've just come up to me and asked me what was going on, and I would've told him what I knew and that the deal would take care of itself. Our relationship was completely poisoned and I was left with the job of finding the money he had lost. On top of the $500,000 he had thrown in the bin thanks to our reduced deal with Jim Beam, we also had to foot James's ridiculous wage.

We tried to cut budgets and save where we could, but motor racing is not a cheap sport and you can't financially forecast the unknown. Motorsport is unlike any other business. You can't keep to a budget because of one simple fact: drivers crash cars. What may seem like a little shunt will cost you $30,000. A complete wreck, and I've had more than a few, can cost you hundreds of thousands. And it's not like you can tell your driver to go out and simply bring the car home because you have no cash. You need them to take risks and do well to service your sponsors and guarantee income. It's a razor-sharp double-edged sword.

Charlie and I basically didn't talk from that point on. We had to on occasions, for the sake of the team, but we kept conversations short and terse. Our relationship was slowly disintegrating and I think it began to poison the team. Everyone was aware of the political situation and it must have affected them to some degree.

Whatever relationship we had ended when Charlie told me he wanted to sack my brother, daughter and son. In the greatest insult he could possibly make, he walked into my office one day and told me they all had to go.

'We need to replace Steven with another driver,' he said. 'I reckon I can get someone else who will do a better job.'

'Oh yeah,' I said. 'And who would that be?'

He looked at me nervously. 'Steve Owen.'

'Over my dead body,' I said. 'No one is replacing my son.'

Charlie also had it in for my brother Dyno. Charlie would walk through the entire factory and say hello to everyone but him. He ignored Dyno completely.

Dyno was a jack-of-all-trades who had been with me since day one. He built all the diffs and the gearboxes and also drove and maintained the truck. Both a carpenter and a motor mechanic, he was an invaluable part of the team. Dyno knew that Charlie was after him and had asked me to let him go.

'I'm not going to put up with this shit,' he'd said. 'It just isn't worth it. I'm out of here.'

After more than 30 years by my side, Dyno called it a day. He was so popular, not just within the team but within the sport, that he was given an almighty send-off by the entire pit-lane at his last race in Bahrain. He is still missed.

Charlie also forced out my daughter, Kel. He'd told me she wasn't needed and we had to downsize. Kel looked after the media, ran the shop and worked in the office. At the end of the day she decided to go too. She knew where it was all going and didn't want to get caught up in the nasty politics. Kel wound up getting a good job elsewhere and is doing well.

On top of that, Charlie wanted to get rid of Steve, but I wouldn't have a bar of it.

There's no doubt that the tense atmosphere worsened going into 2010. Charlie and I only talked when we had to and we were skating on thin ice when it came to money.

We didn't have what we needed to get through the year and made do with what we had.

Despite all this, Adrian Burgess was the man who really held it together. He was firmly focused on the job of going fast and rallied the troops for the common aim. Adrian and his family had moved from the UK to start a new life in Australia. He was committed to making our team a success, working long and stressful hours and improving the cars in ways that had never been seen.

When it came to politics, Adrian was on whatever side he had to be on, jumping fences to appease both Charlie and myself. James, on the other hand, was very much on Team Charlie. He was, after all, the man who had brought him to the team and they got along well.

Now, I've spoken a lot about Adrian Burgess and what he did for the team, but I must also give credit to a silent player who was every bit as important.

Mark Woolfrey was an engineering genius. He had been with me for ten years and was brilliant at whatever he did. He was the best CAD drawer I had ever seen and took James's engineer, Scotty, under his wing. Scotty absorbed everything he could from Mark and did a good job. But it was Scotty and Adrian who were given all the credit for the good results when Mark was actually the man.

Mark was a non-confrontational, stand-in-the-corner type of bloke, who tended to let others push him aside. It's quite sad because he deserves as much credit as anyone for the remarkable results we achieved that year. Unfortunately, Mark is no longer with us.

It might amaze you to think we were on track to win the

championship given the shit that was going on behind the scenes in 2010, but we got to a point where DJR was a real contender, following a string of podiums and a couple of race wins. It became clear that we were in with a mighty shot and James Courtney and Jamie Whincup were going to fight it out for the title.

Given the tension between Charlie and me, I found it very hard fronting up to races around that time. We were having our best season in years and outsiders thought all was good, but it was the complete opposite. Charlie and I continued to be as cold as ice to each other but put on a show for the media and the fans, and though this was certainly uncomfortable for the team, they still tried to enjoy the year. Winning is an extraordinary thing and it can put a bandaid over even the deepest of cuts. The team ignored all the shit that was flying and ploughed on with their job. Well, until Bathurst . . .

The Bathurst Bombshell

The smouldering campfires filled the air with the sweet smell of exhausted wood. The early morning frost sent my nose numb as the sun edged over the top of the Mountain, stirring the hangovers and frozen tents to life. People rose, yawning and stretching, grabbing at their chairs and eskies, dragging them down to the edge of the track to witness the latest instalment of crashes and carnage, of heartbreaks and horrors. Of glory and legend.

As always, Bathurst was electric. The picture-perfect scene of restless punters and fading frost evoking memories of all the trials and tribulations that have defined my life.

I stopped for a moment and savoured the sights. I thought I was walking into one of the best chapters of my career. We were leading the championship, but I didn't care about that. I was at Bathurst and we had the car, the driver and the team to win. I wanted this one . . . more than anything.

And then I was floored.

'I'm not going to be here next year,' said Adrian Burgess, the man who had given us the cars capable of winning the greatest race in the world, now just three days away.

'I've had an offer from Triple Eight, and I'm taking it. Sorry.'

I was stunned, shocked into silence. The energy and excitement I was feeling a moment before rushed from my body and sent me white. I stood there, not knowing what to say, a thousand voices buzzing at once.

'Fair enough,' I said, silencing the chaos in my mind. 'But why tell me now? WHY TELL ME NOW?'

Adrian shrugged before walking away to work on a car.

The knots in my belly, the ones that had momentarily gone, twisted tight. My arms tensed, my fists hardened, knuckles clenched white. I felt like spewing. I sat down and attempted to collect my thoughts.

I was angry.

Why now? I thought. *Why would he tell me before Bathurst? Why is he going? Things are just coming good, and he's on the verge of winning a championship with us.*

I fumed for a minute. Then my sympathetic side took over.

Adrian has been through a lot. More than any man deserves. I don't blame him for wanting out. After all, he's going to the best team in the sport.

Truth be told, Adrian probably saw the end.

DJR were underfunded in 2010, and to make ends meet we had dipped into the budget for 2011 and 2012. It was a decision I didn't agree with. DJR were screwed from 2011 on.

Still, I couldn't forgive Adrian's timing. It was inexcusable. I later found out that his UK working visa had ended on that very day. He was now eligible for permanent residency and made his move knowing he was no longer reliant on me employing him to stay in the country.

I tried to forget about it and decided to get on with the job. I didn't want anything affecting our Bathurst campaign, so I pulled myself together, walked back into the garage and pretended Adrian and I had never spoken. We prepared the car, and I left the track in a good mood, thinking we could win the race.

Later that night, I received a call from the *Daily Telegraph*'s James Phelps (who has co-written this book).

'Dick,' Phelps said. 'This is a courtesy call. I'm just letting you know that I'm running a story in tomorrow's paper. You don't have to say anything because everything's been confirmed. I'm just ringing to give you the opportunity to comment.'

My heart sank.

'Do you have to?' I asked. 'Do you really have to write about it? This will kill us.'

He said he did and that there was nothing he could do. Phelps knew about Adrian. He also knew that Charlie and I were not on speaking terms and that he was trying to sell his share of the team.

'I've written that James Courtney and half your team are going to walk at the end of the year,' he said.

'What?' I replied.

That was news to me. Phelps went on to say that James had a get-out clause in his contract and was set to activate it. Apparently, James had been fielding offers from rival teams and was ready to leave. The story was going to print on the back page of the paper.

'Don't do it,' I said. 'Don't write it. You have no idea the damage this will do.'

He did it anyway.

I hung up the phone and the pain returned, intense and crippling. I sat on the side of the bed, an utter mess. I knew the story would kill off our Bathurst campaign, maybe even our hopes for a championship win. I was also sure it was going to ruin the deal that was about to save my team and get rid of Charlie. (More on that shortly.)

I thought about picking up the phone. But who would I call and what would I say? Instead I grabbed a bottle of Jim Beam, had a couple and went to bed.

I arrived at the track at about 5.30 the next morning. I didn't buy the paper on the way, deciding I would ignore everything and get on with the job at hand. I wanted to pretend that nothing was wrong, to give my team a chance of winning this race.

I walked into the garage and a giant kid with flaming red hair jumped me at the door.

'Dick,' he said. 'I'm Tyson Otto from the *Daily Telegraph*. What do you have to say about James Courtney wanting to leave your team?'

I looked at him and growled.

'Get out now!' I yelled. 'You're not welcome in here. And if you come back, I'll knock you out.'

I shouldn't have blown up but I did.

My dreams for championship glory were shattered; my house of cards had been blown away. After my pre-dawn showdown with the journalist, there was no denying our team troubles were big news and there was nothing I could do. The atmosphere in the garage was cold, and no doubt the increased tension as a result contributed to the loss of our Bathurst campaign. We wouldn't stand a chance now that the cat was out of the bag.

The story about me threatening to punch a journalist also hit the stands. What a disaster.

Nathan Tinkler

Mining magnate Nathan Tinkler sat in his private helicopter as the engines warmed. He had a cheque for $1.5 million in one hand and a copy of the *Daily Telegraph* in the other. He grabbed the paper and flipped to the back page.

'Turn the engines off,' he said. 'We aren't going to Bathurst.'

Tinkler had booked a suite in a hotel in Mount Panorama and was due to arrive at Bathurst on the Friday. He was coming down to pay Charlie out and buy a half-stake in my team. All that changed in a moment, when he picked up the paper and read about the shit that was going on in the team.

I was screwed.

Tinkler never called that morning. I tried to reach him on his mobile, but it went straight to message bank. Deep down, even before I had gathered the truth, I knew why, but

I was hoping he had been delayed or called away on other business.

I eventually got through to him on the Monday night. Tinkler told me he had read the story and was having second thoughts. He didn't rule out buying the half-share in DJR, but it didn't look good. I never gave up hope, though, not until later that year. Charlie had been desperate following the no-show. He had got in touch with Tinkler and had slashed $500,000 off his asking price, but the big man had fobbed him off.

I first met Tinkler in a hotel car park at Bathurst earlier that year. It was a hot morning and he was about to strap down in a GT Falcon and race the 12-hour drive with my son, Steve.

'G'day, Dick,' he said, his wife by his side and his kids running around. 'Bloody good to meet you.'

He was wearing thongs, shorts and a T-shirt, and seemed like my kind of bloke. I had no idea who he was or what he was worth at the time. All I knew was that he was running a GT at Bathurst and he was obviously wealthy enough to support a race team and had a passion for motorsport.

Call me old-fashioned, but I am not one of those people who googles others. I don't study the life and times of anyone on a computer; I prefer to make my judgements about them and learn their history face-to-face. I'm not much of a believer of résumés, either – you can't learn anything about a person from a piece of paper. You have to make your judgements solely on the person you meet and your interactions with them.

I ended up having dinner with the man, and it turned

out he was a good bloke who loved Newcastle, rugby league and his cars. 'Tinks', as he quickly became known, was a huge motor racing fan, having grown up watching the sport, and absolutely loved his Fords. His dream was to drive, knocking about in the lower categories. Tinks had the money to do it and I applauded him for having a crack.

I found Tinks to be straight up and down, what you see is what you get. There's no bullshit about the bloke and he's the polar opposite of Charlie – he's in the sport because he loves it, not because he wants to hang out with the 'big names'. Tinks, an electrician who struck it lucky in the mining game, doesn't want a thing to do with the media, and is shy and reclusive, doing his best work behind the scenes. That's the thing about Tinks – he doesn't get involved for attention; he does it because he's passionate. He went on to buy the NRL Newcastle Knights and the A-League Newcastle Jets and has copped a lot of flak over it, but I can tell you right now that the only reason he bought those teams was because he cared about them and had the money to help. He knows how much sport means to his community and it was his way of putting back into the region he loves so much.

I didn't speak to Tinks for a couple of months after we'd first met. He and Steve had become good friends; they were about the same age and had similar tastes. Steve invited me to dinner one night, telling me that Tinks was coming along. It was there we first discussed him buying out Charlie and becoming my partner. It wasn't anything concrete. I told him of the situation with Charlie and he told me he was interested. At the end of the day it really had nothing to do with me. Charlie owned 50 per cent of my business and if Tinks wanted it, he'd have to buy the share off the forklift man. Secretly, though, I was hoping Tinks would pursue it. I considered him to be the perfect potential business partner, and I wanted Charlie out. I couldn't stand the bloke, let alone work with him.

Tinks and Charlie knew each other in a roundabout way. Charlie wanted to cut and run, and he thought this cashed-up millionaire was an easy way out. He'd put a huge amount on his share of the DJR business and offered Tinks a deal. I don't know the full details because I wasn't directly involved. I just know Tinkler came up to Queensland and inspected the factory. He also sent a team in to examine the books on another occasion and had them interview our staff.

Not long before Bathurst he agreed to buy Charlie's stake in the business for $1.5 million. I was over the moon. The amount didn't really concern me because it wasn't going into my pocket – he could've bought it for $5 or $5 million, for all I cared. I was just relieved to be getting rid of Charlie and becoming partners with a bloke who was passionate, influential and well backed.

Tinks had the money for the half-share in a trust account when he boarded his Bathurst-bound helicopter. The deal was to be finalised over the weekend, but then he'd read the paper and the true state of our team had been revealed. To be fair, it would've been enough to make me want to walk too.

So we had no money, had owners that didn't talk to each other, and had half the team, including the gun driver and engineer, about to quit.

But there was still the 2010 championship to consider, and the future of DJR at stake. I was left with no choice but to stick my hands up and punch on. As you should know by now, I am not a quitter and never will be.

30

FROM CHAMPIONS TO CHUMPS

Titles and Torment

'Don't bullshit me,' I screamed. 'Just tell me. If he's going, I need to start planning for next year. You can't leave me in the lurch.'

Alan Gow, James Courtney's manager, lied through his teeth.

'I don't know,' he said. 'I have no idea.'

Crap.

'Mate, you're the one doing the deals,' I said. 'What the fuck is going on?'

Jillie was in the car with me while he was on speaker. My wife is adamant she has never heard anyone treat me with such disrespect. Gow was damn right rude.

I suspected our driver James, the championship favourite, was about to walk out on his contract, but I couldn't get a straight answer from him or his manager.

I was being squeezed by our major sponsor Jim Beam, who wanted answers – and so did I. Everyone was telling me James was set to walk, and I needed to know the truth. Our future depended on it. We were two races away from winning an against-all-odds championship, but my team was being ripped apart. I was a wreck and couldn't enjoy our success for a moment.

The get-out clause in James's four-year contract meant he could officially break his terms if there was a significant management change. Race team manager Adrian Burgess's looming departure would give him his out. I'd read the reports and heard the speculation, word being HRT had offered him a million dollar deal.

I finally cracked it when we got to Sandown. I walked out of the garage and saw the flashes, the lights from the cameras going off.

James Courtney was sitting on a bunch of tyres, posing for a front-page shot. I stood in the background, arms crossed, fuming.

Reporter James Phelps was there, directing the shoot, which was to appear in the *Daily Telegraph* ahead of the final championship bout. I waited until they were finished before letting Phelps have it.

'You are an arsehole,' I attacked. 'A complete prick. You've cost me my team. Do you have any idea what you've done?'

'You did it to yourself, buddy,' he fired back. 'I just report the facts. Why did you wait until now to tell me how you felt? I didn't think we had a problem. Go and get fucked.'

No surprise we didn't speak for a while after that.

I also fell out with other journalists, such was the pressure.

Gordon Lomas, who was formerly with the *Courier Mail*, is a tremendous reporter. We'd been mates for years, but I ended up giving it to him too. At this point in time, I felt that I was being targeted by the media; I was in the foetal position while these people I knew and respected were whacking me when I was down. I expected them to support me, not to swing at me and land cruel blows.

Sandown was a terrible round. The shit was hitting the fan and I lost my cool. I was facing a walkout from my very own team members, but no one would give it to me straight. Adrian was technically gone (having already given me his notice of resignation), James was apparently on his way out and so was half my staff. I didn't know if I was even going to have a team for next year – let alone whether I could pay them given the huge hole in my budget.

I never fronted James about the situation. He is a politician and would never have given me an answer even if I tried. He left that all to his manager, a bloke I was already pretty cautious of. I was completely frustrated and desperate. I knew the talk, and most of the time it's true. You can't hide anything in our sport: pit-lane is a see-through door.

I'd been told that James had been to so-called secret meetings in the back of the HRT truck. He had also been spotted with Ford Performance Racing. Others had told me that my staff, engineers, mechanics and crew had been submitting résumés to rival teams, bracing themselves for the fall. James had come out and said DJR was in such a bad way he hadn't received an upgrade since the middle of the year. He'd told the press he was fighting with bad tools and was doing the best he could. I wasn't happy with his remarks, nor were the team.

In Sandown, James finished up 90 points ahead of Jamie Whincup in the championship, and I think he was setting himself up for a win–win situation. It was going to go down to the wire, winner at Sydney taking all, and James gave himself a get-out, an excuse. If he lost, it would be because of the team and their financial struggles; if he won, he'd be seen as a legend who had defied the odds.

The Sydney 500

The Saturday of the 2010 Sydney 500 went down as one of the most dramatic days in Australian motor racing history. And I think few will disagree. It was out-of-this-world, superpower stuff, fights and feuds forgotten, if only for a moment.

We arrived at the final race of the year, the team still a complete wreck. Charlie was off at the whole team and had not been sighted for months. He hadn't been brave enough to go to the workshop and was turning up to races but refusing to come near us. He was unwelcome and disliked by the entire team.

We still weren't too sure whether James was going or staying, even though at first we thought he was going to defect to FPR. Charlie had done a deal with Pepsi and was ready to take his licence to FPR. In fact, he was so sure he had James signed and secure, he even had Pepsi agree to print a limited number of cans with James's face all over them. Meanwhile, the DJR team were preparing for life without Charlie and

James, manoeuvring to get another licence so we could run a second car the following year.

I had understood that the contracts with Pepsi, James, Charlie and FPR were signed and it was a done deal. But James and Gow had different plans. And they fell out with Charlie in spectacular fashion. I don't know the full details because I wasn't involved, but I do know Charlie and James stopped talking not long after Bathurst. The wonder kid who Charlie had adored snubbed him and was off talking to HRT.

It became clear that something between James and Charlie was off. Just before the championship-deciding event at Sydney got underway, I saw Charlie walk bravely up to the grid and stick his hand into the cockpit to shake James's hand. James slapped it away, refusing to swap flesh with the forklift man who had paid him $800,000 a year to steer.

I wish they got that on camera. The once inseparable duo was at war, and poor Charlie had to buy back all those cans of Pepsi he'd printed! I'm sure it was both costly and highly embarrassing for the self-declared 'smooth operator'. I later heard that Charlie was trying to sue James for breach of contract.

The uncertainty among our staff didn't do any favours for team spirit. Adrian was leaving, that had already been confirmed, but I didn't know how many team members would follow him out the door. We suspected it would be a lot. In short, our team was a mess and bursting apart. I had no idea how we'd all arrived at the track, let alone how we would fight to win a V8 title that was going right down to the wire.

2010 was a little bit like 1981: it was driver vs. driver, car vs. car, team by team. It was one of the few championships that was going to be decided by the final race, but instead of me and Brock going for it, it was Courtney and Whincup.

James went into the race with a 90-point lead. Each race was worth 100 points, and a DNF or a poor run would have finished James and given the title to Whincup, who was in ominous form. The Sydney 500 is the last place you want to be worried about a DNF because it is an absolutely brutal track of concrete and broken dreams. We were seriously nervous heading into the weekend, and had genuine concerns about Whincup storming it home and stealing the crown.

Hollywood couldn't have written a better script for what came next.

James and the DJR team had done a magnificent job all day. Our job wasn't to beat Whincup, but to keep him in sight. We didn't need to win this race – we just had to finish near him in both races to ensure we'd secure the title.

The race was challenging and hectic, and with the end in sight, we thought our job was done. It wasn't. James was third and Whincup first when all hell broke loose. If I hadn't been in a similar situation before, I wouldn't have believed what had happened next.

It was lap 59 when a safety car was called. A freak storm cell was hovering above the track and there had been an incident. It was raining on one side of the 3.5-km circuit – around about where ANZ Stadium and Olympic Park are – and bone dry on the other. The rain was heavy enough for any driver to want wets. But according to the radar, it appeared as though the storm would be gone in an instant, the rainfall to be very little, so the wet half of the track would soon be dry. If you came in for wets, the rain could have been gone by the time you strapped them on. You would have had one lap on the rain-friendly rubber before going back to dry tyres – that would've meant two pointless time-consuming stops.

It was a heads or tails situation. Some drivers took their chances and came in for wets, while others stayed out. For us, it wasn't our decision to make. We had to follow Whincup.

'Is it going to keep on raining?' he asked his engineer over the radio. 'We might need wets.'

'I don't know,' his engineer said.

'Let's push on.'

We moved away the tyres stacked in the lane, and retreated to the garage, knowing Whincup had decided to go on despite the rain.

It was a terrible decision. And one that almost cost us the crown.

On lap 60, the charging leaders hurtled on: Whincup was first, Mark Winterbottom second and James was hanging on in third. They made ease of the straight and the first couple of corners, all dry and untouched, but then, just behind the Olympic Stadium, the heavens unloaded. Rain bucketed down, effectively turning the track into a river. Water gushed across the slippery street, which looked more like an ice-skating rink.

Winterbottom went first, completely losing control and passing Whincup through a chicane. He couldn't pull himself out of the way after making the move and speared into a concrete wall. James looked as though he was making a move and edged up on Whincup, who passed him on the inside but had no control and bounced off a wall before reaching a heartbreaking stop.

But the damage seemed to be minor and Whincup flew on by. We thought there was still hope for him even though he'd been stalled. Just as James was recovering and was about to motor on . . .

Bang!

Craig Lowndes speared him straight in the arse. It was a brutal hit that we thought had ended our chances of winning the championship. I was furious.

Whincup kept on going, seemingly unhurt, until we heard his voice on the radio.

'I'll have four wets,' he said. 'And something's wrong with the front right.'

Whincup's car was damaged. Thank God. We looked back to the screens, and seeing James continue on the track renewed our hopes. He pushed and pulled, revved and roared, and his car moved. We smiled – all was not lost.

'He's OK,' I said. 'He's going to get back.'

My optimism seemed to have uplifted the mood in the garage from a sense of silent defeat into roaring action. The team yelled for him to move. And he did. James managed to find a gear and began pushing the twisted piece of metal across the track. The car looked like a snowplough. We all cheered and clapped, willing the ruined car home. It was touch and go; the injured beast could have stopped at any time.

'Get ready,' Adrian shouted. 'He's coming back in. Let's fix this thing.'

What happened next was utterly amazing. A true testament to the human will. James's car shouldn't have been able to move, yet he got it back to the pits, all scorched rubber and twisted steel. But that wasn't what defied belief. It was the team and what they did to get it back out.

Whincup's car was back in the Triple Eight garage too. This meant that whoever made it back onto the track and earned points would win the 2010 championship, which was going to be decided in pit-lane.

I didn't think we had a chance. Our car was a wreck, James barely got it going, and Whincup appeared to be driving with no serious problems. But now it was life or death. Chumps or champs.

There was little time to prepare and Adrian worked the team into a frenzy. He was like a general at war, George Washington, Robert Lee and George Patton all rolled into one. He shouted orders, and the rest of the team followed every word. They grabbed at red-hot steaming brake rotors with bare hands, pulled them off, flesh searing, and threw them to the ground. Others ripped off razor-sharp panels, skin cut, blood splashing.

I sat back and smiled. It reminded me of the time an air spike ripped through my arm while I was standing in the pits. One of the crew rammed the spear clean right out of my arm and JB helped clean me up. I was ordered to go to hospital, but I told them to get nicked. Instead, I jumped straight back behind the wheel. I couldn't make a fist with my left hand, such was the damage, and I spent the rest of the race changing gears with my wrist, which eventually became bloody and bruised.

What I saw before me was a perfect example of adrenaline and commitment for a common aim. Blood poured, the blisters and bruises rose, and I welled with pride. Here was a bunch of blokes that had been through the shit. Some were leaving soon after this race, others didn't know if they had jobs the following year. But in this moment they operated as one, working tirelessly to get our driver back on track to win the championship.

Finally, the car rolled out and we cheered. We were back in the race, and Triple Eight, the big guns of the sport, who had raced problem-free, failed. Whincup eventually made it on the track but couldn't finish. We won the championship there and then.

It was an amazing end to a horrible year. We didn't celebrate until the following night, when we went back to the hotel and I downed one too many Jim Beams with the team. They were all there, minus Charlie, and we had a final fling. I eventually passed out. What I do remember is that Adrian is one bloke who certainly knows how to celebrate, getting everyone going. I'm pretty sure it was him who set off the fire-extinguishers and left us with a hefty cleaning bill.

I've already made it pretty clear that I didn't like the way Adrian left. He shouldn't have told me he was resigning days away from Bathurst, but regardless of this, I have to pay the guy the credit he deserves. I don't want to blow smoke up his arse, but he is a true professional and one of the best mechanical minds in the sport. When everything went haywire on the Saturday, he rallied the team to fix the car. It appeared hopeless but he got the job done. The thing about that effort was he was racing the very team he was set to join – Adrian was on his way to Triple Eight the following year, and could have easily handed them an early present by gifting them the championship. I think it shows a lot about the bloke. He dug in and did his job. He is a true competitor, full of pride.

What a highlight. A brilliant flash of lightning in a dark and stormy night.

31

SACKING MY SON AND
SAVING MY TEAM

Dark Clouds

I should have left Sydney celebrating. We had just won the 2010 championship and enjoyed our best year on track since John Bowe reigned supreme. Merchandise was going out the door, our sponsors had been splashed across back pages and televisions screens and all should have been good.

But it wasn't.

I had a headache like you wouldn't believe and didn't know how I was going to pull a team together for 2011. I should have been thinking about cashing in on our success and consolidating the team for the future, not worrying about whether or not I would still have one the next week. The first thing I had to do was get some answers. I needed to find out what Charlie was doing with his licence and who from my team – apart from James and Adrian – was going to walk out the door.

It turned out Charlie didn't actually know what he was doing the following year. Believe it or not, he was still negotiating with Nathan Tinkler in Sydney, the mining magnate renewing his interest to buy a half-share of my team. I'd still been hoping that they would be able to work it out. It was clear Charlie and I had a very strained partnership, and I needed to run a two-car team, given that one-car teams are expensive and simply don't have much in the way of success.

I soon found out that Charlie had once again botched another potential deal with Tinkler – they couldn't come to an agreement. Charlie was in limbo. He had a licence, but nowhere to run his car. The bloke wouldn't know an engine from an exhaust and had no hope of setting up an operation himself, let alone enough time to do so. He had no chance of doing a deal with another team.

Enter Steve Brabeck. Steve has been a mate of mine for years and a huge supporter and sponsor. The managing director of Crimsafe, a company that manufactures security screens – yep, I'm in a couple of his TV ads, all safe and secure in my home – suggested I do a deal with Charlie to rent his REC for a couple of years. It wasn't an ideal situation, but Charlie and I had little choice. He needed someone to run his car and I needed another licence, not only to give me the two-car team I wanted but also to fulfil my commitments with sponsors based on the provision of a two-car outfit.

So Steve went in and made the deal. There was no way in hell I was talking to Charlie. I didn't want to give him a cent either, but I was between a rock and a hard place. Steve negotiated to rent Charlie's licence for two years. We agreed on paying him $200,000 for the REC in 2011 and $230,000 to have it again in 2012. Now that I'd secured both my cars, what about the rest of the team?

James Courtney soon announced his deal with HRT. He was going to Clayton to become the outfit's latest $1 million man. I was totally over him and the situation by then and was just happy to finally have an answer. I wished him the best and sent him away. To be honest, I was quite glad to be rid of his $800,000 annual salary because we would have struggled to pay it if he stayed.

As I said, we were in a world of hurt when it came to money, having eaten into our funding for 2011 and 2012 early on in 2010. We were looking at a giant black hole and were desperate to come up with some sort of feasible budget. This ultimately meant we were in no position to sign a big-name driver; in fact, we couldn't even contemplate paying for a steerer. We had nothing.

James Moffat stuck his hand up and said he was looking for an opportunity. He was Allan's son of course, and it seemed fitting to have the child of one of my greatest on-track rivals coming to race for my team. My son Steven Johnson in one car, Allan's James Moffat in the other. But the reason he got the gig was because he was willing to drive for free. He also brought money with him in the form of sponsorships from Norton and Toshiba.

So now we had the cars and drivers sorted. But did we have a team?

Unfortunately, no. More than half my team quit after the last race for 2010. Adrian took a couple of key members of DJR – my best No. 1 and No. 2 mechanics, highly skilled guys – with him to Triple Eight. James also took his engineer to HRT. We also had Jonathan Webb run his car out of our factory in 2010, but he left in 2011, taking several of our best guys with him. Others pulled up stumps and went to work for Paul Morris, who was promising big things with some Triple Eight deal.

I was left in the lurch and had to scrape together a team. I called my mate Malcolm Swetnam, an English whiz who I knew back in the Sierra days, to become my team manager. Malcolm was initially reluctant to make the big move to Australia, but after speaking to his family he finally agreed. The Englishman was instrumental in pulling a team together for 2011, and although it was a skeleton crew, it was enough to get us on track.

But we didn't have a hope.

2011 and 2012 were always going to be horrible years. We didn't have the budget to compete with the big teams and were treading water. We did what we could to find cash to make the cars as fast as possible. But nothing worked and we were a shadow of the team we used to be.

For 2012 we decided to go for a four-car outfit. Dean Fiore came over with his licence and Paul Morris pulled the plug on his Norwell-based operation and joined DJR, with Steve Owen behind the wheel.

I thought it was going to be a good thing for us, but it turned out to be an absolute disaster. We just weren't prepared for an operation that size and struggled to service all the sponsors and meet their demands. We also didn't have enough money to make the cars a real force to be reckoned with and I think they ended up costing us more than what we had coming in. Running the four cars really set DJR back, and gave me no hope of consolidating, let alone preparing for what was to come.

Things were about to get a whole lot worse, those hovering clouds finally unleashing thunder, striking us to the ground.

Left in the Lurch

The first crack of thunder came, shaking us to the core.

Towards the end of 2012 Jim Beam officially told us that they were ending their sponsorship after five years. We'd tried our best to convince them to stay, but they felt as though the partnership had run its course, and our $1.8 million a year deal with them would be finished.

We needed to find a replacement – fast. Thankfully the guys at Jim Beam, complete professionals and all above board, kept us in the loop throughout the year, having made their decision early enough for us to prepare for life when they left. It was a major blow, but we were confident of finding a replacement. We were sad to lose Jim Beam – they had been a huge part of the DJR team and my life.

It didn't take us long to find another backer. Hungry Jack's had been involved in our team in a minor way. The fast-food giant came forward and said they were interested in taking over from Jim Beam, and after some serious negotiations the burger chain was prepared to offer us a five-year deal, with an annual pay of $3 million. It was an absolute godsend and our future was a step closer to being assured.

The paperwork was organised and we had an agreement. There was one stipulation that didn't appear to be major: Hungry Jack's wouldn't sign the contract unless the new V8

Supercars TV deal was done before 7 January 2013.

I never thought that would be a problem. The sport had known the TV contract was up for some time and had been working feverishly behind the scenes, hiring former Fox Sports boss David Malone as the governing bodies' CEO to ensure the best deal was done. The V8 Supercars season started in March, and I couldn't see them not having a deal done by January. In fact, it should have been completed well before 2013, as all the other codes had already locked down their deals.

So with $3 million a year set to come in, we stopped looking for a major sponsor. It was all but done. But we still needed more money in order to be considered real competition and I wanted to secure DJR's future. I never wanted to be in this position again, where I'd be left financially vulnerable. It was clear that my business skills were not up to the mark and I was ageing and unwell. I wanted to bring some smart minds in to help alleviate the crippling pressure that was making me ill.

I organised to sell two-thirds of my business to a couple of clever operators who I had known for years: my good mate Steve Brabeck and Maurie Pickering of South Coast Automotive. Steve had a brilliant mind and was a true motorsport man with a huge knowledge of business. He was keen to officially come into the fray and immediately agreed. Maurie was also a motorsport enthusiast. He was looking at giving two young guys a start and wanted to buy my cars to run them in the 2012 Dunlop Development series. I thought the best way forward was to restructure the business, each of us getting a one-third share.

We all signed a heads of agreement on 12 November 2012. Both Steve and Maurie agreed to buy a one-third stake in my business for $1.5 million each. This amount as a result of the new partnership, along with Hungry Jack's $3 million for the following year, was going to ensure we had a big enough budget to rise from the dirt. Having Steve and Maurie involved in DJR was also going to help take the pressure off me and allow me to step back and let others take control.

So everything was looking good. I sat back at the end of the season and enjoyed my break, finally relieved of the stress that had been ruining my life. But it was short-lived. The clouds and thunder were back – blacker, more devastating and louder than ever before.

The new storm just might strike down my team, once and for all.

I began panicking just after Christmas. Despite their promises and assurances, V8 Supercars hadn't signed off on a TV deal. I couldn't believe it. What was the hold-up? Our sport was booming and the NRL and AFL had just doubled their deal to over $1 billion, yet here we were, with less than two months before the first race of the season without a free-to-air deal. My deal with Hungry Jack's was in doubt.

And so, 2013 rolled in and no decision had been made. I put my hands up and braced for the worst. I called V8s and demanded to know what was going on. I was told that they were nearing towards an agreement, but it wasn't near enough. January 7 hit and Hungry Jack's pulled out. I told them the TV deal was just around the corner and assured them that V8 Supercars were set to sign with either Channel 7 or Channel 10. They couldn't take my word and an upcoming change of management in the fast-food company meant that the deal was off.

Shit.

And with that, I lost $15 million in one day, a phone call sealing my fate. I now had just 53 days to secure a major sponsor to save my team. Believe it or not, the TV deal was announced just eight days later. At least I had the $3 million that Steve and Maurie were putting in. Or did I?

Maurie pulled out just after the Hungry Jack's deal fell through and the heads of agreement we had signed to secure DJR's future was off. He didn't even have the balls to call, sending his news in a terse and matter-of-fact email. His reason for backing out was because of some missing invoices his team had picked up when they'd audited the business. (He'd sent a crew in before the deal had been made official and some idiot who worked for me had stashed a bunch of receipts in a drawer and hadn't filed them electronically.) I suspect Maurie pulled the pin because the deal with the major sponsor had fallen through.

Either way I was screwed.

My son Steve and Dean Fiore were all set to strap down and drive at the Clipsal 500 in Hungry Jack's cars, their futures secure. Now we didn't even have the money to make it to the following week. We couldn't pay wages, let alone think about building the costly cars. To his credit, Steve Brabeck stuck strong. Even though the deal was off, he agreed to loan me the $1.5 million he had pledged. Without that I was a shot duck. Thanks, mate.

Another big part of my problem was the so-called 'Car of the Future'.

In preparation for 2013 we were to scrap the cars we currently had, and design a cheaper, new and improved car that would allow other manufacturers to join the sport. It would be a 'revolution', they said, that would secure our future. At first the V8 officials told us the car was going to cost no more than $275,000 to build, which was fine because that's what we budgeted for. But guess what? The car ended up costing $620,000 without an engine – and we had to build two.

This was the final insult and I thought it was mission impossible for DJR. I was sure we were going to fold.

So here we were, just two months before the race. We didn't have the money to build these 'new generation' cars, nor did we have the cash to pay wages. Again I thought about chucking in the towel, but I looked around the garage and couldn't fathom sending anyone from my team out on the street.

So the team knuckled down and came up with some solutions to at least make sure we made it to the first race of the season.

One of these deals cost my son his job.

Sorry, Steve, You're Out

I have made some hard decisions in my life, but none harder than sacking my own son.

I sat Steve down, looked him in the eye and told him it was either him or the team.

'I know, Dad,' he said. 'I wasn't born last week. Do

whatever you have to. I want this team to survive and I'll do whatever it takes.'

We were desperate, and the only way to move forward was to get in drivers who could pay some of the bills. We had lost funding from Jim Beam, Norton, Toshiba, Hungry Jack's, Coca-Cola, V.I.P. Petfoods and Ford, to name a few. I had to hire a driver with some financial backing, and Kiwi V8 SuperTourer Jonny Reid agreed to come along and bring cash with him. It wasn't a lot, but it was something.

It killed me having to tell Steve he could no longer drive. It was just gut-wrenching and one of the most painful things I've ever experienced, something a father should never be forced to do. I was ending my son's career – at least for now – and I felt like a complete piece of shit. I still struggle to sleep knowing what I've done and I just hope he can get back into the game soon. I won't be able to live with the fact if that's it for him. He deserves so much more.

Dean Fiore was also forced to step aside for Tim Blanchard, who also brought in a deal – another blow that was sad for both Dean and the team.

But even then, we still didn't have enough cash to make it to the first race. We were locked in a desperate battle and it was only an eleventh-hour deal with Wilson Security that got us over the line and has been able to secure our future – until the second race of the year, that is.

The guys at Wilson are terrific. They are big supporters of motor racing and the sport has also been good for their business. We're talking about furthering the partnership going forward, but by the time you read this, I may or may not have a team . . .

In short, I'm in the shit, and I don't know if I can dig myself out. Not this time. I need another $2.5 million just to make it to the end of the year. We've also had some assistance from the great people at Shell and Cabcharge, but I'm not sure if our team will still be able to pull through with all of this. Only time will tell.

Regardless, I have had enough. It has become too much for me and I want out. I am nudging 70 and should have retired a long time ago. Mentally, this is all killing me, and physically I am a wreck.

But I'm not about to leave my team in the lurch after 33 years. It would kill me to see it collapse. Ideally, I want to get DJR back up on its feet and sell it with me as an ambassador. I will go to races, act as a figurehead – I'll do whatever it is the new owner wants.

I am determined to get DJR up off the floor, one way or another.

Steve has taken over as the company's general manager and is doing a great job. He's fantastic with the staff, a class-A motivator and he also has the ability to make the hard decisions that I couldn't. I really want to see him back behind the wheel next year, and maybe down the track he can take over the family business – and run it for another 33 years.

One thing's for certain – I will be devastated if DJR disappears. It's my life's work. It means as much to me as any of my Bathurst or championship wins.

The G.O.A.T.s

When I look back at my career, I can't help but think that despite the crap I've been through, all the triumphs over adversity have made everything worthwhile. The competition I've encountered in this sport has made me a better driver, challenging me to improve on my weaknesses, feeding my drive to succeed.

I'm often asked who the greatest-of-all-time drivers are. It's a difficult question I tend to shy away from, given the different eras, cars and what each and every driver was up against in their day. But I suppose I can't write a book without giving you an answer . . .

I'm not going to rank drivers – that's just impossible – but I will give you my top five of all time. In no particular order, they are: Peter Brock, Jim Richards, Allan Moffat, Ian Geoghegan and John Bowe. I think that they've shown the most skill, determination and guts behind the wheel.

Brock was an absolute freak. He was a well-rounded driver, talented and judicious. His great results at Bathurst make him the most revered driver in our sport. Brocky always had good gear but didn't make the most of it at times during the Touring Car championships. Brocky never played dirty and was always fair, and I will always love and respect him for his attitude. He was a legend and will forever be missed.

Richards was the complete pro, Mr Cool, although he did lose his shit at Bathurst once, calling everyone a 'pack of arseholes'. Jim was a bloke who really showed his class in both good cars and bad. He is a gentlemen and an accomplished driver who deserves every bit of his success.

Moffat was another freak. He was unstoppable in his Ford in the 1970s. Allan had a flawless technique and style, and was a guy I looked up to. No doubt he's one of the best drivers in motorsport history.

Geoghegan was another man with boundless natural skill, showing his talent in a number of different cars. He won his first Australian Touring Car Championship in 1964 and would go on to win five, a record I matched. He is one of my idols and deserves his place in the V8 Supercar Hall of Fame. There are few better than this man.

JB just might be the most skilful of the lot, but maybe I'm just biased. I got to watch Bowe close up when we worked together and knew exactly what he was fighting with and what he was capable of. Sometimes his cars weren't great, but JB really knew how to extract the best from the beasts. He was one of the first drivers to really get on the wheel and give it a shake. It's a shame he never got a decent car after he left me. He would have won plenty more.

Craig Lowndes is a driver who could easily be in my top five. He has had a lot of good gear, and he's up there with Brock when it comes to natural talent. Much like his nickname, he drives like a king, wringing the hell out of whatever he's got.

Jamie Whincup might just go on to be better than them all – at least where records are concerned. With his Triple Eight weapon, he is marching relentlessly towards my five-title record, and I'm sure he'll eventually break it if he sticks around and stays with a good team. He has been blessed with good cars and has made the most out of them. He often wins against Craig Lowndes, which just goes to show how talented he is. Will Davison and Mark Winterbottom could be just as good in the same car, but that's a debate best left for the pub.

I reckon the next big thing's going to be Shane Van Gisbergen. He is a driver through and through, and I can't wait to see him develop even more.

And as for the future of motorsport . . . who knows? I'm not the only one who's been left bleeding, and I have fears for the category going forward.

Midway through 2011, a private equity group called Archer Capital bought a majority stake in V8 Supercars. At the time I thought it was a godsend, but now I'm not so sure. Before the sale, team owners held a 75 per cent share of the business and a company called Sports & Entertainment Limited, led by Tony Cochrane, owned 25 per cent. Now team owners have a 35 per cent stake and Archer, the new mob, have 65 per cent. As team owners, we got about $4 million straight up per REC to sell our share. For me, that eased a lot of my personal debt and saved my house. I thought it was also a good thing for the sport.

We were getting about $800,000 a year per REC as a return on our ownership. Archer promised that by 2013, despite having a smaller share in the company, team owners would be receiving the same. We were recently told we would get nothing this year. Not a cent, which means that the current system isn't working – it's all going backwards.

The problem with Archer is they have no experience in motorsport. They are an investment company and have come in swinging the axe, taking everything to the bottom line, cutting jobs, budgets and events. That is not how this sport works – you have to invest money in order to make it a success and there are no short-term fixes.

It's hard to understand the direction that the sport is heading. The teams have delivered – we have 28 cars of the future on track and the racing has been competitive. The status quo has been well and truly shaken up. It's been a tough battle getting to this point, and with any luck the sport's new management has learnt a few valuable lessons. However, the teams have every right to feel let down by Archer. Financial promises and assurances haven't been met and they have a long way to go to secure the future of the sport.

We need to reinvest in the sport. We need to spend it to really make it work.

So I think that's about all I have to tell. What you've read here is my life – all the triumphs and the wins, the pain and the losses.

I started off as a young kid who liked cars and dreamed big, and against all odds become a race car driver who did pretty well for himself. And while I had my share of spectacular battles, I also got to experience glory beyond my wildest dreams.

I got to marry Jillie, the most wonderful woman in the world, and together we have Steve and Kel, who I'm both so proud of. My grandchildren Lacy and Jett are the best, and I have great mates across the globe. Sure, I might have fallen out with some, but I'm blessed to have such wonderful people around me, who are always there to help no matter what.

I also need to thank Ryan Story. He's a remarkable man who's been instrumental in keeping my team alive. Ryan is a bit of a genius. A mathematician, he does strategy for F1 teams and runs a successful business. He has helped me behind the scenes by keeping a watchful eye over my affairs, stumping up cash to get me through.

Above all I have my fans, and without them, my racing career would have been over even before it began. They are the most loyal and staunch people you could ever hope for. And this book is for them.

DICK JOHNSON STATISTICS

Years active as driver: 1964–2000

Teams: Holden Dealer Team
Bryan Byrt Racing
Dick Johnson Racing

Starts: 202
Wins: 22

Championship titles

1981   Australian Touring Car Championship
Bathurst 1000

1982   Australian Touring Car Championship

1984   Australian Touring Car Championship

1988   Australian Touring Car Championship

1989   Australian Touring Car Championship
Bathurst 1000

1994   Sandown 500
Bathurst 1000

1995   Eastern Creek 12 Hour
               Sandown 500

Previous series
1982–91   Australian Endurance Championship
1989–90   NASCAR Australia
1990   NASCAR Winston Cup

Awards
2001   V8 Supercar Hall of Fame

JAMES PHELPS is a senior sports reporter for Sydney's *Sunday Telegraph* and is also News Limited's chief motor-sport writer in Australia.

Loved the book?

Join thousands of other readers online at

AUSTRALIAN READERS:

randomhouse.com.au/talk

NEW ZEALAND READERS:

randomhouse.co.nz/talk